*Also by Henry Kissinger*

# FOR THE RECORD

# FOR THE RECORD

*Selected Statements*
*1977–1980*

# Henry Kissinger

Little, Brown and Company — Boston–Toronto

FIRST EDITION

"Henry A. Kissinger: The Lessons of the Past: A Conversation with Walter Laqueur"
reprinted from *The Washington Review of Strategic and International Studies,*
Volume I, number 1, copyright © 1978 by the Center for Strategic and International
Studies, Georgetown University, Washington, D.C. (later *The Washington Quarterly*).

LIBRARY OF CONGRESS CATALOGING IN PUBLICATION DATA
Kissinger, Henry Alfred.
    For the record.
    Includes index.
    1.  United States — Foreign relations — 1977–
— Collected works.  I.  Title.
E872.K57        327.73        80–25341
ISBN 0–316–49663–4

MV
*Designed by Susan Windheim*
*Published simultaneously in Canada*
*by Little, Brown & Company (Canada) Limited*
PRINTED IN THE UNITED STATES OF AMERICA

*To my parents*

# CONTENTS

# FOREWORD

THIS book makes available some of my speeches and other public statements since I left office in January 1977. I have chosen what I think are the most important, and they cover a range of current topics: the fall of the Shah of Iran; the SALT II treaty; human rights as a goal of foreign policy; the ups and downs of Middle Eastern diplomacy; the energy crisis; the future of NATO; East-West trade; Communist parties in Western Europe; appreciations of remarkable personalities I have known; and other subjects.

Until 1945, Americans had the habit — and the luxury — of treating foreign policy as something with which we concerned ourselves only sporadically, as a matter of choice when we saw fit or as a matter of immediate self-defense when directly attacked. After a period of exertion, we withdrew into comfortable isolation. Since World War II we have had to get used to the unpleasant reality that our challenge is now unending. We no longer have the option of turning our backs on the world. Our security is not self-ensuring; our preferences do not automatically prevail; our interests and values require vigilance and effort if they are to survive. Indeed, as the world becomes more complex, our safety and well-being require more commitment at an early stage if the challenges are not to grow overwhelming. When the scope for action is greatest, the challenge is bound to be ambiguous. When the nature of the problem becomes unambiguously clear, the scope for creative action may well have disappeared. The task of statesmanship is to attempt to shape events according to a vision of the future, with the moral fortitude to act boldly even when consensus and certainty are often unattainable.

This is a particular problem for a democratic society, in which all fundamental commitments require a base of public support if they are to be sustained. We solve this problem as we solve all problems: through debate and discussion, through contests in the political arena, through the perennial tension between the Executive Branch's imperative of leadership and the Congress's imperative of setting the broad policies. It is an untidy process, but it is the essence of a free and vital society.

Having served in government, I have sympathy for the burdens of those who today occupy high positions of responsibility. They face few easy choices; all the simple problems are resolved at lower levels and only the difficult ones are passed to the top. In office I often spoke of the need for national unity and a spirit of nonpartisanship in foreign policy. This was not a ploy to disarm opposition but a recognition of reality. It is the only possible basis for a vigorous, successful, and sustained foreign policy.

Thus, out of office, I sought to live up to the same standard. Readers of these speeches and statements will note that I supported efforts of the Administration on a number of issues and attempted to express whatever disagreements I had on a philosophical plane. A new President of a different party is hardly obliged to carry out the preferences of the Administration he replaces. At the same time, America's position of leadership in the world imposes some responsibility of steadiness; America should not itself become a major factor of instability in the world, shifting course radically after every year divisible by four. Nor do the realities of the world, or our national interests, change at quadrennial intervals. Therefore, some continuity is essential. And a loyal opposition has the duty to perform its critical task with the attitude that we are all engaged in a common enterprise. The world's future, and our own, is at stake.

I would like to thank Little, Brown and Company, publishers of my memoirs, for the suggestion to produce this volume. I am grateful to Genevieve Young of Little, Brown for her contribution to this book. Betsy Pitha of Little, Brown applied her copyediting genius in preparing the material for publication (polishing the texts somewhat for stylistic consistency and better presentation). William G. Hyland and Peter W. Rodman of my staff assisted me in the original preparation of the speeches and statements.

HENRY A. KISSINGER

*August 1980*
*Washington, D.C.*

# COMMUNIST PARTIES IN WESTERN EUROPE

## *Challenge to the West*

*Remarks made on June 9, 1977, in Washington, D.C.,
at the Conference on Italy and Eurocommunism
sponsored by the Hoover Institution on War, Revolution
and Peace and the American Enterprise Institute for
Public Policy Research*

THE COHESION of the industrial democracies of Western Europe, North America, and Japan has been for thirty years the bulwark of peace and the engine of global prosperity.

This unity has been the keystone of our foreign policy in every administration from President Truman to President Carter. The first permanent peacetime security alliance in American history was with the democratic nations of the Atlantic community; it was soon followed by our commitment to the security of Japan. Since then, the agenda of cooperation among the industrial democracies has spread from collective defense to common action on energy policy, economic recovery, the international economic system, relations with the Communist countries, and with the Third World. This cohesion rests not simply on material considerations of wealth and power but on a common moral foundation as well — on the shared conviction that the consent of the governed is the basis of government and that every individual enjoys inalienable rights and is entitled to constitutional liberties.

It is ironic that at the moment when the industrial democracies are most cohesive in their opposition to external threats, at a time when our cooperative efforts cover a broader range than ever, the unity developed with so much effort and imagination over a generation should be jeopardized by an internal danger — the growth of Communist parties and the danger of their accession to power in some of the countries of Western Europe.

In *Italy*, in the parliamentary elections of June 1976, the

Communist Party obtained 34 percent of the vote, strengthening its position as the second largest party and as a powerful rival of the Christian Democratic Party, which has governed Italy throughout the postwar period. The Communists' growth since the 1972 election has been primarily at the expense of the democratic socialist groups, and is part and parcel of an increasing and dangerous polarization of Italian politics. The Communists have already achieved a virtual veto over government programs in the Italian Parliament.

In *France,* in the presidential election of April 1974, a coalition of the Communist and Socialist parties came within one percentage point of victory on the final ballot. A majority for this coalition in the parliamentary elections which must take place by March 1978 would bring Communist leaders into key ministerial positions. It would do so, moreover, in conditions of constitutional crisis, for the constitution of the Fifth Republic has not yet faced the test of a president and a prime minister from different parties.

In *the Iberian peninsula,* where hopeful steps are being taken toward democracy, Communist parties have fought with ruthlessness and disciplined organization to increase their already considerable influence. Portugal is a member of NATO; Spain is strategically crucial and tied by special agreements to the United States. Communist participation in the government of either country would have serious consequences for Western security.

And these Communist challenges do not exist in isolation from each other. There is no doubt that a Communist breakthrough to power or a share in power in one country will have a major psychological effect on the others, by making Communist parties seem respectable, or suggesting that the tide of history in Europe is moving in their direction.

Most of the causes of this phenomenon are indigenous to the individual countries. And by the same token, the response to this challenge must come in the first instance from European leaders and voters who are persuaded that democracy is worth the effort. America cannot make their choices for them or decide the outcome of free elections.

But America *must* recognize the significance of what may lie ahead. We must not delude ourselves about what the accession of Communist leaders to executive power will mean to the most basic premises of American foreign policy. We must not confuse either our own people or those in allied countries who take our judgments seriously about the gravity of the threat. We must not weaken their resolve either by treating a Communist victory as inevitable — which it is not — or by imagining that a Communist electoral victory would be an accidental, transitory, or inconsequential phenomenon. The ultimate decisions are for the voters of Europe to make. But they — and we — would be indulging in wishful thinking if we all did not acknowledge now:

- that the accession to power of Communists in an allied country would represent a massive change in European politics;
- that it would have fundamental consequences for the structure of the postwar world as we have known it and for America's relationship to its most important alliances; and
- that it would alter the prospects for security and progress for *all* nations.

## THE COMMUNIST PARTIES AND WESTERN DEMOCRACIES

Those who take a less grave view of these prospects often claim that the European Communist parties are independent of Moscow, that they have been effectively democratized and assimilated, and that they therefore pose no international issue in the broader East-West context.

It is true enough that the centrifugal and polycentric tendencies in the Communist world are among the most striking developments of our age. These schisms, moreover, are made doubly intense by the passions of a quasi-religious battle over what is true dogma and what is heresy. Symptomatic is the fact that the Soviet Union has used military force in the postwar period only against other Communist countries — in East Berlin, in Hungary, in Czechoslovakia, and on the Sino-Soviet border. The Sino-Soviet conflict may indeed be the most profound and potentially explosive current international conflict. Nor is there a serious observer who disputes that the Communist parties in Western Europe have in fact occasionally demonstrated some degree of independence from the Soviet Union.

But this hardly exhausts the issue. For we must ask: In what sense and on what issues are they independent? And what are the objective consequences for the West of their policies and programs?

We are entitled to certain skepticism about the sincerity of declarations of independence which coincide so precisely with electoral self-interest. One need not be a cynic to wonder at the decision of the French Communists, traditionally perhaps the most Stalinist party in Western Europe, to renounce the Soviet concept of dictatorship of the proletariat without a single dissenting vote among 1,700 delegates, as they did at their Party Congress in February 1976, when all previous Party Congresses had endorsed the same dictatorship of the proletariat by a similar unanimous vote of 1,700 to nothing. Why was there not at least one lonely soul willing to adhere to the previous view? Much was made of this change as a gesture of independence. Now it turns out that the new Soviet constitution, in preparation for years, drops the phrase as well.

Throughout their existence, the guiding principle of the

Communist parties has been their insistence that a minority had to seize power as the vanguard of the working class and impose its views on the rest of the population. This disdain for democratic procedures — whether it is presented in the traditional form of the "dictatorship of the proletariat" or wrapped in Gramsci's more elegant phrase, "the hegemony of the working class" — is precisely what has historically distinguished the Communist from the Socialist parties. I find it hard to believe that after decades of vilifying social democracy and treating it as their mortal enemy, especially in every Communist country, Communist parties have suddenly become social democrats. Whether or not they are independent of Moscow, Communists represent a philosophy which by its nature and their own testimony stands outside the "bourgeois" framework of Western constitutional history; they are a movement that appeals to a different tradition and uses a largely misleading vocabulary.

To be sure, the French, Spanish, and Italian Communist parties have all recently declared their resolve "to work within the pluralism of political and social forces and to respect guarantees and develop all individual and collective freedoms." Enrico Berlinguer and Georges Marchais pledged their devotion to national independence and political pluralism at a conference of Communist parties in East Berlin in June 1976.

But can we take these declarations at face value? After all, Marchais has listed Bulgaria, Poland, and East Germany as countries having a "pluralistic" party system. As recently as 1972, French Communist doctrine was that "there can be no return from socialism to capitalism." And a few weeks ago, to the great irritation of their Socialist allies, the French Communists estimated the cost of the economic program of the two parties at over 100 billion dollars. The Communist program — by definition — calls for the radical transformation of society; by the very nature of their beliefs Communists will be driven to bring about institutional changes that would make their ascendance permanent.

Moreover, are these professions of the national road to communism and of devotion to democratic principle really so new? Let me read some quotations from European Communist leaders.

*First:* The crux of the matter, and we Marxists should know this well, is this: every nation will effect its transition to Socialism not by a mapped-out route, not exactly as in the Soviet Union, but by its own road, dependent on its historical, national, social, and cultural circumstances.

That was from a speech by Georgi Dimitrov, leader of the Bulgarian Communist Party, in February 1946.

*Second:* We take the view that the method of imposing the Soviet system on [our country] would be wrong, since this method does not correspond to present-day conditions of development. . . . We take the view rather that the overriding interests of the . . . people in their present-day situation prescribe a different method . . . , namely the method of establishing a democratic anti-Fascist régime, a parliamentary democratic republic with full democratic rights and liberties for the people.

That is from a proclamation of the (East) German Communist Party in June 1945.

*Third:* The great national task facing the country cannot be solved by either the Communist party or by any other party alone. The Communist party holds that it does not have a monopoly, and it does not need the monopoly, to work among the masses for the reconstruction of the new [nation]. The Communist party does not approve of the idea of a one-party system. Let the other parties operate and organize as well.

That is a statement by Erno Gero, Communist Party leader of Hungary, in November 1944.

*Fourth:* In [our country] there is a division of functions, and State power is based on parliamentary democracy. The dictatorship of the proletariat or of a single party is not essential. [Our country] can proceed and is proceeding along her own road.

That is from a speech by Władysław Gomulka, Communist Party leader of Poland, in January 1946.

*Fifth:* The Communist party seeks to attain socialism, but we are of the opinion that the Soviet system is not the only road to socialism. . . . The coalition of the Communists with other parties is not opportunistic, a temporary limited coalition, but the expression . . . of all strata of the working people. . . . We seek at present to make certain that our new democratic parliamentary methods . . . be expressed in constitutional law. If you want the view of the Communists, I can only say that they will be the strictest guardians of the new Constitution.

That is a statement by Klement Gottwald, Communist Party leader of Czechoslovakia, in January 1947.

*Sixth:* Marchais speaks of "Socialism in the colors of France." But in 1938, George Orwell described French Communist strategy as "marching behind the tricolour."

In short, what the leaders of the Western Communist parties are saying today about their affection for the processes of democracy is not significantly different from what East European Communist leaders declared with equal emphasis in the 1940s — before they seized the total power which they have never relinquished since.

Certainly Communist parties are willing to come to power by democratic means. But could they permit the democratic process to reverse what they see as the inevitable path of "historical progress"? Would they maintain the institutions — press, parties, unions, enterprises — that would represent the principal threat to their power? Would they safeguard the freedoms that could turn into instruments of their future defeat? No Communist Party that governed alone has ever done so, and the vast majority of those democratic parties which entered coalitions with European Communists are now in the indexes of history books rather than in ministries or parliaments.

The Italian Communist Party, to be sure, left the government following its disastrous defeat by the Christian Democrats in 1948. But the situation today is greatly changed. In 1948, the Communists were a far smaller party, with little regional or municipal power. They had to contend with a younger and more united Christian Democratic Party, a strong Socialist Party, and a determined Western Alliance alarmed by Stalin's adventures in Greece and Czechoslovakia. Today, Italian Communists participate in the governments of most major cities and regions, have enormous trade union strength, substantive support from intellectuals and the popular culture, and have reduced the strength of the Socialists to a fraction of what it was three decades ago.

The French Communists were similarly removed from the government in 1947, following the intensification of the Cold War. But, just as in the Italian case the following year, the popular revolt against the Communists took place within the framework of a united West with a clear perception of an external and internal threat to its survival. By contrast there are now many people on both sides of the Atlantic who have permitted themselves to be convinced that European communism is only social democracy with a Leninist face.

We cannot know with certainty whether a fundamental change has occurred in these parties' traditional goals and tactics. But their internal organization and management speak against such a view. It is not democratic pluralism but the stern Leninist precept of "democratic centralism" which continues to guide the internal structure of all European Communist parties. This is a doctrine of iron discipline, not a principle of free and open dialogue. It is a system of dogma, of a "party line," of authority and obedience, of suppression of dissent and purge of dissenters. There are too many recent instances of resorts to violence, attempts to censor newspapers and broadcasting, and efforts to control the functioning of universities to be optimistic about their character.

Only in *Western* Europe and the United States are there still illusions about the nature of Communist parties. In Eastern Europe, boredom, intellectual emptiness, inefficiency, and stultifying bureaucratism have been obvious for decades. Countries which used to be leading industrial powers have been reduced to mediocrity and stagnation; nations with long democratic traditions have seen the destruction of civil liberties and democratic practices. The countries of the West would mortgage their future if they closed their eyes to this reality. Societies that try to avoid difficult choices by making comforting assumptions about the future win no awards for restraint; they only speed their own demise.

## COMMUNIST PARTIES AND THE ATLANTIC ALLIANCE

It is sometimes asked: If the United States can deal with Communist governments in the Soviet Union, China, Eastern Europe, and even Cuba or Vietnam, why can we not accept and learn to deal with Communist parties seeking power in Western Europe? Is not the Soviet Union uneasy about the prospect of new Communist regimes that it may not be able to control?

These questions miss the central point. There is a crucial difference between managing conflict with adversaries and maintaining an alliance among friends, particularly when the prospects for stable East-West relations depend vitally on the cohesion of the Western Alliance. And even if some West European Communist parties should prove more difficult than the better disciplined satellites of East Europe, and thus pose new problems for Moscow, they would pose far more serious problems for the West.

For the key issue is not how "independent" the European Communists would be, but how Communist. The dynamics of the Communist parties and the program on which they would be elected suggest that their foreign and domestic policies are not likely to be consistent with the common purposes of the Atlantic Alliance.

The solidarity of the great industrial democracies has maintained global security for thirty years. Western collective defense provided the shield behind which the United States, Western Europe, and Japan developed the institutions of European unity and the progressive world economic system. All these relationships would be severely jeopardized if Communists came to power in allied governments.

Specifically:

*The character of the Alliance would become confused to the American people.* The signatories of the North Atlantic Treaty pledged in 1949 that "they are determined to safeguard the freedom, common heritage and civilization of their peoples, founded on the principles of democracy, individual liberty and the rule of law." If Communists entered governments in allied countries, the engagement to help maintain the military balance in Europe would lack the moral base on which it has stood for a generation. The American people would be asked to maintain their Alliance commitment on the basis of two highly uncertain, untested assumptions: that there is a new trend of communism which will in time split from Moscow, and that the West will be able to manipulate the new divisions to its advantage.

Both of these propositions are open to the most serious

doubt. No major Communist split has ever been generated or maintained by deliberate Western policy — in fact, the Soviet Union's disputes with Yugoslavia and with China had been festering for months and even years before the West became aware of them.

But even such a split — which would surely take years to develop — would hardly diminish the danger to current allied relationships. By the time it occurred, the damage to the NATO structure would probably have become irreparable. And the character of the Atlantic relationship would be totally transformed, even should the United States, for its own reasons, eventually decide to support a revisionist communism. While the United States can never be indifferent to the extension of Soviet hegemony to Western Europe, the permanent stationing of American forces in Europe could hardly be maintained for the object of defending some Communist governments against other Communist governments. Such a deployment could be justified only on the crudest balance of power grounds that would be incompatible with American tradition and American public sentiment.

This is not a personal recommendation as to a desirable policy but a judgment of stark reality. Significant participation by Communist parties in West European governments will over time undermine the moral and political basis for our present troop deployment in Europe.

*The effect on Alliance cohesion generally would be disastrous.* The Western Alliance has been held together by a system of close consultation based on shared goals and compatible philosophies. President de Gaulle cherished France's independence from the United States, but in major crises over Berlin or Soviet missiles in Cuba, he stood firmly with his allies. By the same token, Communist governments in Western Europe, however independent of Moscow they may be on intraparty issues, can be expected to demonstrate their basic Communist convictions on major international issues.

If Communist parties come to power in Western Europe, significant divergences on foreign policy would be bound to develop between Europe and the United States, and between European states in whose governments Communists participate and the others.

In February 1976, Italian Communist leader Berlinguer stated to a London *Times* interviewer that "the Soviet Union's peace policy is in the general interest of mankind." The Italian Party newspaper denounced NATO last year as "one of the fundamental instruments for American manipulation of the politics and economy of our country and Western Europe," and urged that "the relations between the countries of Western Europe and the two superpowers must be rediscussed." A leading member of the Italian Party's Central Committee was asked in a recent interview with Radio Free Europe: If the French and Italian Communist parties were in power, what would you do in the event of "a grave international crisis between the Soviet Union and the West"? He answered: "We would choose the Soviet side, of course." Such "support" of NATO as is expressed is explicitly tactical, and rests upon a distortion of détente. It is coupled with the proposition that a Soviet threat against Western Europe is inconceivable. No European Communist Party suggests that it wishes to be part of a Western Alliance to withstand Soviet expansion. And, indeed, how could Leninist parties dedicate themselves with any conviction to a military alliance whose primary purpose was and remains to counter Soviet power?

To be sure, these parties have had their differences with the Soviet Union, but in practically every case it has been on a matter of relations *within* the Communist movement. They have rarely, if ever, diverged from the Soviet position on an international issue. The Italian Communist Party has hailed the Cubans in Angola as "freedom fighters," condemned the Israeli rescue of hostages at Entebbe as an "intolerable violation of Uganda's national sovereignty," applauded Soviet policy in Africa, and denounced

America's diplomatic efforts in Southern Africa as an attempt to "save the neocolonial and military-strategic interests of imperialism."

At best, West European Communist parties can be expected to steer their basic policies closer to the so-called nonaligned bloc and in an anti-Western direction. Yugoslavia — whose independence from Moscow on East European issues is by now traditional — has emerged as a champion of anti-Western and anti-American positions on most international issues outside of Eastern Europe. Why should we expect that Communist parties in Western Europe would be more friendly to us than the most independent East European state which has been engaged for nearly three decades in an open dispute with Moscow and whose government the Kremlin has sought repeatedly to undermine?

The strong role our allies play in defending Western interests in many regions of the globe — such as President Giscard's courageous actions in Zaire — could not be expected from a nation where Communists share power. In the Middle East, in Southern Africa, in relations with the Third World, on Berlin, on arms control and European security, the parallelism of views that has existed between the United States and its European allies would almost certainly be eroded. Indeed, active opposition especially in regions of traditional European cultural and political influence is probable. In our common efforts to improve the world economy and stimulate progress in both the developed and developing worlds, in the OECD, in the Paris Conference on International Economic Cooperation, and at heads of government summits, divisions would soon be apparent. How could Atlantic unity possibly be maintained in such circumstances, even on the security issue?

*The military strength and unity of NATO would be gravely weakened.* The Communist parties of Western Europe pay lip service to NATO. In fact, it is hard to visualize how the present NATO structure could continue, with its exchange of highly classified information, its integrated military planning, and its political consultation, if Communists had a significant share of power.

The participation of Communist parties in West European governments would force a major change in NATO practices, as occurred temporarily with Portugal, which had to exclude itself from classified discussions within the organization when its own political future was in doubt. These parties are unlikely to give NATO defense a high budgetary priority. Communist parties would surely use their power to diminish the combined defense effort of Western Europe and inevitably sap our own will to pay the costs of maintaining US forces in Europe.

Furthermore, if Communists participate in a significant way in the governments of key European countries, NATO may turn by default into a largely German-American alliance. This specter could then be used in other Western European countries to undermine what remains of Atlantic cohesion. With NATO thus weakened, while the Soviet Union continued to increase its strategic and conventional strength and maintained its grips on the Warsaw Pact, the essential equilibrium of power between East and West in Europe would be fundamentally threatened. The freedom of many European countries, allied or neutral, to chart their own future would be diminished in direct proportion as the fear of Soviet power grows. Eventually, massive shifts against us would occur, not because a majority freely chose such a course, but because the upsetting of the overall balance left them no alternative.

*The hopeful progress toward European unity would be undermined.* The French and Italian Communist parties opposed the creation of the European Common Market as a conspiracy of monopoly capitalism. Until quite recently, they have consistently fought progress toward European unity. Lately they have come to accept the European Community as a fact of life; they now say they seek to make it more "democratic" and to transform it, by "a process of innovation . . . in the spheres both of institutions and of general orientations," as Berlinguer expressed it. They can be counted on to reorient the Common Market toward closer relations with the state economies of Eastern Europe and toward the more extreme of the Third World's demands for a "new international economic order." It can be assumed that they will not encourage European political unity to foster cooperation with the United States; rather they will urge it, if at all, to encourage Third Force tendencies. And over time either governments with Communist participation will pull the others toward them, or deep fissures will open up between the traditional Atlanticists and the "New Left" in the European Community. Either outcome would be destructive of European unity and Atlantic solidarity.

Thus whatever hypothesis we consider, Communist participation in governments of Western Europe will have a profound impact on the international structure as it has developed in the postwar period. We cannot be indifferent or delude ourselves that the advent of Communists to a significant share of power in Western Europe would be less than a watershed in Atlantic relationships.

## THE AMERICAN RESPONSE

The attitude of the United States toward such developments must of necessity be complex. The crucial role must be that of European governments; the final decision must be that of the European voters. We cannot substitute for either.

In the end, the Communist parties in Western Europe find their opportunities less in their inherent strength than in the demoralization, division, or disorganization of their opponents; they succeed only when the democratic system seems unable to solve the social problems of the day; when the center does not hold and societies become polarized. Violence — such as that currently tor-

menting Italy — drives many to support communism in despera-
tion, convinced that drastic remedies are required to end a state of
siege which has now spread to the press and other media.

The basic causes of Communist gains thus go deep and are
not easy to remedy. In many European countries disillusionment
with democratic government and democratic leaders is pervasive.
In an era of peace, in a world of bureaucracy and mass production, there is no galvanizing crisis and little opportunity for heroic
performance. A relativist age debunks authority and puts nothing
in its place as an organizing principle of society. Massive impersonal bureaucracy disillusions the citizen with the responsive-
ness of his government, and simultaneously makes the task of
elected officials more difficult. In too many democratic countries
the young are offered too little inspiration; their elders too often
have lost confidence in their own values. Too frequently democratic leaders are consumed by winning and holding office and are
unable to demonstrate the force of conviction and philosophical
self-assurance of their radical opponents.

The very success of Western societies in maintaining prosperity at a level undreamed of even forty years ago sometimes
contributes to their malaise. Intellectuals condemn society for ma-
terialism when it is prosperous and for injustice when it fails to
ensure prosperity. The widespread economic difficulties of the last
four years — recession and inflation unparalleled in a generation,
to a large extent induced by the extraordinary increase in oil
prices — fuel the frustration of all whose hopes for economic ad-
vancement are rebuffed. The interdependence of economies causes
inflation and recession to surge across national boundaries, compounding the sense of individual impotence.

And yet, with all these difficulties, the democratic forces of
the West have it in their power to determine whether the Communist parties have opportunities to succeed. They have the capacity to put their economies on the path of steady noninflationary
expansion. They have the intellectual capital and the resources to

usher in a new period of creativity. Anticommunism is not enough; there must be a response to legitimate social and economic aspirations, and there must be a reform of the inequities from which these antidemocratic forces derive much of their appeal. With able leadership — and Western cohesion — the democracies can overcome their challenges and usher in a period of dramatic fresh advance.

In this process it is vital that the United States encourage an attitude of resolve and conviction.

First of all, we must frankly recognize the problem that we will face if the Communists come to power in Western Europe and we must understand the practical decisions this will impose on us as a nation. We must avoid facile projections which seek to escape difficult choices by making the most favorable assumptions about what might happen. We must have a program for encouraging the forces of moderation and progress in this critical period and for rallying them should a Communist Party nonetheless prevail.

Second, we must avoid giving the impression that we consider Communist success a foregone conclusion by ostentatious association or consultation with Communist leaders or by ambiguous declarations. Communist success is not a foregone conclusion; United States hesitation or ambiguity can, however, contribute to it. Communist parties are riddled with weaknesses and internal strains, and marked by a fundamental flaw: parties that do not speak for the humane values which have inspired the peoples of the West for centuries are unlikely to appeal to a majority in a Western nation except in a moment of unsettling crisis. In no Western European country has the Communist Party ever fairly won more than about a third of the vote. Their most powerful weapons are fear, distrust, and discouragement; their principal asset is the myth of their inevitability. Therefore, we do our friends in Europe no favor if we encourage the notion that the advent of Communists and their allies into power will make little or no difference to our own attitudes and policies. I am talking less of formal statements — which depend on tactical judgments difficult for any outsider to make — than of a clear and unambiguous US attitude.

Some have argued that such a policy would be counterproductive, that it would encourage Communist protest votes. I believe the opposite to be true. On balance, I consider it important that Europe know of America's interest and concern. Many voters in allied countries value the friendship of the United States and appreciate the security supplied by the Atlantic Alliance. We should not ignore them, or demoralize them, or undercut them. The gradual gains scored by the Communist parties over the past years occurred — by definition — at the margin, among voters who had not voted Communist before; who did not vote by anti-American reflex; who for one reason or another were persuaded that the Communists have now become acceptable or indispensable.

There is no evidence that voters are influenced to vote *Communist* by American attitudes. On the contrary, the real danger may well be the other way; many usual opponents of the Communist parties may be lulled by voices, attitudes, and ambiguities in this country implying that our traditional opposition has changed. Paradoxically, we even weaken whatever moderate elements may exist in Communist movements by settling too eagerly for verbal reassurances.

If the United States has a responsibility to encourage political freedom throughout the world, we surely have a duty to leave no doubt about our convictions on an issue that is so central to the future of the Western Alliance and therefore to the future of democracy. Human rights is not an abstraction concerned only with judicial procedures and unrelated to basic questions of political and geopolitical structure. We cannot fail to reckon the setback to European freedom that will result if Communist minorities gain decisive influence in European politics; we must not close our eyes to the effect on freedom throughout the world if the global balance tips against the West.

Thirdly, the United States should conduct its policies toward its allies in a way that strengthens the moderate, progressive, and democratic governments of Western Europe. We must, on the one hand, avoid demands or lecturings which, whatever the intrinsic merit, magnify domestic fissures in European countries or the sense of impotence of European governments. At the same time, the United States can contribute to a sense of accomplishment by offering vigorous cooperation in joint efforts to solve common problems in the fields of diplomacy, arms control, energy, and economic growth. This was the purpose of the economic summits among Western leaders begun by President Ford at Rambouillet and Puerto Rico, and continued so successfully in London by President Carter.

The unity and cooperative action of the democracies are crucial to all that America does in the world. Western unity defends not only our security but our way of life and the most basic moral values of our civilization. On this we cannot be neutral. To foster these principles deserves the same dedication and commitment that inspired the most imaginative periods of American diplomacy.

The stagnant societies of the East to which I have referred serve as both a warning and a hope. They remind us that the West's latent intellectual and political vitality, even more than its material prosperity, is the envy of the world. The winds of change are ultimately blowing from the West. The men and women of *Eastern* Europe are certainly aware that the West, for all its doubt and sense of spiritual dilemma, is the vanguard of modernization, the vital source of learning and of much of modern culture, and the haven of the free human spirit. The developing countries yearning for progress also turn to the West, not the East, for assistance, support, and the measure of what man can achieve when he aspires. Our technology, our creativity, our unequaled economic vigor, not some bureaucratic doctrine of economic determinism, are the forces that will shape the future if we mobilize the energies of free peoples.

This is not the time for resignation or aquiescence. It is a time for confidence, determination, and hope. The power of free men and women and free nations acting in concert, confident of their strength and of their destiny, cannot be matched by any totalitarian regime or totalitarian movement. The spirit of freedom can never be crushed. But freedom can be lost gradually. Such a danger exists today in Western Europe, and that threat could have consequences not only in Europe but throughout the community of democracies and the world.

If we cherish freedom, we will face the peril, marshal joint efforts to overcome it, and begin a period of new fulfillment for our peoples. Western Europe, our closest partner and the cradle of much of our civilization, is too precious to us for us to do otherwise.

# THE FUTURE OF BUSINESS AND THE INTERNATIONAL ENVIRONMENT

*Address given to the first Washington meeting of the Future of Business Project of the Center for Strategic and International Studies, Georgetown University, on June 28, 1977*

N O ISSUE is more important to the future vision of international order than the ways in which the world will manage the output and distribution of goods and services. International economics has become a crucial foreign policy challenge. Central to this issue will be the relationship of business to the management of public affairs. I want to thank the Center for Strategic and International Studies for inviting me to inaugurate its Future of Business program.

A generation ago, in the period from the Great Depression to the Marshall Plan, economic concerns were at the heart of international order. The issues which we will face in the decades ahead are at least as urgent and far more subtle and complex. And the most decisive of these issues are at the intersection of economics and politics, of national and international policies, of the public and private sectors. It is essential that both policymakers and businessmen understand these important new interrelationships.

We have come a long way, and very rapidly, to the axiomatic proposition that international business depends decisively on international politics. We have come a long way, that is to say, from the day when Adam Smith could suggest that government should content itself with the modest responsibility of the maintenance of justice and the construction of good roads and otherwise serve mankind by remitting the management of the wealth of nations to the unseen land of private decision. We have come a long way from the nineteenth century, when the United States accounted for very little in the scale of world economics.

We have come a long way even from the decades between the wars, when we strode big on the world economic scene, participated actively in world economic issues, and yet stolidly maintained an isolationist foreign policy in all other respects. We shall never forget the paradox of Cordell Hull's championing free trade at the same time that the Congress insisted that we ignore the darkening clouds across the Atlantic.

We have learned that America's neglect of the requirements of political stability was a major contributor to the disasters of the 1940s which shattered the economic as well as the political order. We have understood that a strong American role — political, military, and economic — in world affairs is indispensable to peace, security, and prosperity. Enlightened American leadership in international diplomacy is equally vital to world order *and* to the flourishing of the world economy. A coherent public policy must address with equal insight the requirements of security and the management of the economic system. Thus the future of American business will require the highest degree of sensitivity to the political framework in which it functions and to the great coming changes in the world political process.

The map of the world's economy has changed as radically as the world political map. A generation ago, 51 countries joined to form the United Nations; today the world community numbers nearly 150 nations. Each country is, or attempts to be, a discrete economic unit, each with its balance of payments problems, its trade policies, its attitude to investment, and its hopes and aspirations for a better life for its people. The global economic system has grown massively in scale and complexity.

A generation ago, only one major nation, the United States, had emerged from World War II with its economy intact and flourishing; today, Western Europe and Japan have joined us as major producers of the world's manufactured products and as centers of finance. The Bretton Woods conference established the institutions of an international monetary system after World War II. Today, the colossal expansion of world trade and the dispersal of economic power have compelled major restructuring of that system. Whereas George Kennan thirty years ago in his seminal "containment" article could suggest that there were only five small pockets of significant economic activity in the world, today the oil producers have become major contenders in the economic arena, the Communist nations are factors in the world economy, and aspiring economic powers like Mexico, Brazil, and Korea are gaining new importance in world affairs.

Thirty years ago, the Marshall Plan was launched with American resources and European effort to rebuild Western Europe from the devastation of war. Today, the experience of the Marshall Plan is clearly inadequate for the vast enterprise of economic development in scores of new nations. In Europe and Japan, the social forms and technical skills of a modern economy were already present, and only capital had to be replaced. Political stability was threatened above all by the gap between expectation and reality. It is now clear that in the less developed parts of the world supplying capital is not enough; there is a desperate need for technology and trained manpower. And the relationship between economic progress and political stability has emerged as anything but automatic.

We are in the midst of a revolution that we have only begun to perceive. The distinguished sociologist Daniel Bell has recently observed that forty years ago the response in every country to the Great Depression was to strengthen the nation-state; national government came into its own as the manager of economic and social policy. Today we see citizens in many societies losing faith in the relevance of government to their personal concerns, and there are tendencies of fragmentation; at the same time economic problems such as inflation surge across national boundaries and are at the margin of governments' ability to control. Bell observes that the national state has become too small for the big problems in life, and too big for the small problems. We face a pervasive challenge to the adequacy of the institutions and principles by which we have governed ourselves.

The next decade will determine whether the industrial democracies will be able to manage their economic policies and keep social peace in the face of a probably lower long-term growth rate in the 1980s; whether and in what fashion the developing countries will advance their economic, social, and political well-being, and on what terms of confrontation or cooperation with the West. It is not yet clear what long-term role the Soviet Union, East Europe, and China will play in the world economic system. The full implications of the looming energy crisis have yet to work themselves out. We cannot know perfectly how any of these developments will affect political events.

But we can be certain that economics and politics will be closely related, and that American decisions and American leadership, for better or worse, will shape the response of the industrial democracies and thereby of the rest of the world. Without us there can be no progress; if we fail, we risk recession, confrontation, and chaos.

Modern economic history also suggests that the contribution and creativity of the free enterprise system will be central to that response. Wherever countries of comparable resources have run the race together — Austria and Czechoslovakia, West and East Germany, Greece and Bulgaria, South and North Korea — the economy with a significant private sector has clearly done more in fulfilling the aspirations of its people than has its Socialist counterpart. The world community cannot ignore the affairs of business if it is successfully to shape a new political structure that serves peace and the well-being of mankind. Conversely, the private sector can no longer ignore the political environment if it is to make its contribution to an expanding world economy in which it can flourish.

I would like to discuss a number of current economic issues, drawing attention to their political significance, the imperative of international cooperation to address them, and the role of business in helping to solve them. Specifically:

- the common economic problems of the industrial democracies;
- the emerging relationship with the developing countries; and
- the beginnings of interaction between the industrial democracies and the nonmarket economies of the Communist world.

## THE FUTURE OF BUSINESS AND THE INDUSTRIAL DEMOCRACIES

The future of business is inseparable from the future of industrial democracy. Western Europe, North America, and Japan produce 65 percent of all the goods and services generated in the world. They account for 75 percent of its trade. Their economic performance drives international commerce and finance; their investment, technology, managerial genius, and agricultural productivity are the dynamic force of prosperity everywhere. They are the world's bankers and the world's inventors. Critics of the West, in the Communist world and elsewhere, have disparaged our system for decades, but they have not solved any of their own problems. Ironically, they now turn to the industrial democracies for the technology, the techniques of analysis, planning, and management, the industrial systems, and the marketing skills which their own systems seem incapable of generating.

But this relative success story is no guarantee for the future. Realism compels us to note the signs of strain. The political future in several nations of the West may well be clouded by shortfalls in the output of goods and services, or breakdowns of the financial system. In too many countries demands for real increases in wages, coupled with the insistent pressures to expand public services and public sector expenditures, have generated increasingly complicated inflationary pressures at the very moment when the increase in the cost of imported energy has added its own impetus to both inflation and recession. These demands cannot possibly all be met simultaneously. An attempt to do so is bound to disrupt and ultimately to demoralize the political system. There is a grave danger of an erosion of the legitimacy of government and a prospect of basic changes in the domestic structure in Europe and perhaps even in Japan.

It is not beyond the realm of possibility that one or more of the Communist parties of Western Europe will gain entry into national governments — an event which would mark a watershed in postwar relationships. It is not beyond imagination, either, that some nations will find the discipline required to establish priorities among levels of demand too burdensome to permit their continued adherence to the liberal trading system, and that they will instead revert to protectionism and isolationism. Finally, it could happen that because of disparities of growth rates, balances of payments positions, and international competitiveness, the momentum of European unification would further decelerate and the political cohesion of the West in international negotiations and institutions would break down. The consequences for business would, of course, be ominous.

The future of the world economy and indeed of Western political cohesion will depend on the capacity of the industrial democracies to meet these challenges. No one country can hope to address its problems alone. The unity of the democracies, demonstrated in substantive cooperation on concrete issues, is one way — perhaps the only way — to restore the self-assurance of Western societies and their confidence that they are the masters of their destiny. This must therefore be one of the fundamental priorities in our foreign policy, which has been eloquently stated by President Carter at the London summit a few weeks ago.

The United States cannot possibly carry all the burdens, devise all the programs, or provide all the resources, either for international security or for economic development. But the other industrial democracies, who are also our major trading partners, have grown in strength to the point where a sharing of leadership and responsibility becomes both necessary and desirable. American policy in every administration of both parties for over thirty years has therefore been to encourage Europe's strength and economic and political unity as well as a close relationship with Japan. This solidarity, which began with collective defense, has deepened in recent years to embrace, in addition, common problems of economic policy, arms control, diplomacy to reduce tensions with the East, and initiatives in the dialogue with the Third World.

This cohesion rests not only on pragmatic grounds but also on a common moral foundation. It is no accident that our closest partners and interlocutors on every international issue are the countries that share our most fundamental values.

One of the central tasks on the agenda of the industrial democracies must continue to be the vitality of the global economy and the harmonization of growth policies among the economies of the West. Consistent expansion without inflation requires not only sound national policy but an increasing coordination among the nations in the industrial world. We must learn more effectively to synchronize our national decision-making so that national policies can complement and reinforce each other, and not be at cross-purposes.

This was the purpose of the economic summit meetings at Rambouillet in 1975, in Puerto Rico in 1976, and most recently in London. This was the task which Secretary Vance pursued last week in the ministerial meeting of the Organization for Economic Cooperation and Development, the permanent economic grouping of the industrial democracies. These were not mere ceremonial exercises. They represented the beginnings of systematic consultation among the economic powers of the free world. We must now consider how we can move beyond consultation to real coordination of growth strategies and of other basic economic policies.

For it is important to face the fact that the industrial democracies have been more effective in devising the procedure than the reality of coordination. They have been torn between the knowledge of interdependence and the temptations of shifting their problems to their partners. They have invoked the rhetoric of cooperation, but they have been unwilling to subject what have traditionally been domestic decisions to international agreement. As a result, they have not been able to mount with full effectiveness the coordinated attack on the twin pressures of demand and inflation that must succeed if democracy is to survive. To achieve a true coordination must be a major goal of our foreign policy.

## THE NORTH-SOUTH DIALOGUE AND THE FUTURE OF BUSINESS

In the last several years, the poorer nations, in a variety of forums and with varying levels of stridency, have stated their demands for the renovation of international economic relations. They claim a greater voice in the decisions that affect them and a more just share of the global prosperity. The industrial nations, in response, have reiterated their continued commitment to the open system of world trade and investment. As the final ministerial meeting of the Conference on International Economic Cooperation in Paris made clear, the North-South dialogue has so far failed to establish an agreed frame of reference. And it is plain enough that if it deteriorates to a level of confrontation and conflict, the gulf between the rich and the poor will widen ominously.

This prospect would be unfortunate for all. The United States, as the world's strongest economy, would be injured less than others by an environment of hostility and autarky. But the outbreak of economic warfare between North and South would damage even our own well-being. It would be a long-term threat to the open economic system which has nurtured our prosperity and that of the world for a generation. And it would be, as well, incompatible with basic American values and the fundamental American instinct for a world of peace and cooperation.

Although the developing countries would suffer the most, it is their stale rhetoric of confrontation, their adherence to Marxist doctrines that have never worked in countries where they have been implemented, and their insistence on bloc tactics that are at the heart of the problem. At the same time, we must be careful to avoid the conclusion that because the developing world is given to overstatement, all its concerns are unfounded. The developing nations do have legitimate demands for equity, for a greater voice, and for increased opportunity. But they cannot escape the reality that their future depends on the vitality of the world economic system. Attempts to wield bloc economic power and to frame the issue as one of guilt and retribution will undermine both the receptivity of governments and the public support which are essential if the industrial democracies are to respond creatively and compassionately to the legitimate aspirations of the developing world.

Overestimation by developing countries of their ability to manipulate raw material prices, following the model of the oil cartel, has been one of the causes of the recent failure of the North-South dialogue. But oil is a special case. It is unlikely that even the most imaginative schemes could alter the long-term market prospects for any other commodity. One basic reason is that the industrialized countries, particularly the United States, Canada, Australia, and the Soviet Union, are themselves major producers of commodities like iron ore, nickel, copper, cotton, and sugar. In addition, there are technological possibilities for substitution which make it difficult to assert in other commodities the kind of control over supply and price which the oil cartel enjoys.

Thus, it is high time to face the fact that the issue of new market schemes for raw materials will not be determined primarily through economic pressure from developing countries. It will also depend on what happens in the industrialized countries — how private producers or brokers or investors in those commodities react; whether governments on political and moral grounds are prepared to take account of the inequity of excessive fluctuations in prices for countries dependent on a single commodity; and whether the developed nations perceive that they have an interest in proposals which would stabilize prices around a market trend, avoid artificial limits on supply, and increase new productive investment. Tactics of confrontation are likely to be counterproductive; both developed and developing countries have a major interest in improving the atmosphere of the dialogue, as well as the system itself. It remains to be seen whether their domestic imperatives permit them to do so.

The business corporation which functions across national borders has been at the very heart of the North-South debate. In many developing nations, it is charged with basing production and export decisions on global strategies rather than on individual national interests; it is accused of corrupting life-styles toward the wasteful and conspicuous habits of more wealthy societies, of manipulating profits by artificial transfer pricing between subsidiaries, and of suffocating local competitors.

It would be wrong to pretend that there has never been any evidence to support these charges. Some of the criticism has a basis in fact. But many of the critics do so out of a philosophical bias that makes the facts of individual cases superfluous or irrelevant. The distinguished Brazilian economist Roberto Campos has called the inflamed rhetoric "escapism and demonology" —

escapism, as an effort to externalize the responsibility for poverty; demonology, to lay the blame on the multinational corporation. It is irrational to fear the multinationals for their vast supposed powers of manipulation, when those corporations are far less inclined to such adventures than are governments; with all due respect, they are institutionally and conceptually incapable of managing such efforts consistently or effectively.

Nor have we in our own country settled on a balanced view of how to deal with international business. The revelation two years ago that some firms had made illicit payments sparked a regulatory race between several public agencies to assert jurisdiction and capture public attention. The destabilizing effects in Japan and elsewhere are matters of historical record. One need not condone bribery or ignore the need to improve international business ethics to prefer a system of domestic business regulation which avoids such assaults on the interests and domestic structures of our closest allies.

The multinational enterprise as we know it today is, in fact, an effective vehicle for the development of science and technology, for the application of new knowledge to the world's resources, for the management of the international capital markets, and for the promotion of trade and commerce among nations. No foreseeable increase in public assistance can come close to meeting the needs of the developing countries. Private capital alone can close the gap and without many of the conditions and restrictions that governments are likely to attach. Moreover, no government or group of governments can possibly deal with *all* of the developing countries. But *many* developing countries by their own initiative can create conditions to attract private capital whether or not donor governments look with favor on every aspect of their national policies.

Public assistance to development will continue to be important. The flow of resources through the international financial institutions such as the World Bank and IDA, as well as bilateral aid, can and should be increased. The United States has a responsibility to raise its inadequate levels of official development assistance and to remove the encumbrances that successive Congresses multiply.

But it is increasingly plain also that public aid cannot be expected to do the whole job. The developing countries must look increasingly to private investment for the capital resources they need for growth. Latin America, for example, has progressed further and faster in the last decade than any other region of the developing world. It has done so while shifting from public to private sources of external capital, and probably for that reason. In the era of the Alliance for Progress in the early Sixties, most of Latin America's external capital was public; today, more than 80 percent of it is from the private sector.

To suggest that the nation-state lacks the capability to discipline the multinational corporation, by either negotiation, persuasion, or compulsion, is a counsel of despair and runs counter to all experience. All developing countries have the power to ensure that private business, including foreign private business, comports itself in accord with public priorities. Yet no country can hope for real, long-term growth if it isolates itself from or systematically attacks an instrument so well suited to deal with the commercial, financial, and technological tasks of the modern world.

In fact, the conflict over the role of the private business firm in the developing world threatens to turn into a vicious circle. Excessive suspicions of the purposes and policies of the foreign firms treat business as an enemy rather than a collaborator. Managers of transnational enterprises are thereby given an incentive to maximize short-term profits and bury income by fictitious transfer pricing.

A serious responsibility thus falls first on business firms and secondly on governments. Business must show sensitivity to the social purposes and political goals of the countries in which it is established. It must represent what is best in America; it must not lend itself to discriminatory practices based on race or religion; its conduct must reflect this country's standards of fair play, honest dealing, and goodwill. It must make a serious contribution not only to the economic but also to the social development of the host country. The few notorious cases of illicit payments have stirred apprehension and undermined support for international business both at home and abroad; they cast a cloud over the vast majority of firms whose conduct is beyond reproach.

At the same time, it is one of the urgent tasks of governments to make clear, on an agreed basis, the ground rules for foreign investment. Developing countries have a right to ensure that private capital is admitted in areas or ways consistent with the national priorities and legitimate regulations of a sovereign government. But investors and the industrial nations have a right to know in advance what the ground rules are, and not to have them altered arbitrarily and capriciously in the middle of the game. Both sides clearly have obligations; both sides can benefit from agreed principles cooperatively achieved.

These agreed principles should focus on the instruments of public policy which can minimize the temptation to collusive market practices. They should strengthen the incentives for multiple firm markets, effective competition, local entrepreneurship, and domestic financial institutions, and lay down clear and predictable guidelines and rules of the road. By turning to these practical steps, we can open up new and important opportunities for transnational enterprises to serve what have become the two commanding concerns of the developing countries — access to capital resources and the transfer of technology.

To an increasing degree, it will be the private firm that will be the vehicle for the technology transfer which the developing world requires and demands. This concept — the *quality* of capital investment — is a major concern of those developing nations that have already made significant progress and have become important actors on the world economic scene. Most of the new knowledge, skills, and techniques that will be needed by developing countries in the years to come are in the inventory of private industry. The bulk of that technology is in the West. Thus, it is in the interest of the industrial democracies as well as in the interest of the developing countries to enhance the incentive of our private sector to adapt its storehouse of know-how and skills to opportunities in the developing world.

It is clear that the solution to technology transfer will not be found exclusively in the relationship of the private firm to the host country. Governments of the industrial nations must assume a major responsibility. New agreed practices of international cooperation and new institutions which have the confidence of all parties are needed to provide a framework of public commitment and private incentive within which the multinational corporation can make a constructive contribution to development in the decade ahead.

There will be ample room for creative thinking. If I may refer again to the question of raw materials, the dependence of most developing countries on commodity export earnings is painfully obvious. And yet, because of the tensions and uncertainties which attend the question of private foreign investment in new commodity projects, the vast bulk of mineral investments today is being made, not in the poor countries of the world, but in the industrial democracies. If the trend continues over the long term, commodity earnings for the less developed countries will be far below what they might be, and prices will be higher for everyone. We need, not stagnation or investment, but policy initiatives to assist the developing countries to mobilize the capital, technology, and management skills to produce the commodity resources they have in such abundance.

At the Nairobi meeting of the UNCTAD [United Nations Conference on Trade and Development] last year I suggested an International Resources Bank, which could act as intermediary or partner with the host countries and foreign investors; there is some interest now in exploring ways in which the World Bank might play that role in a similar pattern of triangular relationships. Whatever the institution, it is important that we search for new ways to reduce the noncommercial risks for resource investment, and thus promote greater flows of investment capital for worthy projects on reasonable terms, in the interests of both producers and consumers.

In this and in a host of other areas, it is time the world community accepted the legitimacy of private capital flows. Business has an immense future, of opportunity and responsibility, in helping to meet the development challenge. There is no more serious issue for the prospects of private commerce than its role in the relationship between rich and poor in the years to come.

## BUSINESS AND OUR FUTURE ECONOMIC RELATIONS WITH THE EAST

New trade and financial relationships with the nations of East Europe, the Soviet Union, and the People's Republic of China will also transform the landscape for business in the next several decades. In recent years the Communist countries to a greater or lesser degree have abandoned their traditional insistence on autarky and begun to move toward greater economic interchange with the industrial democracies. As their economies have become more sophisticated, their demand for consumer goods, high technology, food grains, and a variety of other products has grown comparably.

A rapid and sudden expansion of East-West trade has come about — and a consequent explosion of Western lending to finance that trade. Estimates of the total new debt, public and private, to finance the flow from the West to the East have ranged from $27 to $45 billion.

The desirability of East-West trade and its impact on overall East-West relations have been the subject of intense debate. One school of thought holds that trade and finance automatically serve to restrain Soviet policy. Hence the more intense the mutual interaction between the industrial democracies and the Communist nations, the more likely that the Soviet Union will show a sense of responsibility in international affairs. The opposing view argues that *any* trade will inevitably strengthen the Communist economy and ultimately its military potential. Therefore it should be tied to specific conditions, especially the humane evolution of the Soviet domestic system. This was the basis for Congressional action linking Most Favored Nation status to Soviet emigration practices.

I believe *both* approaches to be one-sided. The relation between increased trade and a responsible foreign policy is *not* automatic. After all, World War I broke out under conditions of nearly free trade. Only if the balance of power is maintained and Soviet adventurism is resisted can economic relations be expected to have an impact on Soviet conduct. A great deal depends, moreover, on what the trade consists of, what long-term domestic commitments it implies, how open-ended is the nature of the credit, and whether the industrial democracies or the Communist nations would suffer more from its interruption.

Many opponents of increased East-West trade also vastly oversimplify the problem. There is no question that because of the many possibilities of the diversion of resources inherent in the modern economy, almost any kind of trade can indirectly benefit military potential. But this must be weighed against the fact that a carefully and prudently designed trade and credit policy is bound to create vested interests that can act as an incentive for responsible conduct. The balance can best be struck if projects are approved on an individual basis, rather than through open-ended credits, through long-term projects whose possible termination involves a serious cost, rather than through the delivery of integrated plants in a very brief period of time.

There is no question that Communist nations are prepared to pay *some* price for increased trade. But it is important to understand what this price is and not to act as if it could be exacted mechanically in every field by unilateral demand. As a general proposition public concessions are more likely to be obtainable in the field of international conduct, with respect to which foreign countries have a defined interest and legal standing, than in matters traditionally considered the subject of domestic policy.

The following principles should, in my view, guide East-West trade:

1. East-West trade cannot be "free." It must be subject to some political control and some political conditions. All of the industrial democracies have agreed to this principle, though they have applied it with varying degrees of conviction.

2. It is the responsibility of governments to make certain that these controls make sense, that they promote clear-cut and attainable objectives in both what they prohibit and what they permit.

3. Uniform standards must be applied by the industrial democracies so that self-restraint in some area by one country does not turn into a windfall economic opportunity for another to the detriment of both.

4. Credits should not be open-ended but tied to specific projects.

5. Projects should be sufficiently long-term so that there is a serious penalty in their termination, and they should be decided on the basis of whether their termination is a greater penalty to the industrial democracies or to the Communist side.

6. Conditions should be related in general to foreign policy

actions and not to demands that sovereign nations will never accept as a result of public pressure from foreigners.

Such a strategy requires a high degree of discipline and public understanding. American business must reflect these qualities, which I am frank to say it has not always done. On the one hand many businessmen encourage a rhetorical anticommunism that seems more concerned with liturgical obeisance than practical achievement. On the other hand they tend to resist — in the name of free enterprise — any attempt to control the level of trade or the rate of credits or to relate them to concrete foreign policy developments. I remember with a well-suppressed nostalgia how the Administration of which I was part, after years of being attacked for "selling out" on the grain deals of 1972, was castigated unmercifully in 1976 for injecting itself into grain sales when it did so for the purpose of bringing about a long-term agreement, rather than a one-time sale, and also responsible Soviet conduct in trouble spots such as the Middle East. I hope a more sophisticated approach will be possible in the years ahead.

Equally important is a unified strategy on the part of the industrial democracies. When the restraint of one becomes the windfall of another, it encourages not Communist responsibility but a strategy that divides the industrial democracies and uses their short-sighted obsession with immediate gains to undermine their long-term security. For years there was an intense debate in the United States about extending credits to the Soviet Union, which were never planned to exceed one billion dollars and would have been tied to specific projects and conditions of international restraint. Within two years of the enactment of the Stevenson and Jackson amendments, other industrial democracies had extended open-ended credits exceeding ten billion dollars.

The need for a conscious and deliberate strategy among the industrial democracies for East-West trade will become ever more urgent as the scale of East-West trade grows. It was to the end of developing a common strategy that in 1976 the United States suggested to the OECD a comprehensive study of the entire East-West economic relationship and its implications. One result was the agreement that the OECD nations would restrain for one year their temptation to compete on export credit terms. Another result was an OECD study to look into both the economic and political implications of the new trade relationships.

These are questions which require an urgent answer: What are the real sources of financing for East-West trade? To what extent does the increased debt of the East to the West mask payment risks? How do we ensure economic reciprocity? How do we prevent dumping and other unfair trade practices? How should Communist countries relate to international economic institutions? Are we now effectively coordinating export policies or are some nations evading the gentleman's agreement? At what point does the West become vulnerable to demands that it extend special favors to East European exports? Will the East European nations argue that they require favored treatment if they are to repay their debts? What are the consequences to the sensitive political relationship between the industrial democracies and the Soviet Union?

The economic strength of the industrial democracies is one of our greatest assets in relations with the Communist countries. It underpins our military strength as well as the cohesion of the democratic nations. If managed with wisdom and prudence, it also offers prospects for affecting Communist conduct in a constructive way. But it can also hasten demoralization and confusion if driven by short-term considerations of domestic or national advantage rather than by a clear-cut strategy. Trade with the Communist countries may be a matter of business, but it also involves international issues of the gravest consequences. How the governments of the industrial democracies deal with this challenge will determine the international environment in which foreign policy as well as private business is conducted for years to come.

# CONCLUSION

America's economic vitality is our greatest asset. It is the product of the creative spirit of a free and industrious people and of an economic system that gives opportunity to private incentive. It is the foundation of our prosperity, our military strength, and constructive relationships in a world of peace.

I have discussed some of our foreign policy concerns — the great importance of our economic cooperation with the other industrial democracies, the role of private enterprise in economic development, and the implications of doing business with Communist countries. In every area, political and economic objectives intersect. In every area, private enterprise, with sensitivity to the broad national framework and by doing what business is good at, can make a vast contribution to the world's welfare and to international peace. It is more essential than ever that American private enterprise understand the political context — not only the political conditions in the host country where it does business, but also the overall framework of America's international responsibilities.

As a nation we must understand that we can neither dominate the world nor escape from it. For the first time in our history we are permanently involved in international affairs. This is a heavy responsibility, but also an historic opportunity. Our fellow democracies look to us for leadership. Our adversaries watch for weakness or a flagging will, which to them spells opportunity. The developing world needs our assistance, our advice, our understanding, and our compassion. This is a challenge that summons the best qualities of Americans — ingenuity, dedication, pride, confidence, and moral stamina.

Much of the world now bears the imprint of the creative American spirit. We have achieved great things, and even greater achievement is needed to master the future. In a world of new complexities and high hopes, Americans can show once again that we will meet our challenges.

# THE ENERGY CRISIS AND WORLD ORDER

*Remarks made on August 3, 1977, to the annual meeting of the National Conference of State Legislators in Detroit, Michigan*

M Y SUBJECT today is the energy crisis — a problem that is at the intersection of the public policy concerns that you wrestle with from day to day, and the global and strategic issues with which I have been involved.

A Gallup Poll in the spring of 1977 produced the startling result that only half of the American public knew that the United States must import oil to meet its energy needs, and only 17 percent had a perception of just how great our dependence is. When such a large proportion of our population is unaware of one of our most urgent national problems, it is difficult to gain public support for a major program even when our peril is already clear and in another decade could become overwhelming. We face a massive challenge to leadership at all levels of our society. You in this audience have a major role to play. However much national and state leaders may debate about specific aspects of the energy problem, we all have a major responsibility to educate the American public about its reality, its gravity, and about the urgency of a coherent strategy.

The energy crisis is not just a technical problem; it is not an abstract playground for specialists. It has wide-ranging implications for our daily lives and some of our deepest values. Energy is central to our own economy. It affects our jobs, prices, and prosperity. And internationally the energy crisis has global dimensions; it is one of the most fundamental challenges to international stability in a generation. It threatens the vitality of the world economy. And for the first time in our history, a small group of nations controlling a scarce resource could over time be tempted to pressure us into foreign policy decisions not dictated by our national interest.

The question is quite simply whether energy will bring about the destruction of the system of world order we have been building slowly and painfully over the last two decades, or whether it will serve as the instrument and vital proof of our common progress. The energy crisis therefore goes beyond the technical problem of establishing a better balance between supply and demand. It is the supreme test of nations' ability to live together on this shrinking planet, to prevent this increasingly scarce resource from leading to major conflict, and, above all, to understand and act upon the mutual dependence of different nations — of producer and consumer, developed and developing nations, the wealthy and debt-ridden.

I believe that in the final analysis the interests of the nations of the world are, though different, complementary. But that complementarity is not self-evident; a new commitment to international cooperation will not emerge from the crisis of the last four years automatically. It is the supreme task of statesmanship for our age to create out of the elements of our mutual dependence a new dedication to positive collaboration, and in this way to turn the energy challenge into a powerful positive force for world cooperation, order, and progress.

## THE ENERGY CHALLENGE AND ITS CONSEQUENCES

What is the energy crisis?

The last three decades have been a history of our increasing dependence on imported energy. In 1950, the United States was virtually self-sufficient in oil. In 1960, our reliance on foreign oil had grown to 16 percent of our requirements. In 1973, the year of the embargo and the massive price increase, America's dependence had doubled to 35 percent. Since then our dependence has *grown*, not diminished; in the winter months of this year, oil imports for the first time in our history reached 50 percent of our oil consumption — a development which only two years ago was not expected until the 1980s.

When the United States was self-sufficient, or a net exporter of oil, not only were we invulnerable to embargoes but we also had some influence over the world price. We could go far toward ensuring that the world economy had available to it adequate supplies of oil at reasonable prices.

In the last two decades conditions have changed dramatically. We have become net importers of oil and on a growing scale. Western Europe's and Japan's energy needs increased rapidly. Developing countries around the world began their own efforts toward industrialization, and in consequence became for the first time major consumers of energy. Prices remained low. And so for two decades the world economic system was based on the expectation of cheap and plentiful petroleum, while supply, except in the Middle East, fell far behind the explosive energy demand.

The effect on the United States of this structural change in the world energy market was dramatic. As we grew increasingly dependent on outside oil, we became vulnerable to external manipulation of price and interruption of our supply.

It was against this background that OPEC began to make its influence felt. Forged into an effective mechanism for agreement on prices and production among the few nations in the world that were oil exporters, OPEC embarked on what in 1973 became a successful effort to quadruple the world price of oil. In the same year, in an added demonstration of the central role of petroleum in the world's economy, the major producers cut off their exports to certain countries during the Arab-Israeli war.

These events made explicit the energy crisis which had been building for decades. They caused an immediate economic crisis both in this country and around the world. A drop of only 10 percent of our imported oil, lasting less than half a year, cost Americans half a million jobs and over ten billion dollars of national output. The massive price increases of 1973 added at least five percentage points to the price index, contributing to our worst inflation since World War II. It set the stage for a serious recession, in this country and worldwide, from which we are only now recovering.

Internationally, the energy crisis reduced the annual growth rate of the industrial countries by 1.2 percent and accelerated the average rate of inflation in the industrialized world by 3 percent. It has also had a massive adverse effect on the balance of payments of all the industrial nations. Since 1973, the oil-consuming countries have paid $367 billion in oil import bills to the thirteen OPEC countries; this is the equivalent of a huge excise tax and constitutes one of the greatest and most sudden transfers of wealth in human history. Today, each 10 percent price increase adds an additional $14 billion to the OPEC balances. For the United States, the quadrupled oil price worsened our balance of payments by $36.4 billion in 1976 alone. To put it another way: President Carter has stated that this year our balance of payments deficit is running at a rate of $25 billion a year; without oil imports, we would be running a surplus of $20 billion a year. Oil imports mark a $45 billion difference, which over time could spell an economic disaster.

The enormous surplus earnings of the oil producers overhang the world economy. They are a factor of instability even if not manipulated for political motives. In another Middle East crisis the vast accumulated petrodollars could become a weapon against the world monetary and financial system.

Since the dramatic events of 1973, America's dependence

on imported oil has increased by nearly 50 percent despite the efforts of three Presidents to mobilize an effective national response to the energy challenge. This growing dependence is intolerable. Even when the oil producers behave responsibly and seek to be moderate — as they have in recent years — their decisions are determined by *their* conception of their interests, priorities, and political choices, and not by ours. Our ability to conduct a fair and responsible foreign policy according to *our* values and *our* choices is constrained. Our country's freedom of action in foreign policy is to that degree circumscribed.

If the economic and political consequences of the energy crisis are severe for the United States, the impact on other countries more dependent on imported oil is correspondingly greater. Simultaneous recession and inflation — stagflation — has created severe problems in many countries, including many of our allies in Europe. Political and social difficulties that were already at the margin of governments' ability to manage threaten in some cases to get out of control. Economic crisis was a rude shock to large numbers of ordinary people in Western Europe whose aspirations had been raised so dramatically in the years since the war.

Thus, too much of Western Europe of the Seventies has become fertile ground for social friction and political turmoil within nations, and for economic conflict between them. The energy crisis has hampered the progress of European unity. It has strengthened the hand of opponents of democracy as democratic governments and moderate leaders have come under severe attack for failing to solve their economic problems, to a degree not experienced since the Twenties and Thirties. If Communist parties come to power in Western Europe, it will mark a tragic watershed in America's relationship to its alliances, transforming the North Atlantic Alliance as well as the purposes and practices of European integration. The irony is that some of the most conservative and anti-Communist governments in the world will have contributed to this state of affairs.

Even short of this prospect, the consequences for the cohesion of the Western Alliance are grave. Nations in economic travail are inevitably tempted to resort to protectionism in a desperate effort to keep jobs and markets at home. The result can be a vicious spiral of shrinking trade and further economic deterioration for all nations. Today, even while the industrial democracies are embarked on the difficult process of recovery, protectionist pressures are high and still mounting. This is because the recovery is uneven, and unemployment remains a problem almost everywhere.

Nor is the impact of the oil crisis confined to the industrial nations. In fact, it is the nations of the developing world that suffer most from the massive balance of payments deficits caused by the oil price rises. Indeed, the severest blow to the economic development of new nations has come not from the "imperialist exploitation" so loudly assailed in international forums but from an arbitrary price increase by their Third World brethren. The developing countries do not have the means, as the industrial nations have, to pass on the price rises to some extent to other nations in exports of manufactures. If they are to be able even to feed themselves they must achieve agricultural modernization, which depends on chemical fertilizers that are petroleum-based. The higher energy costs are to the developing nations permanent, chronic, and massive. The increase in their energy costs now in fact equals the total flow of external economic aid they receive. The entire world's assistance thus barely enables them to stand still.

In short, the energy crisis has placed at risk the entire range of our foreign policy. It mortgages the prospects of our own economy; it weakens the industrial democracies economically and potentially militarily; it undermines the world economy; and it frustrates the hope for progress of most of the new nations.

# RESPONDING TO THE ENERGY CHALLENGE

Many of the challenges this country faces in international affairs are unavoidable, as other nations grow inevitably in strength and as the specter of nuclear warfare overshadows the planet. But the threat that oil, and its price and supply, pose to the national interest and world order can be significantly reduced by determined action — at home and in cooperation with others. The failure to do so will be a blow to *all* our national purposes. To be sure, the crisis will evolve slowly, almost imperceptibly, and its full consequences may not be apparent for a decade. But when our vulnerability threatens our standard of well-being and when our destiny and that of our allies has become hostage to unpredictable decisions, shall we then tell our people that, knowing our peril, we absorbed ourselves in sterile domestic debate and were afraid to put before them the relatively minor sacrifices and inconveniences that could have avoided a calamity?

The United States is in a unique and fortunate position which imposes on us, for that very reason, a responsibility of leadership and a duty to be resolute. Our allies cannot aspire to reduce their dependence significantly by their own efforts. We can — and in so doing we are in a position to affect the condition of all nations psychologically as well as materially. The United States has the opportunity to create a new unity of purpose among the democracies on an issue of vital common concern; to give direction to the world's tentative steps toward wider patterns of fruitful cooperation.

The United States needs, most of all, an energy strategy. First, there must be recognition of the severity of our present circumstances — by leaders, legislatures, and public. The steps that are taken must not be random responses but elements of a coherent strategy that links both domestic and foreign concerns.

Such a strategy requires above all a determined national energy program for the United States. It must mobilize the solidarity of the industrial democracies. It must address the international financial implications of the crisis. It must accommodate the needs of the developing nations. And it must engage the oil-producing nations as constructive participants and partners in a thriving global economic system.

In the absence of such a program, diplomatic attempts to persuade the cartel to be moderate in pricing policy are at best a stopgap measure. "International jawboning," as it were, is a weak basis on which to rest the future of the world economy and the autonomy of our foreign policy. It puts us in danger of being supplicants instead of equal partners in constructing a world order based on equity. It adds to the temptations to set the price on political grounds and to ask a political price in return. The price of oil will be restrained only by objective market conditions; energy crises can be averted only if the industrial nations' dependence on imported oil is diminished by determined national programs.

Thus we in this country should set ourselves a clear goal: We should seek to reduce our oil imports, within a reasonable period of time, to a point where our lessened vulnerability to supply interruption and our reduced balance of payments drain restore balance to the international energy dialogue.


## ELEMENTS OF AN ENERGY STRATEGY

An effective national energy strategy to bring about this result must include the following elements:
- conservation;
- development of new supply;

- collaboration among the consumer nations, including safe-guarding the world financial system; and
- shaping of a reliable long-term relationship between the consumers and producers.

President Carter in a series of public appearances in April called attention to the urgency of the energy challenge. He also vigorously advocated *a determined program for energy conservation.* Whatever the merit of specific elements of the program, the President's objective deserves the support of all Americans. To discover new sources of oil and to develop alternative supplies of energy will take years. In the near-term future, only conservation will enable us both to absorb the present burden of energy costs and to begin to restore balance between supply and demand.

President Carter's conservation aim is to reduce the annual growth of national energy demand to less than 2 percent by 1985, from the present 4.6 percent; to limit gasoline consumption to 10 percent below its present level by 1985; to reduce oil imports from a potential level of 16 million barrels per day to 6 million; to establish a Strategic Petroleum Reserve of 1 billion barrels as insurance against emergencies; to increase coal production by two thirds to more than 1 billion tons annually; to insulate 90 percent of existing homes and all new buildings; and to install solar energy in more than 2.5 million homes.

The United States is theoretically capable of reducing its energy consumption by as much as 30 percent *without* affecting the rate of growth of our GNP or our standard of living. In 1975, Americans *wasted* more fossil fuel than was *used* by two thirds of the world's population. Energy is wasted whenever energy expenditure can be reduced without higher economic or social costs. To give but one example: In the past two decades architects have more and more tended toward sealed constructions, that is to say, buildings whose windows cannot be opened — especially office constructions. But in most cities of America, temperatures for many months each year are comfortable. Thus, in sealed buildings a great deal of energy is wasted in achieving a temperature that already exists outside and that would be available for free if windows could be opened. This simple conservation measure would obviously impose no hardship and could be rapidly achieved by changing building codes.

Given the high cost of energy, conservation is in the clear self-interest of every hardheaded businessman or every cost-conscious homeowner. It is a classic example of how the national interest can be exactly consistent with self-interest. Conservation is not a new burden to be imposed on our pocketbooks; it is the discipline and effort required to *ease* the burden of energy costs on the national economy and on individual families.

Conservation requires above all the more efficient use of the energy now available. It means getting thirty to forty miles to the gallon instead of seven; better insulated houses with more efficient heating systems; a national commitment to eliminate waste by turning out unneeded lights, television sets, and air conditioning, and the greatest possible use of public transit.

If we fail to take these relatively simple measures, we doom ourselves to 50 percent or even greater dependency on imported energy. We will have delegated crucial decisions to foreign countries to whom our prosperity is not in all circumstances an overriding objective and who cannot be expected to show a greater concern for our well-being than we do.

It is imperative that Congress and the President reach agreement on a comprehensive, far-reaching conservation plan. If we are to restore balance to the world energy market, an effective conservation program *must* be enacted and soon.

The second essential element of an energy strategy is *development of new and alternative energy supplies*. Conservation alone, crucial as it is, cannot permanently reduce our dependence on OPEC oil. Even the most ambitious conservation plan could not expect to do more than reduce our dependence on imported oil to the level of 1973 — when an embargo caused the most serious recession since the 1930s.

The Administration has, frankly, been much less energetic in pressing for new sources of energy and in fostering cooperation with the industrial democracies than in stressing conservation. We should urgently complete a coherent national energy program.

Much more can and must be done to develop new sources of oil. We should provide every incentive to maximize domestic production. We should also pursue a conscious policy of diversification of foreign sources. Any new source of oil is additional insurance against an embargo and a contribution to equilibrium in the international energy dialogue.

It is clearly in the interest of the United States and all the industrial democracies to diversify technologically as well as geographically. It has been said that the United States is the Saudi Arabia of coal, so vast are our deposits. Moreover, the industrial democracies have the technical skill and resources to create fuels from shale oil, tar sands, and coal gasification and liquefaction. And much progress has been made — and more can be made — on advanced methods such as nuclear power, fusion, and solar power.

It is important to face the fact that nuclear power represents one of the best hopes to close the gap between supply and demand, especially for some of our allies in Western Europe and Japan. They are committed to civilian nuclear power as a matter of urgent national policy, and they will not be easily dissuaded. It is time to end the disputes triggered by our very legitimate worries about the proliferation of nuclear weapons and to work with the industrial democracies on a coherent nuclear energy policy. If the United States uses its ability to supply nuclear fuels as a form of pressure, it may only accelerate the temptations to develop autonomous national nuclear programs.

The investment required to develop new and alternative

sources in the near-term future is as massive as it is essential. A serious review of the incentives and disincentives for energy development provided by our tax system and environmental policies is therefore in order. Such a review should also address the question whether existing incentives can work rapidly enough to produce the alternative energy sources in the time available. If the answer is in the negative, government-guaranteed financing should be considered.

## THE COHERENCE OF THE INDUSTRIAL DEMOCRACIES

Our own national effort must be part of an international strategy which has these additional elements:

- a coordinated program among the industrial democracies that are the major market for international oil production, including measures to protect and strengthen the international financial system;
- assisting the non-oil-producing developing countries whose development plans are shattered by exorbitant energy costs;
- and for the long term, shaping a productive relationship of economic cooperation in which the oil producers become ready partners, with a shared stake in a common global effort.

First, as to the nations bordering the North Atlantic and Japan, *cooperation among all the industrial democracies* is required to influence world energy markets decisively. We cannot do the job alone, but we are the crucial element since we consume half the oil of the industrialized world.

We, who are blessed with greater resources than any of our allies, who are less vulnerable to outside pressures, have a responsibility to take the initiative to organize the collective effort by our example and by our leadership. With a major American effort, the field of energy can in the Seventies give a new impetus to the unity among the democracies that in the immediate post-war period spurred common defense, diplomatic cooperation, and progress toward European integration.

For these reasons, the United States took the initiative in 1974 first to organize the Washington Energy Conference and then to help bring about the International Energy Agency. This body, the IEA, has been in operation for three years now. It is the principal institution of energy cooperation among the nine-teen leading industrial nations of the democratic world. It is a firm foundation on which to build the future common effort of the industrial democracies.

The IEA has set conservation targets for its members to encourage and coordinate national conservation programs. The goal for 1977 is to hold collective oil consumption to 35 million barrels per day or 3 percent above 1973 levels. Additional goals will be set for 1980 and 1985. A successful joint effort can mark a major step toward reducing the vulnerability of the industrial-ized world.

IEA programs, secondly, call for joint projects drawing on capital, technology, and manpower from IEA members to develop new energy sources. Priority areas have been chosen for research and development. Pooling the research efforts of the most advanced industrial nations will multiply the prospects for breakthroughs in technology and exploration.

The capacities of the industrial countries to develop new energy sources vary widely. Some have rich untapped deposits of fossil fuels; some have industrial skills and advanced tech-nology; some have considerable capital available for investment. Few have all three. Nothing would do more to encourage a sense of common purpose among the industrial democracies than to find ways to undertake joint energy development programs.

Thirdly, an emergency program has been approved by all IEA members to maintain reserve stocks and to share supplies during any future oil embargo. The significance of this program cannot be exaggerated. It greatly reduces the impact of selective embargoes against individual countries. And it eases even the impact of a general embargo, which, in any event, involves such political risks that it could be invoked only in the most extraordinary circumstances. The emergency sharing program thus serves as both insurance and deterrent against any new embargo.

The IEA represents a collective response to one of the most serious challenges the West has faced in a generation. It demonstrates the recognition by the democracies that their destiny is shared, and that their best hope of a solution is through unity and common effort. It is of major political importance because it enables the new Administration to make energy conservation a further stimulus to the strength and cooperation of the democracies.

At the same time, our international energy strategy must include measures to *safeguard the global financial system against disruption.*

There are two enduring consequences of the oil crisis: the creation of massive petrodollar surpluses in the OPEC countries; and the need of consumers, both rich and poor, to overcome the grave balance of payments difficulties created by the high price of oil. It is essential that we guard against the possibility of instability, arising either from the inability of one or several consumer countries to meet their balance of payments needs, or from manipulation of petrodollar surpluses by the producers.

Two measures have been explored in recent years to meet that need. One was a $25 billion Financial Support Fund, negotiated in 1975 by the industrial democracies for mutual assistance in an oil payments crisis. The failure of the United States Congress to ratify the Fund — the only legislature among the industrialized countries to do so — was unfortunate. But the negotiation for the Fund served an important purpose in giving the world assurance that as a last resort the industrial democracies had the resources to defend the financial system.

Within the next few days, the major financial powers are meeting in Paris to discuss a new facility within the International Monetary Fund, which would provide additional resources to countries that suffer balance of payments emergencies. It would draw on important contributions from OPEC members, and be available to borrowers if they were making satisfactory efforts at home to curb inflation and to reduce imports.

Provided its funds are available without conditions dependent on the solution of regional conflicts, the new facility in the IMF will serve an important function and should be implemented rapidly. It is an important first step. Early consideration should be given to arranging a second tranche, perhaps with less rigid dependence on OPEC funds than the presently discussed 50 percent. If this should prove difficult, or if burdensome political conditions are attached by the oil producers, new and urgent consideration should be given to resurrecting the Financial Support Fund of the democracies which was designed to safeguard their economies independently of OPEC.

## THE ROLE OF THE DEVELOPING COUNTRIES

If international order is to be made secure against instabilities caused by energy, the needs of the developing countries which are not blessed with oil must be addressed by the world community.

These developing countries were caught in the middle by the 1973 oil crisis. Because of the energy-induced recession in the industrialized countries, their oil import bills shot up, and their export prospects sharply declined. They seek desperately to resume their advance toward a more hopeful future, but they do so now under less hopeful circumstances. From 1973 to 1975, the foreign debt of those countries nearly doubled, from $67 billion to $117 billion. They need relief from the enormous blight of high energy costs on their development hopes and plans. Relief for the poorer developing countries is an appropriate task for the joint efforts of newly rich oil producers and the industrial democracies. Specifically:

- We should rapidly expand all forms of assistance, capital and technical, to aid developing countries to expand their own domestic energy production. Many developing countries possess considerable promise for oil, coal, and other forms of energy. They have been unable to exploit them for lack of the capital and technical know-how which modern energy development demands.

- The world financial system has performed remarkably well in channeling some of the petrodollar surpluses to the needy developing countries. Now, however, is the time to consolidate their debt structures and expand the flow of official, longer-term capital. The development assistance resources of the World Bank and other international financial institutions must be expanded.

- In the final analysis, the long-term solution to the developing countries' payments problems is trade. We must stem the retreat to protectionism, and complete the Tokyo Round of trade negotiations, if we hope to offer any permanent prospects of development to the poorer nations of the world.

## THE ROLE OF THE OIL PRODUCERS

Every one of the tasks enumerated here calls for a joint effort by the oil producers and the industrial democracies. This brings me

to the fourth, but perhaps most challenging, element of any international energy strategy: the role of the oil producers in the
emerging world energy order.

Clearly, the democracies must safeguard their economies
against the hazard of conflict. But, in doing all we can to reduce
our vulnerability to pressure and threat, we must take care not
to make it inevitable. On the contrary, the basic reality of the
present situation is the economic and political interdependence
between the energy-producing nations and the energy consumers.
The challenge to creative diplomacy in the years ahead is to
mold this mutuality of interest into a stable and positive long-
term relationship.

What are these mutual interests?

First of all, obviously, the producers need markets for their
oil. Disruption of the economies of the industrial democracies
reduces world growth and world demand for energy. In 1975,
as the result of the recession in the industrial democracies, market
conditions were depressed to the point where some producers
committed to ambitious development programs found themselves
in difficulty and were looking for means to sell their oil surpluses
despite the production restrictions of OPEC.

Secondly, the producers have a stake in the financial stability of the industrial democracies which are, after all, the only
places where they can productively invest their payments surpluses. The global economy cannot be disrupted as it was in 1973
without severe damage to the interests of the oil-producing countries themselves. Under present conditions, a world economic
crisis would have a massive impact on the oil producers because
their overseas investments would be in severe jeopardy.

Thirdly, the industrialized world is the only source of the
technology, capital goods, training, and management skills which
the oil producers require to develop their economies. In a climate
of confrontation, the governments and publics of the industrialized world have little incentive to support such programs.

Fourth, many of the oil producers are concerned about their own stability and safety. A cooperative relationship with the West enhances their security. They cannot be eager to shatter ties which might expose them to the designs of avaricious and hostile countries; they have a major political interest, therefore, in the friendship of the industrial democracies.

Thus, most of the oil producers can have no interest in confrontation; indeed, if they understand their interests, they have an important stake in the ability of the industrial democracies to solve their energy problems. Some of the more enlightened OPEC countries are therefore, paradoxically, leading advocates of energy conservation. They know theirs is a depleting resource and they are eager to extend its life over the longest period of time. They want to use their oil revenues to develop and diversify their economies. Some of them also believe that the world's oil reserves are too valuable to be used up for fuel; they are seeking to switch their own oil resources into new petrochemical industries for their own economic advance.

Thus, energy conservation and the reduction of the West's oil import requirements are as much in the producers' long-term interest as they are in our own. This reflects the basic reality that the ultimate "solution" to the world's energy problem is a thriving interdependent global economy which promotes economic advance in every region through the free flow of trade and know-how and international cooperation.

In building such a world, the industrial nations have an obligation to take serious account of the developing countries' and oil producers' legitimate aspiration for long-term income security and economic growth. The developing countries and producers, in their turn, must recognize that pressure or blackmail will in time backfire on those who use such tactics. The United States, as the world's strongest economy, would be injured less than others in an environment of economic warfare. But this would be incompatible with the open economic system that has nourished the world's prosperity and our own. And it would be inconsistent with basic American values and the American people's hopes for a world of peace, compassion, economic progress, and justice.

A cooperative solution for energy thus merges with the problem of world order. The United States has no more important task than to contribute its creativity to building an international system that all nations have a stake in preserving because they participate in its construction and share in its benefits. In a world of 150 sovereign states, there simply is no peaceful alternative to a cooperative international system.

Consumers, producers, and developing countries should learn from the energy crisis both the dangers of economic warfare and a more hopeful recognition of their common stake in a flourishing and just world order.

For the United States particularly, this is an extraordinary moment. For a generation we have carried out our responsibility to maintain the world balance of power and to lead the alliances of the free nations. We have behind us an era of great accomplishment. The energy crisis is the challenge of a new era. Republicans and Democrats, Congress and the Executive, the private sector and government — can work together in the great common enterprise of meeting a challenge that faces us not as partisans but as a nation.

The combination of technical genius and moral ideals is the extraordinary quality of the American people. We have the potential to turn energy from a crisis into a new advance toward our traditional goals of peace and cooperation, justice and progress, toward a future in which all nations and peoples come to participate in the freedom and well-being with which we have been blessed.

# CONTINUITY AND CHANGE IN AMERICAN FOREIGN POLICY

*The Arthur K. Salomon Lecture, given on September 19, 1977, at the Graduate School of Business Administration, New York University, New York City*

YOUR REQUEST that I deliver a "major appraisal" of current American foreign policy presents me with a dilemma — a difficult choice between your interest in the subject on the one hand and the imperatives of responsibility on the other. Despite my notorious humility, it would be tempting for me to speculate with you about how I might have dealt with this or that tactical situation if I had been in office these past eight months. But those who have borne the responsibility of high office know too well the complexities, the ambiguities, and the anguish of charting our nation's course in a turbulent period. The new Administration deserves the opportunity to develop its policies without harassment or second-guessing. Eight months is, after all, but an instant in the life of nations.

President Carter and Secretary of State Vance are on the verge of several weeks of delicate and important negotiations — with the Soviet Union on strategic arms limitation, with the Middle Eastern foreign ministers on peace in that crucial area, and with other leaders attending the United Nations General Assembly on a variety of complex issues. The hopes of *all* Americans go with them. The success of the Administration in promoting peace and progress will be a success for the nation. Any setbacks of the Administration would affect the lives and prosperity of all Americans. When a performer is taking careful and complicated steps on a high wire, it is profoundly inappropriate, not to say dangerous, for a spectator in a seat far below to shout at him that he is putting his toe in the wrong place.

So I would like to speak to you today about some of the philosophical underpinnings from which tactical decisions derive: the nature and purpose of bipartisanship in our democracy; the challenge of pursuing our moral values, especially human rights, in a complex world; and the relationship of issues such as human rights to others, the so-called problem of linkage.

## THE NATURE OF BIPARTISANSHIP

The world marvels at America's extraordinary rebound from the agony of Vietnam and the constitutional crisis of Watergate. We have emerged from these traumas with our democratic institutions flourishing, our public debates vigorous, our economy expanding, our pride in our country intact. Our friends around the world were heartened by this, for they know better perhaps even than we do how vital a stake they have in America's confident leadership.

That leadership is not — nor should it be — the esoteric concern of specialists; it is the means by which the nation serves its interests and pursues its highest goals, and it affects all other nations. For thirty years the world balance of power, the cohesion of the democracies, the health of the world economy, the prospects for growth in Africa, Asia, and Latin America, and the hopes for freedom everywhere have been sustained by the United States.

We have learned through many crises that upheavals thousands of miles away can threaten American lives or jeopardize American prosperity. The 1973 Middle East war ultimately forced us into a military alert. The oil embargo, lasting six months, cost half a million jobs and ten billion dollars in national output; it set the stage for a serious recession, in this country and worldwide. And the abrupt quadrupling of oil prices which followed added at least five percentage points to the price index, contributing to our worst inflation since World War II. We have not yet returned to the high growth rate and relatively low inflation which we enjoyed before 1973.

Now that the bitter passions of the foreign policy debate of the last ten years are, we hope, behind us, it is time for thoughtful deliberation on what are, or should be, our basic premises about the world in which we find ourselves today.

Our foreign policy difficulties are often described as the legacy of Vietnam. But the Vietnam ordeal was not a cause but a symptom. The late 1960s, coinciding with Vietnam, marked the end of the period when America was overwhelmingly more powerful than any other nation, when we could assault problems alone and entirely with our own resources, when American initiatives were accepted without serious debate, when we could believe that our own domestic experiences, like the New Deal, were the automatic blueprint for economic development and political progress abroad. It marked above all the end of the era when we could imagine that any problem could be resolved once and for all and that solutions once achieved would permit us to end our international exertions.

Vietnam was a catharsis. It taught us that our power while great is finite, that our influence though crucial can be effective only if we understand our priorities and the world in which we live.

For a century and a half geography and resources combined to give us the luxury of waiting until threats became almost overwhelming before we committed ourselves. We always had the opportunity to compensate for our tardy involvement by the massive deployment of physical power. We could largely leave to others the burden of the day-to-day decisions that over time spelled war or peace, security or fear, for the global system and even for ourselves. We were spared the continuing agony of inescapable decisions that other nations always faced to assure their survival and their values. More than any other nation in history, we could avoid the dilemma of reconciling the ideal with the practical, of accommodating to limited means and contingent ends.

The post–World War II era was a remarkably creative period of American foreign policy. But our initiatives were explicitly justified as temporary measures to restore an underlying equilibrium. The Marshall Plan, our Alliance commitments overseas, our international economic programs, were all conceived as dealing with temporary emergencies which once overcome would excuse us from permanent direct involvement abroad.

The world of today is not the world of a generation ago. Geography no longer assures security. The American nuclear monopoly has given way to nuclear balance and to proliferating weapons capabilities. The United States is now as vulnerable as any other nation; indeed, nuclear weapons confront all peoples everywhere with a threat to their survival unknown to any previous generation.

The world economy has become interdependent; our prosperity is to some extent hostage to the decisions on raw materials, prices, and investment in distant countries whose purposes are not necessarily compatible with ours.

And the structure of relations among nations has fundamentally altered. In 1945, fifty-one nations joined to create the United Nations; today it comprises nearly 150 nations — many ideologically hostile. Just as two world wars shattered the Europe-oriented order of the last two centuries, so the postwar system of Cold War bipolarity has come apart — and a new pattern of world order must be shaped to take its place.

An increasing responsibility has fallen upon the United States. Without our commitment to international security, there can be no stable peace; without our constructive participation in the world economy there can be no hope for economic progress;

without our dedication to human liberty the prospect of freedom in the world is dim indeed.

For the first time in American history we can neither dominate the world nor escape from it. Henceforth this country will be engaged in world affairs by reality and not by choice. America must now learn to conduct foreign policy as other nations have had to conduct it — with patience, subtlety, imagination, and perseverance.

The most fundamental challenge is thus not to our physical resources but to our constancy of purpose and our philosophical perception. Precisely because we can no longer wait for dangers to become overwhelming, they will appear ambiguous when they are still manageable. The case for ratifying the Panama Canal treaties, for example, is not an immediate present danger in Panama but the need to forestall a united front of *all* the countries of Latin America against what they consider an American attempt to maintain inequity by force. The issue in Angola two years ago was not a direct threat to our security, but the long-term danger of allowing Soviet surrogate forces to intervene globally to tip the scales in local conflicts. The argument for a forthcoming American attitude in the North-South dialogue is not to yield to the admittedly limited strength of the less-developed nations but to prevent the polarization of the world into a small minority of the rich isolated in an ocean of poverty and resentment.

It is a paradox of the contemporary world that if we wait until these dangers become realities we will lose the chance to do anything about them. At the moment when we still have great scope for creativity the facts are likely to be unclear or ambiguous. When we know all the facts, it is often too late to act. This is the dilemma of statemanship of a country that is irrevocably engaged in world affairs — and particularly of one that seeks to lead.

America, therefore, can no longer afford the luxury of oscil-

lating as it once did between brooding isolation and crusading
intervention. Our biggest foreign policy challenge is to shape a
concept of our international role that the American people will
support over the long term; we must avoid dramatic swings
between exuberance and abdication. Our responsibility is unending; our accomplishments are likely to be ever-tenuous. We must
change our approach to international affairs from the episodic to
the permanent; from the belief in final answers to the realization
that each "solution" is only an admission ticket to a new set of
problems.

In such an environment the conduct of foreign policy requires a fine balance between continuity and change. This is not
easy for our democracy. Our two-party system, our constitu-
tionally mandated balancing and separation of powers, our open
political process, create temptations for the simplified answer,
the nostalgic withdrawal, or the moralistic sense of superiority.

Yet this free and open political process is also our greatest
source of strength. The alternation of parties in office by free
elections guarantees constant renewal, the infusion of fresh ideas
and new blood into our national life. It presents a striking contrast
with the gerontocracies that run the Communist world. These
systems have no lawful regular process for replacing leaders; it is
no coincidence that the stagnation of their aging leadership goes
hand in hand with plodding bureaucracy and intellectual sterility,
punctuated by periodic crises over succession.

The problem which our society faces is on the whole a far
happier one. Ensuring continuity amidst the constant process of
renewal turns bipartisanship from a slogan into an imperative.

To be sure, all administrations sooner or later appeal to the
spirit of bipartisanship. This is partly because they come to
share much the same perception of the nation's permanent interests as their predecessors and partly because bipartisanship can
be a useful shield against excessive criticim. There is a natural
tendency for the party in power to consider *any* criticism as

excessive. I know these tendencies from experience, having in-
dulged them myself. But the fact that there are also tactical
benefits to the appeal to bipartisanship does not change the
reality that to the world at large we are one nation which can
have only one government.

And we are not just *any* nation. Our country cannot uproot
its whole foreign policy every four or eight years — or imply
that it is doing so — or else America will itself become a major
factor of instability in the world. We must understand that
foreign leaders who design their programs around our policies
are staking their domestic positions on our constancy. Radical
shifts in our course inevitably affect the stability of especially
friendly governments. If these changes are seen to occur largely
for domestic effect, if our elections come to determine as well
the stability of foreign governments, no nation that has a choice
will readily cooperate with us.

Of course, a foreign policy that stresses continuity above
all else would be stultifying and would in time be overwhelmed
by events. A new Administration is obviously not elected to carry
out all the policies of its predecessor. But change in our policy
should be seen as reflecting new circumstances and not change
for its own sake. By the same token, critics have an obligation to
see to it that our foreign policy debates reflect disagreements on
major substance, not a quest for partisan advantage or tactical
second-guessing.

If our foreign policy is well conceived, it must reflect
fundamental national purposes and not personal idiosyncrasy.
Neither the Administration nor the opposition should nurture
differences to score debating points. Both have an obligation to
make clear that our foreign policy is a shared national enterprise. I might add parenthetically that bipartisanship would
come easier if each new Administration resisted the quadrennial
temptation of implying that conceptual insight, creativity, and
moral awareness begin anew every four years on January 20.

Nor should history be rewritten in ways more suitable to faculty debates than to serious national dialogue.

The Administration, when it pursues the national interest, is entitled to the full measure of support from all who cherish the future of the country. For its challenges are great. The new Administration assumed responsibility when hopeful progress was being made in most areas of foreign policy — the Middle East, SALT, relations with both the industrialized and the developing world. But it faces a tremendous task in each, and in continuing to shape the new international order. We are on a journey no single Administration can possibly complete, whose beginning is an understanding of reality and whose goal is a better and more peaceful life for future generations.

## MORALITY AND PRAGMATISM
## IN AMERICAN FOREIGN POLICY

In this spirit, I would now like to turn to one of the basic challenges of foreign policy, the perennial tension between morality and pragmatism. Whenever it has been forced to wield its great power, America has also been driven to search its conscience: How does our foreign policy serve moral ends? How can America carry out its role as humane example and champion of justice in a world in which power is still often the final arbiter? How do we reconcile ends and means, principle and survival? How do we keep secure both our existence *and* our values? These have been the moral and intellectual dilemmas of the United States for two hundred years.

From the time of the Declaration of our Independence, Americans have believed that this country has a moral significance for the world. The United States was created as a conscious act by men and women dedicated to a set of political and ethical principles they held to be of universal meaning. Small wonder, then, that Santayana declared that "being an American is, of itself, almost a moral condition."

At the same time, since Tocqueville, it has been observed that we are a pragmatic people, commonsensical, undogmatic, undoctrinaire — a nation with a permanent bent to the practical and an instinct for what works. We have defined our basic goals — justice, freedom, equality, and progress — in open and libertarian terms, seeking to enlarge opportunity and the human spirit rather than to coerce a uniform standard of behavior or a common code of doctrine and belief.

This duality of our nature is *not* at war with reality. For in international politics, our morality and power should not be antithetical. Any serious foreign policy must begin with the need for survival. And survival has its practical necessities. A nation does not willingly delegate control over its future. For a great power to remit its security to the mercy of others is an abdication of foreign policy. All serious foreign policy therefore begins with maintaining a balance of power — a scope for action, a capacity to affect events and conditions. Without that capacity a nation is reduced to striking empty poses.

But, equally, our nation cannot rest its policy on power alone. Our tradition and the values of our people ensure that a policy that seeks only to manipulate force would lack all conviction, consistency, and public support.

This is why we have been most successful in our relations with the world when we combined our idealism and our pragmatism — from the days when our Founding Fathers manipulated the monarchical rivalries of Europe to secure our independence and launch the great democratic experiment to the creative American initiatives after the Second World War, such as the Marshall Plan. Our modern efforts to achieve strategic arms limitation, peace in the Middle East and Southern Africa, the opening to China, the recasting of international economic relations based on the principle of interdependence have also served both moral and practical ends and can be sustained only by a combination of moral conviction and practical wisdom.

## THE ISSUE OF HUMAN RIGHTS

These considerations come to bear powerfully on the question of the relationship between human rights and foreign policy. The world needs to know what this country stands for. But we cannot rest on this; we must know how to implement our convictions and achieve an enhancement of human rights *together* with other national objectives.

Neither the issue nor the concern is new:

- It was under the two previous administrations that Jewish emigration from the Soviet Union was raised from 400 a year in 1968 to 35,000 by 1973. This resulted from a deliberate policy, as a concomitant to the process of improving US–Soviet relations.
- The release of the courageous Soviet dissident Bukovsky in exchange for the Chilean Communist leader imprisoned in Chile was arranged in 1976 through American intercession. It was but one of many such acts which were not publicized in order to be able to continue to assist hardship cases.
- American diplomatic action in the same period brought about the release of hundreds of prisoners from jails all over the world.
- American foreign policy of the past decade helped enshrine basic principles of human rights in the Final Act of the Helsinki Conference on Security and Cooperation in Europe — providing the indispensable political and

legal basis for pursuing the issue of human rights in East-West relations.

- We also worked to improve the efforts of the United Nations Human Rights Commission; to upgrade the Commission on Human Rights of the Organization of American States. Common human rights policies were forged with the other democracies, and steps were taken to improve the institutional response of the international system to the challenge of human rights.

The accomplishment of the new Administration is not that it originated the concern with human rights but that, free of the legacy of Vietnam and Watergate, it has seized the opportunity to endow the policy with a more explicit formulation. The aim of the Carter Administration has been to give the American people, after the traumas of Vietnam and Watergate, a renewed sense of the basic decency of this country, so that they may continue to have the pride and self-confidence to remain actively involved in the world.

Having had to conduct American foreign policy in a period of national division and self-flagellation, I applaud and support this objective. The President has tapped a wellspring of American patriotism, idealism, unity, and commitment which is vital to our country and to the world. He has focused public concern on one of the greatest blights of our time.

The modern age has brought undreamed of benefits to mankind — in medicine, in scientific and technological advance, and in communication. But the modern age has also spawned new tools of oppression and of civil strife. Terrorism and bitter ideological contention have weakened bonds of social cohesion; the yearning for order even at the expense of liberty has resulted all too often in the violation of fundamental standards of human decency.

The central moral problem of government has always been

to strike a just and effective balance between freedom and authority. When freedom degenerates into anarchy, the human
personality becomes subject to arbitrary, brutal, and capricious
forces — witness aberrations of terrorism in even the most humane societies. Yet when the demand for order overrides all
other considerations, man becomes a means and not an end,
a tool of impersonal machinery. Human rights are the very
essence of a meaningful life, and human dignity is the ultimate
purpose of civil government. Respect for the rights of man is
written into the founding documents of almost every nation of
the world. It has long been part of the common speech and daily
lives of our citizens.

The obscene and atrocious acts systematically employed to
devalue, debase, and destroy man during World War II vividly
and ineradicably impressed on the world the enormity of the
challenge to human rights. It was to end such abuses and to
provide moral authority in international affairs that new institutions and legal standards were forged after that war — globally
in the United Nations and in this hemisphere in a strengthened
inter-American system.

The fact remains that continuing practices of intimidation,
terror, and brutality, fostered sometimes from outside national
territories and sometimes from inside, mark the distance yet
to be traveled before the community of nations can claim that it
is truly civilized. This is why the distinguished junior senator
from New York, Senator Moynihan, is surely right in stressing
that human rights should be not simply a humanitarian program
but a *political* component of American foreign policy.

For the difference between freedom and totalitarianism is
not transient or incidental; it is a moral conflict, of fundamental
historical proportions, which gives the modern age its special
meaning and peril. Our defense of human rights reminds us of
the fundamental reason that our competition with totalitarian
systems is vital to the cause of mankind. There is no reason for

us to accept the hypocritical double standard increasingly prevalent in the United Nations, where petty tyrannies berate us for our alleged moral shortcomings. On this issue we are not — and have no reason to be — on the defensive. "The cause of human liberty," the poet Archibald MacLeish has written, "is now the one great revolutionary cause."

And yet, while human rights must be an essential component of our foreign policy, to pursue it effectively over the long term we must take the measure of the dangers and dilemmas along the way.

First, any foreign policy must ultimately be judged by its operational results. "In foreign relations," Walter Lippmann once wrote, "as in all other relations, a policy has been formed only when commitments and power have been brought into balance."

To be sure, the advocacy of human rights has in itself a political and even strategic significance. But in the final reckoning more than advocacy will be counted. If we universalize our human rights policy, applying it undiscriminatingly and literally to all countries, we run the risk of becoming the world's policeman — an objective the American people may not support. At a minimum we will have to answer what may be the question for several friendly governments: How and to what extent will we support them if they get into difficulties by following our maxims? And we will have to indicate what sanctions we will apply to less well-disposed governments which challenge the very precepts of our policy.

If, on the other hand, we confine ourselves to proclaiming objectives that are not translated into concrete actions and specific results, we run the risk of demonstrating that we are impotent and of evoking a sense of betrayal among those our human rights policy seeks to help. Such a course could tempt unfriendly governments to crack down all the harder on their dissidents, in order to demonstrate the futility of our proclamations — this indeed has already happened to some extent in the Soviet Union.

Nor can we escape from the dilemma by asserting that there is no connection between human rights behavior and our attitude on other foreign policy problems — by "unlinking," as the technical phrase goes, human rights from other issues. For this implies that there is no cost or consequence to the violation of human rights, turning our proclamation of human rights into a liturgical theme — decoupled, unenforced, and compromised. Or else we will insist on our values only against weaker countries, in Latin America or Asia, many of which may even be conducting foreign policies supportive of our own. This would lead to the paradox that the weaker the nation and the less its importance on the international scene, the firmer and more uncompromising would be our human rights posture.

Second, precisely because human rights advocacy is a powerful political weapon, we must be careful that in its application we do not erode all moral dividing lines. We must understand the difference between governments making universal ideological claims and countries which do not observe all democratic practices — either because of domestic turmoil, foreign danger, or national traditions — but which make no claim to historical permanence or universal relevance. In the contemporary world it is the totalitarian systems which have managed the most systematic and massive repression of the rights of men.

In recent decades, no totalitarian regime has ever evolved into a democracy. Several authoritarian regimes — such as Spain, Greece, and Portugal — have done so. We must therefore maintain the moral distinction between aggressive totalitarianism and other governments which with all their imperfections are trying to resist foreign pressures or subversion and which thereby help preserve the balance of power in behalf of all free peoples. Our human rights policy owes special consideration to the particular international and domestic setting of governments important to our security and supportive of free world security interests. There are, of course, some transgressions of human rights which no necessity — real or imagined — can justify. But there are also realities in the threats nations face, either from terrorism at home, such as in Argentina, or aggression across borders, such as in Iran or Korea. And we must keep in mind that the alternative to some governments that resist totalitarianism with authoritarian methods may not be greater democracy and an enhancement of human rights but the advent of even more repression, more brutality, more suffering. The ultimate irony would be a posture of resignation toward totalitarian states and harassment of those who would be our friends and who have every prospect of evolving in a more humane direction.

We must take care, finally, that our affirmation of human rights is not manipulated by our political adversaries to isolate countries whose security is important for the future of freedom, even if their domestic practices fall short of our maxims. The membership of the UN Human Rights Commission, composed as it is of a number of nations with extremely dubious human rights practices, does not augur well for an objective approach to this issue in the United Nations. Cuba and other Communist governments, as well as the more repressive regimes of the less developed world, have no moral standing to bring other nations to international account. We should not hesitate to say so.

Third, there is the ominous prospect that the issue of human rights if not handled with great wisdom could unleash new forces of American isolationism. This could defeat the Administration's goal of using it to mobilize support for continued American involvement in world affairs. That the human rights issue could develop a life of its own, regardless of the Administration's prudent sense of its aims and limits, is already evident from some developments in the Congress.

A distorted or misunderstood human rights policy can become the basis and justification of a modern isolationism. What appeals to many as a useful impetus to resistance to the Communist challenge can be used by others to erase all the distinctions between totalitarians and those that resist them, to induce indifference to European Communist parties' accession to power, or to disrupt security relationships which are essential to maintaining the geopolitical balance. Excuses can be found to deny help to almost any friendly country at the precise moment when it faces its most serious external challenge. If conservatives succeed in unraveling ties with nations on the left and liberals block relations with nations on the right, we could find ourselves with no constructive foreign relations at all, except with a handful of industrial democracies. The end result ironically could be the irrelevance of the United States to other nations of the world. A policy of moral advocacy that led to American abdication would surely condemn countless millions to greater suffering, danger, or despair.

Fourth and most fundamentally, we should never forget that the key to successful foreign policy is a sense of proportion. Some of the most serious errors of our foreign policy, both of overcommitment and withdrawal, have occurred when we lost the sense of balance between our interests and our ideals. It was under the banners of moralistic slogans a decade and a half ago that we launched adventures that divided our country and undermined our international position. A few years later young people were parading in front of the White House carrying coffins and candles and accusing their government of loving war; the national leadership was denounced as excessively, indeed imperialistically, involved in the internal affairs of other nations. A few years later still, the government was attacked for sacrificing our ethical values on the altar of détente and being *insufficiently* concerned with the domestic behavior of other nations. Neither we nor the rest of the world can any longer afford such extreme fluctuations.

Human rights policy in this period of American responsibility must strengthen the steady purpose and responsible involvement of the American people. It can do so only if it is presented in the context of a realistic assessment of world affairs and not as the magic cure for the difficulties and shortcomings of mankind's contemporary experience.

The Administration is surely right in insisting that human rights is a legitimate and recognized subject of international discourse; it is an object of international legal standards — importantly as a result of American initiatives by administrations of both parties. At the same time we must recognize that we serve the cause of freedom also by strengthening international security and maintaining ties with other countries defending their independence against external aggression and struggling to overcome poverty, even if their internal structures differ from ours.

We cannot afford to subordinate either concern to the other. Morality without security is ineffectual; security without morality is empty. To establish the relationship and proportion between these goals is perhaps the most profound challenge before our government and our nation.

There is every indication that within the Administration rhetoric and capacity for action are being brought increasingly into balance. In an important speech in Athens, Georgia, on April 30, 1977, Secretary Vance has wisely pointed out that "a decision whether and how to act in the cause of human rights is a matter for informed and careful judgment. No mechanistic formula produces an automatic answer."

## THE LINKAGE OF FOREIGN POLICY ISSUES

The inescapable relationship of our human rights objectives with other foreign policy goals is an example of a broader, virtually universal phenomenon of our contemporary world. Foreign policy issues are interrelated — "linked" — as never before. A consistent, coherent, and moral foreign policy must be grounded in an understanding of the world in which we pursue our goals.

The concept of linkage — the suggestion that we should design and manage our policy with a clear understanding of how changes in one part of the international system affect other parts — was first put forth in 1969 in the context of US–Soviet affairs. We proceeded from the premise that to separate issues into distinct compartments would encourage the Soviet leaders to believe that they could reap the benefits of cooperation in one area, using it as a safety valve, while striving for unilateral advantages elsewhere. We considered this a formula for disaster.

So strong is the pragmatic tradition of American political thought that linkage was widely debated as if it were an idiosyncrasy of a particular group of policymakers who chose this approach by an act of will.

But linkage comes in two forms: first, when policymakers relate two separate objectives in negotiation, using one as pressure on the other; second by virtue of reality, because in an interdependent world the actions of a major power are inevitably interrelated and have consequences beyond the issue or region immediately concerned.

Of these two concepts of linkage, the latter is by far the more important. It says, in effect, that significant changes of policy or behavior in one region or on one issue inevitably affect other and wider concerns.

Our policy toward the Soviet Union cannot be treated in isolation from our relations with China; our relations with China, in turn, cannot be effective except to the extent that we maintain the geopolitical balance around the world, by which the People's Republic of China measures our ultimate relevance. Displays of American impotence in one part of the world, such as Southeast Asia or Africa, have a direct effect on our credibility in other

parts of the world, such as the Middle East. Our policy toward
Rhodesia and Namibia will inevitably determine the prospects
of a peaceful evolution in South Africa, and vice versa. Our
posture toward Korea cannot be separated from our interests in
Japan and China, and the measures we adopt for one inevitably
affect the other. The decision on the B-1 bomber resulted from
complex and painful budgetary and technical considerations. I
am not here arguing the merits of these considerations, but in
the context of the Strategic Arms Limitation Talks, the B-1
bomber decision did represent a unilateral unreciprocated concession. Finally, either our human rights policy has relevance to
other areas of national policy — or it has no meaning at all.

Perception of linkage is, in short, synonymous with an overall strategic view. We ignore it only at our peril. It is inherent
in the real world. The interrelationship of our interests, across
issues and boundaries, exists regardless of the accidents of time
or personality; it is not a matter of decision or will but of reality.
And it cannot be ended by an act of policy. If we are to have
a permanent conception of American foreign policy there must
be an appreciation of the fact that merits of individual actions
can be judged only on a wider canvas.

As you know, I strongly support President Carter in his
fight for ratification of the Panama Canal treaties. I do so on their
merits but also because of the profound consequences of a failure
to ratify that go far beyond Panama. A defeat of the treaties
would weaken the President's international authority at the beginning of his term. It would suggest to friends and foes around
the world that the United States could not deliver on an agreement negotiated by four Presidents of both political parties over
a period of thirteen years, that it could not perceive its own interests in Western Hemisphere cooperation, and that shifting emo-
tions and institutional stalemates produced erratic behavior in
the most powerful country in the world.

Linkage is not a natural concept for Americans, who have

traditionally perceived foreign policy as an episodic enterprise. Our bureaucratic organization, divided into regional and functional bureaus, and indeed our academic tradition of specialization compound this tendency to compartmentalization. And American pragmatism produces a penchant for examining issues separately: to deal with issues individually, as if they existed as abstractions, without the patience, timing, or sense of political complexity which are so often vital to their achievement; to display our morality in the proclamation of objectives rather than in a commitment to the operational consequences of our actions in an inherently ambiguous environment.

A recognition of the importance of linkage — of the significance and role of the strategic vision to our future foreign policy — thus brings us back to where we began: to the need for patience, continuity, and, above all, for national unity in the conduct of international affairs. This responsibility must be shared by the Administration, the opposition, and the public. Modern foreign policy, by its very complexity, does not lend itself to instant successes. In domestic affairs the timeframe of new departures is defined by the legislative process; dramatic initiatives may be the only way to launch a new program. In foreign policy the most important initiatives require painstaking preparation; results may be months and years in becoming apparent.

Therefore, we should not demand of the new Administration instant results or an unbroken string of early successes; nor should the Administration seek such goals if it wishes to avoid a series of stalemates or worse. Foreign policy, if it is to be truly an architectural endeavor, is the art of building for the long term, the careful nurturing of relationships, the elaboration of policies that enhance our options and constrain those of potential opponents. It requires the coherence that can come only from national unity, a strong leadership, and a political process that reflects the recognition that we are all — the Administration as well as its opponents — part of a permanent national endeavor.

This country has no greater contribution to make in the service of its ideals than to help the world find its way from an era of fear into a time of hope. With our old idealism and our new maturity, we have the opportunity to fulfill the hopes as well as the necessities of a peaceful world. A century ago, Abraham Lincoln proclaimed that no nation could long endure "half slave and half free" and stirred the conscience of the nation. With a combination of lofty idealism and tough pragmatism, he saved the freedom of this nation. With a similar dedication — in a world that is "half slave and half free" — we in this era can be the champion and defender of the cause of liberty.

# GOLDA MEIR

## *An Appreciation*

---

*Remarks made at the presentation of the Stephen Wise
Award to Golda Meir on November 13, 1977, just
before Anwar Sadat's historic trip to Jerusalem*

---

WE ARE privileged tonight to be in the presence of an extra-ordinary human being. Golda Meir led her people with wisdom and courage in their hour of need, and left her mark on history.

I have always admired Golda and loved her for her strength, for her wisdom, and for her humanity. Her life is testimony not only of the history of an individual but of the destiny of a people. It is marked by the faith that made idealists of ordinary men and women and drove them to a wasteland to fulfill an historic vision. It is etched with the fortitude of the survivors of the Holocaust determined that never again would they surrender the ultimate decision over their destiny. And it has been suffused with the compassion and humanity born of the suffering of millennia and the deep instinctive knowledge that man is the ultimate measure of all things.

We love Golda because her values go beyond the bounds of her people. They speak of the worth of all humanity. They remind us that the fundamental aspirations to liberty and justice and service are not realized finally for the Jewish people unless they are realized for all men and women and conversely that they are not secure for mankind unless they are secure for the Jewish people.

Golda always recalls us to fundamentals. She shames the expedient and the second-rate. She reflects a universal conscience — the need for a world in which the weak are protected by a general order, in which justice is not a subterfuge for the dominance of the powerful, and in which peace is based on true trust and reconciliation.

All of us here know that history will record that her term as Prime Minister was a turning point. With sublime courage she led her people through a period of tragic war, and with tremendous vision through two crucial negotiations with Egypt and Syria that will be seen, I am confident, as the beginning of the journey toward real peace.

I had the privilege of working with Golda during some phases of that process. I will not insult your intelligence by pretending that Golda was always easy to deal with. She did nothing to disprove Abba Eban's statement that Israelis define objectivity as 100 percent agreement with their point of view. And on the occasions when I did not immediately embrace the total validity of her considerations she showered on me the outrage reserved for the obtuseness of a specially favored nephew. My wife is fond of saying that some of the best dramatic performances she ever witnessed occurred during debates between Golda and me.

But I am proud that we always came to an agreement — not reluctantly, not based on tests of strength, but on a shared knowledge that the security of Israel is a moral imperative for all free peoples. We never differed in our conviction that a just peace cannot be an imposed peace. A just peace must be a peace which the participants accept and feel a stake in preserving. And therefore the process by which peace is made is almost as important as the final outcome. At each stage the parties must feel that it was their decision and not somebody else's that brought about the result.

We meet in the midst of another debate about peace in the Middle East. Given my own involvement in the conduct of foreign policy over eight years, I have thought it inappropriate since January to participate in a discussion of day-to-day tactics. But I would like to use this occasion to articulate a few general principles.

First, the desirability of peace can never be at issue. No people have suffered more from the absence of peace than the people of Israel, every square mile of whose country is drenched with the blood of its pioneers and whose existence has never been recognized by any of its neighbors. No people can be more aware of how fragile, and how precious, are the restraints that make men and nations civilized.

No people know more vividly that morality must be more than a theory — it must be a constant in human conduct. And no group of men and women understands more acutely that peace depends ultimately not on political arrangements but on the conscience of mankind. History is often cruel, and rarely logical, and yet the wisest of realists are those who recognize that fate can indeed be shaped by human faith and courage. These qualities are what brought the state of Israel into being. This spirit and pride must be nurtured by all friends of Israel, for they are the ultimate guarantee of Israel's future.

But faith and courage are not enough. The people of Israel have seen too much of the transitoriness of human intentions to entrust the destiny of their nation entirely to professions and reassurances however sincere and honestly intended. A peace to be lasting must be founded on the self-interest of all the parties and for peace to be secure it must leave Israel strong enough to protect its future by its own efforts.

Second, the intentions or purposes of the government of the United States cannot be at issue. No President would knowingly risk the future of Israel. Nor would he make a deal to undermine Israel's future for some global considerations. My own acquaintance with President Carter, Secretary Vance, and their senior advisers convinces me that this Administration would not deliberately put Israel's security at risk. But there is always the danger that actions undertaken in good faith may inadvertently produce unforeseen consequences. If such a miscalculation took place either Israel would become totally isolated or diplomacy would become abruptly deadlocked. The art of diplomacy is to move events carefully and shape them toward achievable ends so that neither the United States nor Israel ever face such a stark, impossible choice. A coordination of policies between Israel and the United States is therefore imperative.

Third, the perspective of a superpower and those of a small country may occasionally differ. The United States has enormous strength; Israel has a much narrower margin of safety. The United States can survive trial-and-error diplomacy, because we can always rectify mistakes by redoubling our efforts. But Israeli leaders cannot experiment; they have only one try. If they guess wrong they risk the survival of the nation. We therefore owe the people of Israel an understanding of its special circumstances — all the more so as the country has known only war or the threat of war since its founding. At the same time, Israelis must understand the importance of Middle East peace to the global concerns of the United States and the Western world, which are indeed the essential underpinning of Israel's own security.

Fourth, an overall solution is of course the ultimate prize. But realism forces us to recognize that to achieve it involves issues of enormous complexity and parties with an unequal commitment to peace. It also requires a process that is bound to be protracted. Thus while striving for an overall settlement, we must take care not to foreclose other opportunities that may arise to ease tensions and to enable the peoples of the area to build confidence. We must not give a veto to the most intransigent elements within the area. We must not permit outside powers to emerge as the advocates for a point of view that penalizes moderation.

Fifth, some structures develop their own momentum that cannot be judged by formal declarations or abstract blueprints. A Palestinian state on the West Bank is bound to be an element of instability both for Jordan and for Israel; it will compound the crisis, not solve it. Such a state — whatever the professions or guarantees — must have objectives that cannot be compatible with the tranquillity of the Middle East. It cannot be an accident that no attempt to create such a state was ever made during the twenty years of Arab rule in that territory.

Sixth, any peace settlement must of necessity involve guarantees. But they must be worked out with great care and with a sense for their limits. History should teach us that guarantees by themselves are *not* a substitute for security. No nation should be asked to abdicate its judgment of the requirements of its survival. Care must be taken that guarantees do not provide a pretext for an outside power to intervene constantly in the affairs of the area. With respect to bilateral US–Israeli treaty arrangements there is the danger that the ratification process may produce a debate that paradoxically hazards the friendship and close cooperation which has served so well for a generation. In short, guarantees require the most careful reflection and study; at best they reinforce; they cannot bring about security.

Seventh, whatever the views about the desirability of beginning the process of negotiations with a Geneva conference, so much effort has been invested in it that it has become the touchstone of the prospects of peace. All parties therefore have a stake in bringing such a conference into being. At the same time we must recognize that when it is finally assembled Geneva will be an important achievement, but its primary significance will be procedural. Ahead of us will be complex negotiations about frontiers, commitments to peace, security arrangements, and other issues which will test the wisdom and commitment of the parties.

These issues cannot be left to the pressures of a conference; it is not too soon to explore them actively with the parties. We cannot wait for Geneva to resolve all the complexities that range from the relations of subgroups to the main conference to the concrete outlines of a definition of peace. Especially as far as Israel is concerned it is incompatible with our historic relationship to deal with issues of such gravity in an atmosphere of self-imposed deadlines. And it does not help those Arab leaders who have had the wisdom and the courage to begin the journey toward peace to raise expectations that cannot be fulfilled.

Geneva will be successful to the extent that Israel and the United States end the cycle of fear and reassurance, of outraged protest and soothing generalities, and turn to the elaboration of a common concrete approach. This requires a willingness on one side to give the benefit of the doubt and a readiness on the other to understand the anguish of a people whose historic suffering precludes the abdication of its own judgment, but whose martyrs guarantee that the search for peace, while painful, will be dedicated and committed.

I am convinced that the problems that form the headlines of the day are soluble. In all my efforts in the Middle East, whatever the temporary disagreements, we never failed to develop a common position with our friends in Israel. It was during Golda's term as Prime Minister and that of her distinguished successor that the steps were taken which give us hope for even greater progress now. I have every confidence that the present Israeli government will do no less. And in my experience, at the end of the day, Israel has never rejected a chance to make progress toward a settlement, or to run risks for peace. I have no doubt that we will find a willing — if complicated — partner in a dialogue that emphasizes substance, not procedure, and in a quest that defines specific objectives, not theoretical blueprints. The Jewish people have not survived through the millennia by being found wanting of vision in their hours of need. And the American people have not been the hope of mankind through their history by subordinating moral values to tactical expedience.

So let us end the controversies and turn to the future. And Golda, whom we honor, watchful, deeply devoted, infinitely caring, symbolizes our necessity and guarantees our opportunity.

Golda is an idealist without illusions. She believes in

strength and at the same time yearns heart and soul for peace. Golda was a ferocious negotiator and a woman of powerful convictions. But when she gave you her word, you could absolutely count on it. Once she made up her mind to do something, even if it was difficult and painful, she followed through with enormous courage and extraordinary ability. She was a true leader and a great statesman. And I am proud to say she was and remains a true friend.

Tonight it is appropriate that she is honored by the American Jewish Congress, whose very first convention, in 1918 in Philadelphia, she attended as a twenty-year-old delegate from Milwaukee. No one better represents the indomitable spirit of her people. No one is so universally admired and loved. We owe it to Golda to build a world in which mothers need no longer fear for the future of their children, in which holocausts become attributes of an incomprehensible past, in which the struggles of Golda's generation will be validated by a world in which all peoples will at last live together in genuine security and turn their energies to the tasks of construction.

So you see, Golda, what you have made me do — a long speech without the impatient interruption that would have long since been my lot in that little study in your residence where we spent so many hours that I shall always treasure.

There remains only for me to say: Golda, you have inspired us. May you live a long time, for your life is our glory.

It is a great personal honor for me to invite Golda Meir to the podium to give her this small token of our enormous affection, the Stephen Wise medallion.

The medallion reads: "Golda Meir: For a lifetime of courageous and inspiring leadership of the Jewish people."

# "THEY ARE FATED TO SUCCEED"

*Anwar Sadat and the Middle East*

*Essay in* Time, *January 2, 1978, in honor of Anwar Sadat's selection as* Time's *Man of the Year*

ON A bare hill at Giza, some three miles from downtown Cairo, stands a simple rest house occasionally used by President Sadat. Its principal feature is a wide veranda that overlooks the Pyramids. The light and shadows constantly change the shape of these massive triangles leaning against each other. These are structures at once simple and monumental; they have endured the elements and man's depredations for as close to eternity as man can reach by his own efforts. In no other place in the world is man forced into humility so exclusively by one of his own accomplishments. In this sea of sand split by the green valley of the Nile stretching a man's vision in a thin straight line for hundreds of miles, there is no natural monument to dwarf him. The most breathtaking landmarks are all man-made, defying time and human fallibility. The Egyptian has reared tremendous edifices to remind him of both the finiteness of the human scale and the reach of human aspirations through recorded history.

One wonders whether Anwar Sadat sat on that veranda as he first began to contemplate his journey to Jerusalem — a move at once simple and awesome like the Pyramids themselves. We do know that not far from this rest house Israeli and Egyptian negotiators have been meeting now for two weeks in an old hotel. It is in keeping with the spirit of a region where mirage and reality blend that the negotiators are at a bureaucratic level, which guarantees that no significant progress could be made until Premier Begin and President Sadat had met in Ismailia. But the mere presence of Israeli diplomats in Cairo has lent itself to the symbolic manifestations of public feeling so dear to the Arab heart; the massive demonstrations are significant whether they are spontaneous or government-sponsored. Two great peoples have met again as equals. Through the millennia both have suffered and endured; both have been obsessed with permanence, the Egyptians in architecture and the Jews in moral law. Both have now embarked on the quest for that most elusive of all permanencies: a lasting peace.

And these two eternity-obsessed nations are likely to realize their dreams. The very audacity of Sadat's act, like the artificial mountains which are the Pyramids, dwarfs the small calculations of the recent past. Ups and downs are inevitable in the process; there will be complicated negotiations, but the parties have fated themselves to success.

One need only recall the situation of two months ago: then all was preparation for a Geneva conference. But that conference was distrusted by Egypt and Israel alike. Major procedural problems were unresolved: the scope of the plenary and the working groups, the nature of Palestinian participation, the precise role of the Soviet Union. The procedural deadlock would in all likelihood have been followed by a substantive stalemate as the irreconcilability of the opposing publicly stated positions became apparent. All the most intractable issues were thrown together.

The danger was real that in the very process of organizing the conference the most radical elements would achieve a veto, since no progress could take place without them. In turn, the Soviet Union would be able to exercise a veto over any plausible moderate solution. All the while, Israel, maddened by isolation and the fear of an imposed peace, would withdraw into sullen intransigence. Progress at Geneva would have depended on American pressure on Israel to a degree probably incompatible with US domestic political realities. We ran the risk of being caught between the parties: accused by the Arab side of insufficient exertions and by Israel of excessive pressures. The Soviet

Union would have gained an increasing voice as the frustration of all parties came to focus on us. Egypt — the most eager for peace of the Arab countries, yet treated as just one of a number of participants — was threatened with being reduced to passivity, with losing control over its destiny in a welter of unmanageable and unpredictable claims.

Considerations such as these must have been in President Sadat's mind when he decided to cut through the Geneva minuet that was getting as complicated as it was irrelevant, and go to the heart of the problem — the psychological gulf that had separated Israelis and Arabs since the creation of the Jewish state.

In a recurring irony of history, the Jewish people, persecuted and ostracized for centuries, found themselves again condemned to a ghetto existence of international isolation at the very moment when they had built their own state. The Arabs, their pride stung by the creation of Israel and convinced from the beginning that Israel was occupying their national territories, had refused to accept the very existence of the Jewish state. This created a vicious circle: Israel saw security in purely geographic concessions as the price of a legitimacy that diplomacy turned into legal formulas so esoteric as to be almost meaningless. Intermediaries could help to a certain point. They could lay a foundation. But no nation or leader will ever be totally certain whether an intermediary's account of the views of the opposing side reflects reality, gullibility, or his own preferences. The mere fact that an intermediary was necessary, that direct talks were rejected, reflected and fueled the prevailing distrust.

By going to Jerusalem, President Sadat cut through the mind-set of a generation. He allowed the people of Israel to judge for themselves his commitment to peace; he could see for his part the trauma of a nation that had never known a day without war in its national existence. Sadat was right that the heart of the problem was psychological. By grasping the essence of the issue, Sadat has done more to resolve it than all the wars and negotiations of the last three decades. Matters in the Middle East now can be reduced to a few fundamentals:

*There is no alternative to the Sadat-Begin negotiations.* Geneva as a negotiating forum is dead. This is just as well. It could only have led to a deadlock or to an imposed settlement, and in either case to an enlarged Soviet influence. Were Sadat and Begin somehow to fail to find solutions, lower-level diplomats meeting around a conference table in Switzerland later could scarcely be expected to succeed. In short, failure now would make conflict later inevitable. Israel would return to its ghetto existence; Egypt would face a war its people dread.

The absence of alternatives clears the mind marvelously. Major progress is therefore likely. Geneva could be useful later in ratifying what has been negotiated and to provide a forum for other parties to join the negotiating process.

*An Egyptian-Israeli agreement is not inimical to an overall settlement but the condition for it.* The choice has never been between an overall and a partial settlement, but between a partial settlement as a first step and no settlement at all. A step toward peace is better than the continuation of conflict, all the more so since both President Sadat and Premier Begin have committed themselves to an overall settlement.

*An Egyptian-Israeli agreement should involve principles applicable to the other parties.* Sadat and Begin are too wise not to base progress between Egypt and Israel on principles that have wider application. They know from history that to be lasting a peace must in time reach out to all principal parties and that those parties will support it only if they participate in making it. The day will come when Arab leaders who now denounce the Sadat initiative will be grateful that the largest of Arab nations took on its own shoulders the burden of the first and most difficult decision for peace. By solving the psychological problem,

Egypt has now made it possible to overcome the other obstacles to peace everywhere in the Middle East. This is why coupling the Egyptian negotiations with the Palestinian issue is important both substantively and symbolically. At the same time, on this issue where distrust and hatred have gone so deep, it may be best to set a general course and leave details for later negotiations.

Having had the privilege of working closely with the President of Syria, I am convinced that he will not turn his back on a genuine peace. In the context of Syria's turbulent history and its internal pressures, in the light of its perception of itself as the embodiment of true Arab nationalism, President Assad has sought to keep open the option of negotiation. This attitude should be nurtured.

*The current negotiations will be a test of Soviet policy.* If the Soviet Union genuinely favors a relaxation of tensions throughout the world, it will in the Middle East allow the processes toward peace to occur and not press for formal participation in negotiations which are already under way and to which it can make no contribution. The Soviet Union has nothing to lose from a peaceful solution; indeed, a normalized Middle East should enable all countries to pursue their global policies on the basis of equality. If the Soviet Union encourages intransigence, the motive must be either hurt vanity or an attempt to foster tensions and to improve the opportunities for Soviet penetration. There is no reason to assuage the former, and it is in the interests of all nations to resist the latter.

If the process now under way succeeds — as is likely, even with occasional disappointments — Americans of every persuasion and party will have reason to be proud. We contributed a military balance which foreclosed a military solution. Our nation, because it was trusted by both sides, helped shape a negotiating process which culminated in the breakthrough of Sadat's historic journey. President Carter has handled the sequence of events growing out of the Sadat initiative with wisdom and delicacy, offering assistance but not intruding on the process of negotiations.

The ultimate credit should of course go to the audacious President of Egypt, who dared to smash the psychological mold of a generation; to the courageous Premier of Israel, who seized a unique moment of history; and to all the people of the Middle East, whose inarticulate aspirations, prayers, and sacrifices have created the prevailing climate for peace. Appropriately enough for this season, the barren region of the Middle East, which has spawned in its lonely spaces three great religions, has become once again the focal point of humanity's highest hopes.

# THE LESSONS OF THE PAST

*A Conversation with Walter Laqueur*

*Printed in* The Washington Quarterly, *January 1978*

L AQUEUR: Your studies on nineteenth-century diplomatic history are, of course, well known. You now work on your memoirs. What specific problems do you face in your work on the contemporary period? Or, to be precise, what are in your view the main difficulties facing the contemporary historian, who, unlike you, was not a participant in the events he intends to describe?

*Kissinger:* I have been struck by the difficulties historians will have in forming reasonable historical judgments about the contemporary period. In the nineteenth century, communication between diplomats and their governments was very difficult and it was therefore necessary for the governments to give rather conceptual instructions and for the diplomats to explain the philosophy of their own actions. It was impossible for the participants at the Congress of Vienna, for example, to receive day-to-day tactical instructions on how they should conduct their negotiations. Historians can therefore read the documents — which are mercifully not all that plentiful — and form some impression of what the various individuals wanted to achieve.

Today communication is instantaneous. There is no need for either government or ambassador to give an elaborate explanation of why certain things are being done. Instructions very often simply tell the diplomat what he is supposed to say at a particular session. One result is that an enormous amount of material accumulates that cannot possibly be studied by any one scholar.

The instructions go out in so many different channels and under so many different classifications that it will be next to impossible for somebody who has not been a participant to determine what was crucial and what was peripheral, what was written to keep the bureaucracy quiet, what was written for purposes of later disclosure, and what was written to be implemented.

A second result is that the documents do not provide a reliable guide to the ideas and passions of the participants. This will make it terribly difficult for historians and statesmen of the future to use our records as historians have used those of the past. Whether this will have a deleterious effect on statecraft remains to be seen, for the practice of diplomacy is not something that can be learned from texts, historical or otherwise.

*Laqueur:* It is difficult for the historian to unravel modern diplomacy. This again raises the reverse question, discussed endlessly and inconclusively: Is the knowledge of the past necessarily of help to the statesman?

*Kissinger:* Foreign policy is a form of art and not a precise science, something that some professors have great difficulty grasping. On the other hand, the conduct of foreign policy requires in each instance a recognition of comparable situations. We can talk forever about the "balance of power" or "legitimacy" or the "impact of personalities," and yet as every new case arises, that knowledge will be empty if one does not understand what the elements of power are, how legitimacy is conceived, and what the impact of structure on events can be. That requires an intuitive feeling, which can be partly taught from history but which is partly indefinable.

*Laqueur:* In other words, the statesman is seeking to solve the same type of question as the scholar, but without the benefit of leisurely analysis. But it is also true that the statesman faces problems of verification. More often than not he has to guess at the realities he is dealing with. If so, by what principles should he be guided in analyzing foreign policy and what are the main pitfalls to be avoided?

*Kissinger:* Yes. The statesman has to make a whole series of judgments that he cannot prove while he is making them. He has to deal with other units (whatever they are called — nations, regions, groups, institutions, continents) that are not necessarily subject to his will, and he therefore has to strike a balance between the capabilities of the other parties and their intentions. A statesman can escape his dilemma by assuming that the other party is always benevolent. If his judgment should turn out to be wrong, however, he may have produced something irretrievable. Consequently, one of the purposes of statesmanship must be to seek to restrict the significance of the other's intentions by one's own actions.

In the abstract, it might appear that it is better to gear policy to the capabilities of the other side rather than to its intentions. Yet if this is carried to an extreme, it leads to a policy that seeks empire or hegemony for oneself. The only way to be sure the other side is not capable of harming you is to reduce it to impotence. Absolute security for one side must mean absolute insecurity for all other sides. For example, the debate that often goes on, over whether the purposes, say, of the Soviet Union are defensive or offensive, could be beside the point. The key question may not be merely whether a country feels threatened, but what it takes to reassure it. If a country is reassured only by the impotence of all its neighbors, then the trend of its policies will be toward hegemony, whatever its motives may be. Defensive motives can therefore lead to aggressive foreign policies.

Any statesman must strike a balance between capability and intention. He cannot rely entirely on the goodwill of another sovereign state, because that would be an abdication of foreign policy. He cannot base his policies on physical preeminence alone, because unless he is willing to establish a world empire, this will only tend to unite his enemies and force him to attempt a cynical and dangerous policy of divide and rule, or other such measures. The structural problem of foreign policy is therefore to try to guarantee the relative security and therefore also the relative insecurity of all the parties. Along with this, some common sense of values must be found so that the participants will not constantly attempt to overthrow the international order.

The application of these principles depends on the conception of a sovereign unit, on what the sovereign units are capable of doing to each other, and on what these units want to do to each other. One tremendous change in the international system occurred at the time of the change from the eighteenth to the nineteenth centuries, when the feudal order broke down and the nation-state emerged. Every feudal ruler was threatened, no matter how benevolently he governed, no matter what his intentions were, because the concept of a legitimate political unit had changed. The same was true at the end of the colonial period. It is clear that all these colonies did not feel oppressed at every period in their history. A few thousand Britishers could not possibly have colonized India without the support of a significant proportion of the population. The change in values that made colonialism appear intolerable was brought in part by the colonizers themselves, and it must be recalled that the concept of an Indian nation was unheard of in the eighteenth century. The ideas brought in by the colonizers changed the concepts of legitimate authority, and therefore brought about a revolutionary situation for British rule in India. The same is true in many other parts of the world. If there is a change in the idea of a legitimate unit, you will automatically have a transformation of the international system and a period of upheaval; this is one of the problems of the contemporary period.

The second problem is what nations are capable of doing to each other. In the eighteenth century, it was a matter of total irrelevance whether China was hostile to the West or vice versa. There was no means by which they could interact with each other in any consistent manner. The technical capability for imposing the will of one region on another simply did not exist. The various regions of the world therefore conducted their foreign policy in virtual isolation from each other, without even any real knowledge of each other. Totally different styles of foreign policy were designed in the East and West. In Europe, foreign policy was based on a group of more or less equal sovereign states that balanced off each other's power. In Asia, foreign policy revolved around a hegemonic power, one country that dominated the whole region by its cultural and physical preeminence and which never had to think of balance of power as it was conceived in the West. And the conduct of foreign policy today, by China, for example, is quite different from that in the West.

Finally, any analysis of foreign policy must obviously include an evaluation of other units' intentions: what do they *want* to do to one another? But underlying this are the more fundamental dimensions of analysis I have described.

*Laqueur:* Any newsman who wants to write something even modestly profound about you and the ideas guiding you mentions the enormous debt you owe to Metternich. As a result there has been a veritable Metternich renaissance. I suspect you may not feel altogether happy about this; however intrinsically interesting the Metternich period, he was clearly, after all, within an international system that came to an end a long time ago.

*Kissinger:* The unfortunate problem for the "Metternich theory" is that I really wanted to write a book about Bismarck, and I only started writing about Metternich as a counterpoise to Bismarck in order to understand the context which Bismarck inherited. The discussion of Metternich grew so long, and I was drawn off into so many other things, that I never got around to finishing the Bismarck book, which is still only half written and was published as an article. So it simply isn't true that I was extremely influenced by Metternich, who operated under quite different conditions.

However, there are a number of aspects to that period that I found fascinating. One is that they managed to create an international system that lasted a hundred years, which is a lot better than any of their successors. Paradoxically, all of their successors said they were making permanent peace and they were lucky if it lasted a generation. The people who made peace at the Congress of Vienna thought they would be lucky if it lasted a decade, and it lasted a hundred years, which shows that statesmen are not always the best prophets.

The Metternich period had many of the elements that reappeared in later periods. Hundreds of feudal states were being consolidated into larger national units, which meant that all the traditional power relationships had to be adjusted both physically and conceptually. As always in revolutionary periods, the emerging new forms existed alongside the old ones. Furthermore, when Napoleon's invasion of Russia failed, the question of a major war emerged, because it suddenly became conceivable to defeat French hegemony.

The American approach to war has always been that war and peace are discrete elements of policy: that you fight a war, you defeat your enemy, and then you make peace and live happily ever after. The difference between this romanticism and the approach of the statesmen at the end of the Napoleonic Wars is very striking. At the end of World War II General Bradley wrote in his autobiography, very scathingly, that the British were obsessed with the Balkans and with southern Europe. He said that of course there was no great military goal to be sought, but what the British lacked in military goals they made up in political opportunity — as if it were somehow sacrilegious to seek a political objective in a war.

A problem emerged at the end of the Napoleonic Wars that

was quite similar to the one that existed at the end of World War II. As the Russian armies entered central Europe, they became the dominant factor in European politics; the more territory they acquired, the greater their ability to determine the shape of the settlement. As the end of the Second World War approached, virtually no attention was paid to this issue, and the postwar world has, of course, been profoundly affected by the decisions about the location of lines of demarcation and the exercise of political control in areas occupied by military forces. It has taken us thirty years to establish some equilibrium on the continent of Europe, and even then it has required the permanent presence of American forces to maintain the equilibrium.

The chief actors at the Congress of Vienna would not permit any military operations to be conducted without having some political goals met. They did not fight a war for unconditional surrender: they fought a war in which Russia had to agree to some political structure as a price for military advance. In the postwar period these agreements limited the Russian capacity to impose their will. To be sure, this is not a very glorious way to fight a war, but it has the significant advantage of linking the bargaining that follows a war to the actions that occurred during it.

*Laqueur:* There are interesting lessons to be learned about the relationship between legitimacy, equilibrium, and peace. But I am sure you will agree that the modern period in the history of diplomacy starts with Bismarck.

*Kissinger:* Of course. Without going into the specifics of his diplomacy, Bismarck essentially believed that an international system can be based entirely on the balance of power. The restraints that had been imposed by the common adherence to legitimate principles, along with the convictions that had developed since the eighteenth century, were so much baggage for him. Every state should be free to conduct its own policy based on its own conception of national interest. If it calculated correctly it would understand that there are inherent limits to its strength, and it would produce a rather moderate foreign policy. But at the same time it placed all its energies on the balance of power. Through extraordinarily skillful and extremely moderate foreign policy, Bismarck managed to create a united Germany and maintain the peace for about forty years, even after upsetting the previous system.

Contrary to popular belief, a policy based on pure balance of power is the most difficult foreign policy to conduct. It requires, first of all, a constantly correct assessment of the elements of power. Secondly, it demands a total ruthlessness and means that statesmen must be able to ignore friendship, loyalty, and anything other than the national interest. Third, it requires a domestic structure that will tolerate if not support this strategy. Fourth, it requires the absence of both permanent friends and permanent enemies, because as soon as a permanent enemy exists, freedom of maneuver is immediately reduced.

After Germany defeated France in 1871, the German generals insisted on the annexation of Alsace-Lorraine, which caused Bismarck to say, "I have achieved much more than I thought desirable in this war." He was correct: France became a permanent German enemy, and Germany's freedom of maneuver was greatly reduced. Indeed, the paradox of the German victory was that it, along with the German unification which followed, produced the very structural dangers that Bismarck sought to avoid. A united Germany was a threat to each of its neighbors; its very existence forced them into an alliance. Subsequent German leaders tried to be "reliable" and consistent in foreign affairs, but this only compounded their problems, for the more rigid their policy, the more united their neighbors became.

All of this is crucial in understanding the great tragedy in Western history: the outbreak of the First World War. There was no reason that justified the enormous numbers of casualties inflicted, the destruction of material and human values, and the overthrow of practically all the political systems that entered the war. There was an unfortunate combination of circumstances. First, the entry of a major new power — Germany — into the international system produced a profoundly unsettling effect. This is inevitable, just as it is today in the instance of the growth of Soviet power. When a country acquires enormous additional resources of power in a relatively short period, it forces adjustments on the other participants in the system. When that country has mediocre leadership, unaware of the implications of their actions, the situation can become highly unmanageable. Bismarck's balance of power system rested on the existence of great European statesmen in every generation. Alas, most statesmen are mediocre, and it was not evil intention but mediocrity that produced World War I. None of the political leaders of Europe understood that their system was tending toward confrontation. None of them understood that a war with modern weapons would be violently destructive. None of them understood that they were making military plans that would spread a war over at least all of Europe. None of them understood that they were heading into a four-year conflict.

Each of the European countries had drawn lessons from history that made a catastrophe highly likely. The Austrians, for example, decided that Serbia was like Sardinia, and that they had to knock it out before it organized all of the Balkans. All of them made military plans according to their individual judgments of history, and the military decisions ran away with political judgment in the end.

There is a lesson to this story, and it regards balance of power. A balance is important — perhaps even more so today than during Bismarck's lifetime — but if a balance of power becomes an end in itself it becomes self-destructive. A country without strength will become the plaything of forces out of its control, but a country that makes its decisions only on military grounds will be dragged into adventures with consequences it cannot foresee. We have to learn from World War II, when a preponderance of strength in one country tempted it to attack, but we also have to learn from World War I, when a balance of strength produced a war because nobody got it under political control and put it in the service of foreign policy.

*Laqueur:* Seen in retrospect, what was the purpose (if any) of the First World War and in what way did it constitute the "watershed" you just mentioned?

*Kissinger:* If there was any real purpose to World War I, it was that of destroying German hegemony, but the Versailles peace settlement was more favorable to German expansion than the world that existed previously. Before the war Germany had France on one side and Russia on the other, with Britain commanding the seas. After the peace conference, Germany came to be surrounded by weak successor states of uncertain domestic strength. None of them was capable of resisting Germany. Moreover, Russia — the Soviet Union — was no longer part of the European system, and the weak states were at least as afraid of the Soviet Union as they were of Germany. In short, the diplomats had paid insufficient attention to the structure of the postwar world.

The result was that French vigilance was the only hope for European peace. Peace could be preserved if France had a hairtrigger response and if Germany was permanently disarmed. France had the permanent obligation of becoming the policeman of Europe. But France had just lost two million young people — 5 percent of its population — in the war and was in no condition to carry out this role. Britain was even less inclined to police Germany, because the English had always supported the weaker against the stronger on the continent and were instinctively led to support Germany against France.

Given this political and military problem, the French built

the Maginot line, thus guaranteeing that Germany sooner or later would become predominant in Europe. The Versailles agreement could only be maintained through an offensive French strategy, and as soon as the French withdrew behind the Maginot line, they invited the Germans to expand toward the east. The Versailles settlement was, as we all know, very onerous for the Germans and was bound to inflame Germany, but that is not the issue. The central point is that statesmen can misconceive their structural problems and their balance of power interests. When Hitler took over in Germany, he had a relatively easy task. He had only to rearm and reoccupy the Rhineland, and Eastern Europe lay defenseless before him. When France did not move following the occupation of the Rhineland, it was all over. From a structural point of view, it was just a question of time before Austria, Czechoslovakia, and Poland fell — and indeed a moderate German leadership would probably have brought about this domination without a world war. All of this stemmed from the Versailles agreement, which put a burden on France that could not be met.

*Laqueur:* And then there was the Second World War, another "watershed." But again, as in World War I, few if any people thought at the time of the structure of peace that would follow the war except perhaps in the most general terms of friendship, mutual trust, and the other noble sentiments mentioned in wartime programmatic speeches about the United Nations and related topics. If so, what are the "lessons" of the most recent period of history?

*Kissinger:* After World War II the problem of German hegemony disappeared, but another colossal country spread itself into the center of Europe. In contrast to the period of the Congress of Vienna, none of the statesmen of the war years, except perhaps Churchill, gave any attention to what would happen after the war. Americans were determined not to discuss the postwar period while the struggle was going on. We were determined that we were going to base the postwar period on good faith and getting along with everybody. The victors in World War II would work together in the postwar period. I do not know whether anything else could have been done; we will probably never know. We do know, however, that practically no attention was paid to the issue of the structure of the postwar peace until the Soviet Army was in the center of Europe. Once Eastern Europe was under Communist domination, for the first time in European history there was no chance to balance Russian power through European sources.

In addition to the sudden expansion of Russian hegemony, the elements of power became incongruous with each other. In the past there had almost always been a direct relationship between economic, military, and political power. It was very rare that a country could be very strong economically and very weak militarily. In the postwar world, it is possible to be militarily very strong and economically of moderate strength. It is also possible, as in the case of Japan, to be economically very strong and militarily feeble.

What can be learned from history in the postwar epoch? You cannot learn how to handle the Middle East crisis that broke out in 1973, but you *can* learn from the structural problems that I have very superficially discussed. In each period we must decide which of these structural problems is relevant. History is not a cookbook which gives recipes; it teaches by analogy and forces us to decide what, if anything, is analogous. History gives us a feel for the significance of events, but it does not teach which individual events are significant. It is impossible to write down a conceptual scheme and apply it mechanically to evolving situations. Certain principles can be developed, certain understandings can be elaborated, but it is impossible to predict in advance how they apply to concrete situations.

It is dangerously arrogant to believe that foreign policy can be conducted effectively without knowing something of how other generations have faced comparable problems — the compromises they have had to make, how their best judgments turned out, and how limited human foresight is, even in the best men and under optimal circumstances. We always tend to think of historical tragedy as failing to get what we want, but if we study history we find that the worst tragedies have occurred when people got what they wanted . . . and it turned out to be the wrong objective.

.

# ON WORLD AFFAIRS
## *An Interview*

---

*Conversation between Dr. Kissinger and a group of*
Der Spiegel *editors, published in* Der Spiegel, *July
1978, and in* Encounter, *November 1978*

---

Dr. Kissinger, *in the world at large and in the USA itself there is a certain feeling of dissatisfaction with America's leadership. You yourself have now been out of office for eighteen months. How does it feel to be a man of whom many people inside and outside America are saying this would never have happened in his time, this would never have happened when Henry Kissinger was in office?*

*Kissinger:* In fairness one has to say that the new Administration was not elected necessarily to carry out the policies that I would have carried out. So I think it is correct to say that certain matters would have been handled differently in terms of style and maybe in terms of substance. But then there was, after all, a change in administration.

*You have always been careful not to criticize the present government, except very discreetly. What would be your recommendations to the Presidency to improve its success at home and abroad?*

*Kissinger:* First, let me explain the basic position that I have adopted. I had to contribute to the conduct of foreign policy for eight years, under conditions of near civil war. When I now go through the documents for my book, I realize how anesthetized we were at that time and how we almost took this constant result for granted.

I formed the very strong opinion at that time that what the top leadership of the country needs is an atmosphere in which its motives are not constantly challenged and in which it knows that those who have an influence on public opinion are not just waiting for an excuse to create a "credibility gap."

Therefore, I have been very careful not to make criticisms on essentially tactical issues and to give the Administration the sense that, on those items on which I agree, I will even give it public support. When I do criticize or when I do state a different opinion, I want it clearly understood by our public that this is not an attempt to regain lost power or to undermine the confidence of the public in our government, which I really think is one of the biggest problems of our period.

And this I think has to be understood both for this conversation and for my general public attitude.

*Accepting that, what policy changes would you recommend to the Carter government?*

*Kissinger:* I think what is essential to be done is that there is a clearly articulated concept of American foreign policy which everybody can understand and toward which other nations and our own public can orient themselves.

I think it is not possible to go on indefinitely with these fluctuations which are identified as a contest between this or that personality within the Administration, so that in the period of four weeks you can get very tough talk about the Soviet role in Africa and the Cuban role in Angola, and then the sending of a political envoy to Angola, and each of these contradictory actions will be ascribed to the "victory" of a different adviser.

This I would say is the fundamental requirement of our foreign policy. Whether I would then agree with the results is, to be sure, a different issue.

*You said only recently that the President, every President, must lead rather than simply put suggestions forward and then let them drop again.*

*Kissinger:* I do not say that the President does not lead. I do not contest his proposition that he makes the final decision. But foreign policy is not simply making final decisions on individual cases. Foreign policy is also establishing the relationship between individual cases and developing a sense of nuance among them.

The President has said that he deliberately permits each of his chief advisers, or many of his chief advisers, to articulate different policies so that the public understands what the various issues are.

That is what I question. I think he has an obligation to explain what the different points of view may be; but in a democracy, the different points of view emerge anyway. There would be enough Republicans who would give a different point of view, and for that matter enough Democrats. The President does not himself have to generate a public debate within his Administration in order to teach the public that there are many different points of view.

What is expected of a President is to define clearly what the national purpose is, what the policies are, and to defend this against the inevitable criticisms that a pluralistic society tends to generate.

*The differing point of view of the Republicans was made very plain to him in May in the twenty-nine-page attack of all thirty-eight Republican Senators on the President and his foreign policy, in which they stated: "After 15 short months of incoherence, inconsistency and slovenliness, our foreign policy and the aims of national security are in confusion; everywhere in the world we are being confronted with Soviet presumptuousness."*

*For eight years you were security adviser and foreign minister to two Republican Presidents. Do you agree with this damning condemnation from the Republican faction of the Senate?*

Kissinger: Let me say two things. I did not work on this document. I have established the firm principle that I will not work on "joint documents." If I have something to say, I will say it in my own name, but not together with a group of others.

Secondly, it is in the logic of the democratic political process (and especially of a pluralistic society such as ours) that points of view contrary to that of whatever administration is in office will emerge; and what you have read is a fair statement of what many Republicans believe.

*But you yourself, Dr. Kissinger, have criticized the Cuba policy of the Administration; in the matter of Eurocommunism you are much stricter, very much stricter than the Carter Administration; and on the question of human rights you harbor the fear that this policy is affecting the weaker, smaller allies of the USA more than the strong and powerful opponent in Moscow.*

*Kissinger:* That is correct. I have not agreed with all the elements of our African policy. I think, for one thing, that there is a certain confusion when one first criticizes Cuba for having engineered the invasion from Angola and then sends a diplomat to Luanda within three weeks of making these accusations. I myself would not have recommended that. And I am convinced that we have polarized the situation in Rhodesia by our indifference, amounting to opposition to the so-called internal solution. So it is true that on African policy I have expressed my doubts.

On human rights, I agree with the objective. But the problem in foreign policy is not simply to state an objective but to be able to carry it out over an extended period of time in such a manner that it enhances the impression of other countries that one knows how to achieve one's objective. Otherwise even the noblest goal can wind up creating an impression of impotence.

*Those contradictions you were just speaking of make the foreign policy of the present Administration a mystery to many people. Critics see no concept behind the initiatives and decisions. Do you see one?*

*Kissinger:* I think one has to keep in mind a number of aspects here. As a general proposition the Republican Party has perhaps had fewer experts on foreign policy; but, therefore, when it has been in office it has been able to concentrate power in fewer hands —

*— on Nixon and Kissinger or, later, on just Kissinger —*

*Kissinger:* — but also Dulles and Eisenhower. In any case, it has stood for less diffused concepts. The Democratic Party, on the other hand, has many centers of power, many different views on the nature of foreign policy, and the differences between Senator McGovern and Security Adviser Brzezinski, for example, or between UN Ambassador Young and the more conservative Democrats in the Senate, are very substantial.

So that a Democratic President almost invariably is faced with various claims to a role in foreign policy, and in attempting to meet them all or to reconcile them there is the possibility that the impression is created of a more diffused foreign policy. If you look at the early Kennedy period, I think you will find the same symptoms you find now. I think there *is* a concept, I think the President has some rather clear ideas of what he wants. The problem is, in foreign policy, how you get from here to there, and this is where most of the disagreements are.

*It would interest us as Europeans whether you consider the President acted correctly over the question of the neutron bomb.*

*Kissinger:* No, on that I would have disagreed with the President.

*So you would have approved the building and mounting of the neutron bomb?*

*Kissinger:* With all respect, this is the wrong question. Basically I think the "neutron bomb" is not a wonder weapon, and fundamentally its objectives can be achieved with many other weapons. Therefore, I think the neutron bomb should have been handled as a technical issue to be decided essentially by technicians. I do not understand the moral issue that is raised by a bomb whose radiation damage is less than that of any Soviet weapon now in the Soviet arsenal, and the only "advantage" that the Soviet weapons have is that, in addition to having more radiation, they also have enormously more explosive power. And why to be incinerated in addition to being radiated is a moral advantage eludes me. But this may be a kind of moral blind spot. I just do not understand the moral issue involved in the neutron bomb at all.

Secondly, I do not think the neutron bomb is all that important a weapon.

Thirdly, I think that if we are custodians (or if we think we are) of the nuclear future of the Alliance — then we have to be willing to make the final decisions regarding the most appropriate type of weapon and not ask our allies to make them for us.

And, fourth, I cannot accept the proposition that the Soviet Union can intervene in the matter of what warheads we build — when any attempt by us to make the slightest proposal with respect to the warheads they put on their weapons would be mockingly rejected.

So, for all these reasons, I do not think the neutron bomb was worth making that big an issue about on either side of the Atlantic.

*What would you have done?*

*Kissinger:* I would have either put it into the arsenal or routinely deferred it — almost certainly the former. Now I am afraid that the Soviets may learn from this that they can intervene in the deployment of all other weapons.

*We see what you mean. The Soviets could get the impression — and this is also true for the one-sided American renunciation of the building of the B-1 bomber and the announcement that Amer-*

*ica will withdraw its troops from South Korea — that they are receiving concessions without having to offer anything in return. Would you have insisted on reciprocal concessions?*

*Kissinger:* Let's not discuss what I would or would not have done. I would say that, as a general rule, the Soviet Union does not pay for services that have already been rendered.

*Have the Russians got a stronger foothold in Africa than you would have believed possible five years ago?*

*Kissinger:* Yes; and that, I have to say in fairness, already started when I was in office.

*There are several different interpretations of how the Russians have made such headway in Africa. It began, as you say, while you were still in office, and I'm sure you must have asked the Russians for an explanation. What did they reply to you?*

*Kissinger:* The Soviets claimed that they were only responding to African requests. But we were less concerned with Soviet explanations than with their actions. My concern was to stop this first major Soviet adventure in Africa in fifteen years.

Of course one will never be able to prove these things, and I eventually will write about them in some detail. But, fundamentally, the dividing line began to be crossed in 1975 in two ways.

When the civil war in Angola started between the three factions of Neto, Roberto, and Savimbi, it was like many other African civil wars, in the outcome of which one could have a preference, but one did not need to make it a matter of superpower policies. For example, we accepted the victory of the Frelimo in Mozambique because we concluded that it had been achieved essentially by indigenous efforts with some reasonable ouside support.

But in 1975 we found that between April and June something like $200 million worth of Soviet equipment was introduced on the side of Neto, which was more military equipment than all the rest of the world gave to all the rest of Africa put together.

So, therefore, what the Soviet Union has been doing is, for the first time, massively introducing military equipment and starting a cycle of upheavals similar to the impact of their first introduction of military equipment into the Middle East, into Egypt, in 1954, which led to over twenty years of constantly growing tension.

At this point, we sought to stop this by assisting the black forces that were resisting the takeover. When we did this, the Soviets escalated yet another level by introducing Cubans.

*And you were as surprised by that as the rest of the world.*

*Kissinger:* Yes. By both of these developments; we did not expect either. At that point, by a variety of means, we were in my view on the verge of stopping even that second escalation when the Congress cut off any means of support.

Had we succeeded in Angola, there would have been no Ethiopia. The situation in Southern Africa would today be entirely different, and I think this was one of the decisive watersheds.

*One gets the impression today that you saw your system of the mutual responsibility of the two superpowers as being on the razor's edge. Your criticism of the Soviet Union became stronger than we had come to expect from you. . . .*

*Kissinger:* I think there were a variety of reasons for these actions. One was that you pay for your actions in politics sooner or later. The trouble is you don't usually pay immediately and, therefore, when it happens, people no longer remember what the cause was.

We concluded the Vietnam war under near–civil-war conditions, we went through Watergate, and everybody was saying, "Look, it doesn't affect the conduct of foreign policy at all." But sooner or later the erosion of executive authority reaches a point where somebody tries to test you. You cannot prove what that exact reason was; but this erosion is certainly, in my view, a contributing cause.

The second is that precisely because of the erosion of executive authority a number of the agreements we have made with the Soviet Union, such as the trade agreement, could not be implemented —

*— because Congress intervened and made the trade agreement dependent on freedom of emigration for Soviet Jews and in addition reduced the credit limit to a ridiculous 75 million dollars, almost to a pittance.*

*Kissinger:* That is right; and the Vladivostok agreement could also not be realized as rapidly as possible. So one of our basic thoughts — that we could, through actions of mutual restraint, create inhibitions to Soviet maneuvers of this kind — had been removed.

Therefore, we lost both the capacity to create incentives for responsible behavior and the capacity to create penalties for irresponsible behavior — both as a result of the decline of executive authority. I think this was the reason why the Soviets made their attempts in Angola in 1975 — although I would also say the Soviets were probably surprised by our Congress's reaction in preventing our countermove. I think until then the Soviets were prepared for a withdrawal. That was my strong impression in all my dealings with the Soviets.

*So you think the Soviets suddenly saw that local conditions were favorable to them, and it is not a question of a geographical offensive planned over a long period?*

*Kissinger:* No, I don't think when it started it was intended this way. I think when the Soviets started in Angola, they went further than they normally had but still within limits that would have been containable.

*And Congress is to blame for not stopping them?*

*Kissinger:* Well, the Congress and the way we were playing with our domestic authority for almost a decade.

*Isn't it true that Congress — understandably at that time — wanted to avoid anything that might have led to another Vietnam? And weren't there reasons for the internal loss of authority?*

*Kissinger:* Of course, it is understandable; but in Angola there was no chance whatever of there being a new Vietnam. In fact, it is very important to understand the essence of a problem. There was no intention of sending American troops to Angola under any circumstances; there was no possibility of anybody introducing 500,000 troops into Angola. In fact, it was the Russians through the Cubans who were in our position, that is to say, in the position we were in in Vietnam. We were backing the local population against foreign invaders or at least against foreigners.

*But couldn't you make that clear to Congress?*

*Kissinger:* Well, at that point, I don't think the Congress was eager to listen to this sort of argument. But, again, I would have to say you cannot understand this entirely in terms of 1975. You have to go back to the systematic undermining of executive authority that started in 1967, to the domestic debate that resulted from the Vietnam war and created such profound divisions — whoever's fault it was — that over a period of time it weakened the executive authority of the President.

*Do you accept the Cuban claim that it was their own idea to intervene in Africa?*

*Kissinger:* I think that is possible but not probable. I am sure there are a lot of Caribbean islands that have a dream of global significance. But without Soviet logistics, transportation, and subvention, the Cubans could not have implemented it.

*According to the latest American estimates, Cuba is costing the Soviets more than six million dollars daily in economic and military aid this year.*

Kissinger: I don't doubt that for Castro it is a much more exciting life to be a world figure than to be the president of a "Caribbean Switzerland," which is the best he can achieve if he sticks to his own knitting.

*If someone had come into your office five years ago and said: "Mr. Secretary, we must keep a close watch on what the Cubans will do in Africa," would you have listened to him?*

Kissinger: No, I would have removed him from my foreign policy staff.

*Recently you said: "I simply cannot believe that Cuba, a country with nine million inhabitants, is engaged in world politics and that the greatest industrial state on earth, the USA, can find no way of preventing this. I simply cannot believe it."*

Kissinger: I cannot accept the myth of the invincible Cuban.

*Why then is it that America cannot get rid of Cuban interference in Africa?*

Kissinger: Because there is no consensus of its significance. You have, for example, the views of our Ambassador to the United Nations [Andrew Young], who does not believe that the Cuban intervention in Africa is of any geopolitical significance.

*He even says that the presence of the Cubans in Africa has had a stabilizing effect.*

Kissinger: At first he said it had a stabilizing influence, and on other occasions he has said that one also has to inquire into who really supports the opponents of Neto in Angola —

*— By which he meant the South Africans —*

*Kissinger:* — and then he says he does not consider what has happened in the Horn of Africa to be of geopolitical significance.

*Yes, he said: "When the Cubans suddenly sent troops into the Ogaden Horn Province, we took up this emotional position and decided that these thousand miles of sand were of enormous strategic importance. That is ridiculous."*

*Kissinger:* If you don't believe it is of geopolitical significance, then you have no need to stop it. So it is not a problem of means; it is a problem of thought, and I happen to believe that the appearance — the fact that one is told that we must do certain things, otherwise the Cubans will intervene — could be interpreted by other nations as a sign of American impotence.

*Do you have sufficient information to form a judgment on whether Cuba and Russia really did support the Shaba invasion or not? Castro denies it vehemently.*

*Kissinger:* I have no information whatever whether Cubans actually marched into Shaba but I will say two things, which I keep repeating.

In foreign policy it is important to understand the essence of the problem. The invasion of the Shaba Province occurred by means of the Katanga gendarmes. The Katanga gendarmes have lived where they are now in the northern part of Angola for twelve years. In that whole time they never invaded Zaire. After the Cubans appeared, there have been two invasions in a period of thirteen months. It would be the strangest kind of coincidence if there were not some connection between these events.

Secondly, how would people react if an American President said about a country where we have 20,000 troops either that we didn't know that there was the planning of an invasion of a neighboring country — which is what Castro sometimes claims — or that he did know but was unable to dissuade these people from the invasion? I think if this happened to an American President who has 20,000 troops in another country, the assault by our media on the grounds of "credibility" would be unbelievable. So I have not even asked our government to let me see the intelligence reports on which they based their judgment; it is inherent in the situation that there must be a connection between the Cuban presence and that invasion, and if there is no connection — well, if you put a loose cannon on a deck, you cannot then say you are not responsible when it starts rolling because you didn't predict the particular wave which caused it to roll.

*Was the sending in of French and Belgian paratroopers a reasonable reaction in your eyes?*

*Kissinger:* Yes, and I think we owe France a great debt of gratitude for doing that.

*Were you wrongly interpreted or quoted when you were attributed as saying, at the beginning of April, that the intervention of the Soviets in Africa is comparable with the expansionist policy of Hitler's Germany?*

*Kissinger:* No, I have not said that. The Nazis and Communists are totally different phenomena. What I have said is: Any nation has to make a choice between being psychologically certain and paying a heavy price if it turns out to be wrong, or being psychologically uncertain and paying a low price for taking the necessary precautions. My point is that it would have been relatively easy to stop Hitler in 1936, after the occupation of the Rhineland, but people would still debate today whether he was a misunderstood nationalist or a maniac bent on world domination. By 1941, everybody knew who Hitler was; and it was knowledge for which one had to pay 20 million lives.

Similarly, in Africa in 1975 it was relatively easy to stop the Cubans and the Soviets in Angola. Each successive event will cost more; only in this sense do I compare the problem. I do not think that Soviet strategy is comparable to Nazi strategy. The

Soviets are much more patient; they are much less geared to one individual; and I don't even believe that the Soviets have a clear-cut overall strategy.

I think they have a strategy designed to accumulate strength and a conviction that this strength will sooner or later be translatable into some geopolitical position; but they do not have a fixed plan. Soviet actions are not the result of a fixed plan, but the result of an accumulation of opportunities.

On the other hand, one cannot look at what has happened in Afghanistan, Aden, Ethiopia, and Angola and draw a line between these various countries without coming to certain geopolitical conclusions.

*Geopolitically then, that means that Saudi Arabia, the richest oil country and best friend to the West, is situated in the middle of an area of unrest that can be influenced by the Communists?*

*Kissinger:* I would say that this appears to be the result of this policy. I am not saying this is the design.

*Does the Cuban and Russian activity in Africa present a real threat in your eyes? Will the end result be that the military and political balance will tip in favor of the Soviets?*

*Kissinger:* Again, the nature of these problems is that you cannot prove it until the worst has happened, and by then it will be too late to do something about it. From my conversations with people in the Middle East, I know that they are judging our reaction in a rather gloomy way.

Now, at what point the impression is created that this represents an inexorable wave — and thereby starts a series of events that nobody has planned and that nobody can then control — that I cannot predict. But I believe that such a point exists. I find it hard, however, to believe that the Soviet Union would put $1 billion worth of arms and another 20,000 troops into a country — as it did in Ethiopia right across the Straits from Saudi

Arabia — without promising itself something more than maintaining the borders of Ethiopia —

*— which has meanwhile become the most heavily armed African state through the Soviet supply of arms.*

*Kissinger:* And after all, we have to look at what happened in Afghanistan, contested for over a century. The British considered it important enough to fight innumerable wars on that frontier because they thought that the possession of Afghanistan had some influence on the security of the Indian subcontinent. Afghanistan was 80 percent in the Soviet sphere of influence to begin with. We were not engaged in a very active foreign policy there; and yet we have seen that a government has been established there entirely composed of Communists, and that even that limited balance which existed has now been overthrown. That cannot be an accident.

*Does all this mean that the policy of détente is in a state of crisis from which it will be difficult to extricate it?*

*Kissinger:* Yes, there is a crisis of détente. But it is not insoluble, which, for that matter, has been pointed out both by our President and by the Secretary of State. I think it is possible to solve it; but it will not solve itself.

*What message must one give the Russians to bring about a different situation in Africa?*

*Kissinger:* That it isn't possible to have both détente and expansion.

*But the Russians have said, and not for the first time, that for them détente means on the one hand more or less the end of the arms race in the atomic sector, but at the same time continued support of the so-called progressive forces in the countries of the Third World.*

*Kissinger:* That, as a general principle, is certainly what they have said; but the extent to which that is applied, after all, makes a difference. It makes a difference whether you give some modest support to the Frelimo, which they did in Mozambique, or whether you send $1 billion worth of arms by a forced-draft airlift into Ethiopia.

It makes a difference whether you give some philosophical encouragement to so-called liberation movements (as we give philosophical encouragement to other groups), or whether you send in 20,000 Cuban troops. All of this makes an enormous difference.

And this precise difference will determine whether détente will lead to a real relaxation of tension, or whether it is a cover for Soviet expansionism.

*In any case, it seems that the word "détente" has once more been banished — as it was once by Gerald Ford — from the vocabulary of the West.*

*Kissinger:* Unfortunately, détente became a political issue in the United States, partly as a result of the facts that I described earlier, paradoxically enough by the very people who used to accuse our administration of being "too tough." The fact of a détente policy shouldn't be disputed. Its content should be disputed.

I think every Western government has an obligation to demonstrate to its people that it is making a serious effort to avoid the dangers of war. If it does not do this, it will wind up with all the domestic divisions of the Vietnam crisis.

On the other hand, one must also be sure that peace does not become the only objective because, if it becomes the only objective, it will lead to blackmail. To navigate between these extremes is the art of statesmanship; not to say you are for or against détente, or that you are for or against the Cold War.

*Can we still speak of détente at all at the moment?*

*Kissinger:* I think right now there is no clear-cut concept of East-West relations on either side.

*How would you then define the present situation? As a belligerent peace?*

*Kissinger:* At the moment, we have a tendency to play situations entirely tactically, both on the détente side and on the conflict side; and there is no coherent pattern that is, at this moment, emerging.

*Your successor in the office of security adviser, Zbigniew Brzezinski, recently accused the Russians of damaging the code of détente. But nobody has ever defined together with the Russians what form this code could take, not even you or President Nixon.*

*Kissinger:* Well, that is not exactly true. We signed and published a declaration of principles and a treaty for the prevention of nuclear war, both of which required either side to refrain from seeking a unilateral advantage. Both spoke of consultations regarding matters that might threaten the peace. With goodwill, these clauses could have been interpreted in the right way. So I think it is possible, through a combination of firmness and flexibility, to reestablish the code of conduct; but it requires both. It cannot be done with rhetoric.

*Has détente already survived similar crises?*

*Kissinger:* I would think that going to Moscow in 1972 — after having mined Haiphong and while we were bombing Vietnam — was not a minor matter. As far as the Middle East was concerned, it was our judgment that we were in a stronger position there than the Soviet Union was. Of course, the Soviet Union was not doing everything we would have wanted. Still, we were generally quite confident about being able to manage the crises in the Middle East.

*Ever since the beginning of détente, both sides have continued to build up their armaments. One could go as far as to say, paradoxically, there has to be armament in order for there to be détente.*

*Kissinger:* But the opposite would not be true: that, therefore, in the absence of détente you would have less armament. In the absence of détente, you would have even more armament. The advantage of détente has been that it makes the environment somewhat more predictable.

*Except that the American Congress wants to spend more money on armaments than the American President does at the moment.*

*Kissinger:* This is a new development. Until 1974 the Congress consistently tried to give much less.

*What, in your view, lies behind the massive Russian rearmament? President Carter said in Annapolis that the Russians are arming far beyond their natural security requirements. But who decides what their natural requirements are?*

*Kissinger:* Of course, you have to ask yourself what do the Soviets consider their natural security requirements.

*They have told us many times that they have to be "as strong as the West plus China plus Iran."*

*Kissinger:* Well, the Soviet Union, as the inheritor of Russian history, probably has a very highly developed sense of insecurity. Therefore this produces a tendency to arms. Another factor is the paradox that the Communist states have really no normal method for arriving at decisions except by the contest of bureaucratic forces, and within that contest the military establishment always has a very great voice. Therefore, inevitably, it has a claim on resources.

Thirdly, if you look at Communist industries, Communist economic development, it is generally not the most spectacular success of the Communist system. In fact, you could say that the one thing that the Communist systems do better than any other one thing is the accumulation of arms, and there is an almost inevitable tendency to do those things which a nation does well — to continue doing them.

Anyway, I don't believe that there is a fixed plan for world domination. I don't believe, for example, that the Romans had a scheme to achieve a Roman Empire; all one's study of Roman history would tend to indicate that they fell into one situation after another. Nevertheless, in time they achieved such a predominance that they nevertheless created an empire.

*Do you see a Soviet Empire comparable to the Roman Empire?*

*Kissinger:* I would say that the long-term geopolitical position of the Soviet Union is not brilliant. The long-term domestic evolution of the Soviet Union is not exactly brilliant. Therefore, the temptation to substitute foreign policy successes for the domestic construction must be very great, and very soon they will have the means — and they have already growing means — to do it. Five years ago, certainly ten years ago, they could not have transported $1 billion worth of arms to Ethiopia in a very short period of time.

So, when I say they don't have a fixed plan, it doesn't mean that they will not acquire the power to take advantage of those opportunities that a revolutionary world inevitably generates.

*Some 36 percent of your American fellow countrymen believe that the East is already superior to the West militarily. Can that really be so?*

*Kissinger:* This I don't happen to believe. I think that if you look at the potential strength of the West, that if the Soviets ever triggered us into a real mobilization of our resources, we could still outdo them enough, and, therefore, there is a limit beyond which the Soviet Union will be very reluctant to push us even if their forces-in-being are larger than ours, unless they could knock us out completely, which I do not believe they can do.

To risk everything on one throw of the dice would, in any event, be against the Communist philosophy of having history on their side. I still believe that our potential strength and even our actual strength is not that precarious.

*The Russians think as you do. They themselves say that they are inferior to the Americans worldwide. And they say that they can only compensate for this by maintaining local superiority in Europe by means of their tank concentration which is a factor in the correlation of forces, of the so-called balance.*

*Kissinger:* I think that the Soviet military buildup is reaching a point where in a measurable period of time they will be able to threaten not only Europe, but also many other regions simultaneously, and this is a matter to which we have to pay very great attention.

*Does the stationing of the new Russian SS-20 rockets make Western countermeasures necessary?*

*Kissinger:* Well, I have, from my first book on, and in an interview with you [in 1959] maintained that the time when Europe could rely entirely on weapons and forces stationed far away was drawing to an end, and I have always believed that the regional balance in Europe requires increasingly greater emphasis.

*That would imply that the Russians must withdraw their tanks or the West must set something equivalent against them.*

*Kissinger:* Yes. You know there is a limit beyond which withdrawals really don't do you much good because when they go back 400 miles, they have a capacity to reinforce. I don't know what the studies show; how long it would take them to bring those tanks back. You cannot, in other words, establish the balance only by Soviet withdrawals. There has to be a buildup of Western forces to achieve the balance.

*Would the 11,000 cruise missiles which the Americans may perhaps construct be something with which the Russians would have to reckon?*

*Kissinger:* I have never believed in any one wonder-weapon. The fact is, I saved the missile when the Pentagon wanted to drop it from the budget in 1973. So, I am in favor of it, but I don't think one should say that it is only the cruise missile that can be a counterweight to the SS-20, so long as the decision is made that there will be *some* counterweight to the SS-20. It could be a cruise missile, it could be a ballistic missile. I am a great believer in first making a decision in principle: What is it that you are trying to do? Then the technical implementation of that decision is a secondary question. I am not at all against cruise missiles. I think the cruise missile is one device; other types of missiles could also be considered.

*You also mentioned Soviet air-transport capacity and you said that a few years ago the Russians would not have been able to organize an aerial bridge such as that to Ethiopia now. Have they meanwhile become superior to the Americans in their capacity to transport troops and equipment over long distances in a short time?*

*Kissinger:* First of all, in most areas in question their distances are much shorter than ours. So I would think probably our airlift capacity is still superior if you simply count the number of airplanes and their capacity. But if you relate them to the distances in areas that are likely to be in dispute, they have made very great progress in approaching our capability.

*The Russians repeat that they are in every way inferior to the USA in amphibious warfare. And actually there has been no proof to the contrary.*

*Kissinger:* Well, how do you propose to prove it? You would have to lose a war. . . .

*Nevertheless the argument goes on. But what do you think is behind the gigantic Soviet naval rearmament? Is it a Tirpitz-like illusion, a sort of need to catch up, or do the Russians think that they require this shining weapon for their role in world politics?*

*Kissinger:* Of all Soviet armament efforts, the one that worries me relatively least is their naval buildup, especially their surface navy. It is very difficult for a country that has no sea tradition to establish a preeminent naval position.

*The bear is still the bear?*

*Kissinger:* I mean, after all, Germany, which had a long and outstanding military tradition, never really used its surface fleet with strategic effectiveness.

*Germany was confined within a sea triangle and the Russians are based in the Murmansk fjord.*

*Kissinger:* I was just going to say this. You must consider that a large percentage of the Soviet navy is in Murmansk; the northern fleet is in one port. I am not saying it is insignificant, but I would have thought that in naval warfare we have geopolitical advantages that I would count decidedly on our side.

*But the task which the Russians have set themselves, to maintain a presence in all the oceans of the world, may induce them to meddle in matters which otherwise they would have left alone.*

*Kissinger:* Well, it gives them a capacity to project power into areas where they could not have done it previously. I think it gives them a capacity for intervention, a capacity for harassment that they would not otherwise have had — quite apart from their submarine fleet, which I rate much higher than their surface fleet.

*But a surface fleet presence is visible and committed. The Russians can hardly say that they could not intervene in this place or that because it was too far away.*

*Kissinger:* They can do that better, though, with airplanes than with ships. After all, one should never give the Soviets excessive credit. It is, after all, not impossible that when the Soviets establish their military budget they divide it up among their services the way this has been known to happen in other states — on the basis of the bureaucratic weight of the various contestants — and that they may be building things for which there is no overwhelming geopolitical need. Why should they be immune from these bureaucratic complexes?

*It is conceivable that in regard to Russian armament the West has false information or is working on wrong estimates, that we may be inclined to overestimate Russian armaments as, for instance, the German Luftwaffe was overestimated before the outbreak of World War II. At that time the British thought that Hitler had 10,000 aircraft whereas in reality he had only 2,500.*

*Kissinger:* Yes, although they didn't achieve quite so little. Seriously, it is quite possible that the efficiency of the Soviet military forces is not as high as you would deduce from simply counting their numbers. It is also true that certainly in airplanes (and probably in many other weapons) the West is probably technologically superior. And this helps to establish a certain amount of balance.

There must be some reason why the Soviets at no time since the end of the war have ever run the risk of a direct confrontation with the United States, once they understood that certain actions would indeed produce it. They have usually acted only in areas where there was some doubt about whether it would lead to a confrontation.

Having said all of this, I believe nevertheless that the growth of Soviet military strength in the last ten years, if you project it over another ten years, would create military realities that must have political consequences. The West must, therefore, absolutely strengthen its military capacity.

*The argument is often heard here in Washington that one must show more toughness to the Russians. The argument runs something like this: The Russians' trump card is military power; the West's trump cards are industry and technological progress. If the Russians do not show themselves more forthcoming in the military field (in Africa, for instance) the West must play its economic trump cards.*

*Kissinger:* It is always a mistake to speak of any one card you have as if it were the trump.

The hardest thing to understand about foreign policy is that it has to be extended over time and that there are no decisive individual moves. Within this context, however, I have always believed that there has to be some relationship between the economic assistance that is being given to the Soviet Union directly or indirectly, and its political conduct, especially its foreign policy conduct. Whether that in itself is decisive or not cannot be determined in the abstract, or theoretically. But there is something wrong if the West finances the military expansion of the Soviet Union.

*Does that apply also to the 13.8 million tons of grain which Moscow had to buy in the USA last year and got at preferential prices? The US farmers, after all, have a lobby.*

*Kissinger:* I have always been in favor of relating the agricultural sales to foreign policy conduct.

*During your visit to Hamburg in May you said that it was important, when talking to Brezhnev to Fraktur zu reden [to talk black and white]. What should one understand by that? How can it be done?*

*Kissinger:* I think it is very important not to have ambiguities. These inevitably produce temptations to probe. Since Soviet policies usually are made with some care and always made with complicated bureaucratic compromises, I think it is extremely important to be very clear-cut with the Soviets. We always attempted to do this. I don't say this has to be done publicly, but I think it is important.

*You have spent days and days in very private sessions with Brezhnev and Gromyko. Could you talk toughly, candidly, and frankly? And did they accept that?*

*Kissinger:* I have always thought that to talk directly and frankly is the best method of dealing with the Soviets.

*You once described Russian foreign policy as "basically unimaginative." The strength of Soviet foreign policy lies in their colossal pertinacity, the capacity to play this pertinacity card against our impatience. If, in negotiation, we have not made some new proposal inside three months, then we ourselves become uneasy — and the Russians exploit this. If, however, the Russians are employing, exploiting, or using the Cubans as we think they are at the moment, they are perhaps not quite so unimaginative.*

*Kissinger:* I have to say that the use of Cubans is something that I would not have predicted. On the other hand — I repeat — it cannot be beyond the wit of man to defeat the Cubans; and it could have worked in Angola.

*You have certainly lamented about the Soviet "gerontocracy," about the problem of Russia being ruled by such old men. What difficulties for the West may arise therefrom? Or, perhaps, what advantages?*

*Kissinger:* I think that older men are usually less risk-taking than younger men, although you can't generalize this. One of the problems is that, statistically, it is probable that a large number of the present Politburo will leave within a relatively short time-span — whenever that happens to be. But since they are all of roughly the same age, there will come a period, at some point which I don't want to predict, at which several of the top leaders will be changing within a relatively short time-span, and this will certainly present the West with new problems.

*Many people in the West have become used to differentiating between doves and hawks in Moscow as if they were established parties. The conclusion is then drawn that we must do everything to reinforce the role of the doves and prevent the hawks' gaining the upper hand. Do you regard this approach as correct?*

*Kissinger:* No. First of all, I don't think we know who the doves are and who are the hawks. I think if you look at the history of relations with the Soviet Union, it is usually the current Soviet leader who is considered a dove, and it is always the last Soviet leader who is considered a hawk. For example, when Stalin was alive, he was generally considered a dove in Western commentaries.

*And so he was in foreign policy.*

*Kissinger:* And so was Khrushchev.

*Until the Cuba crisis.*

*Kissinger:* All that I am saying is that undoubtedly there are differences of opinion in the Soviet leadership. Undoubtedly ambitious men will use arguments that relate to policies that do not succeed to advance themselves, just as they do in other countries. I think we know much too little about the "doves" and the "hawks" to know which faction it is.

*We still do not know today with any certainty which of the "doves" or which of the "hawks" were behind the move into Prague.*

*Kissinger:* Precisely. And I don't know which argument would appeal most to the doves. Usually the argument is that you strengthen the doves by making concessions. You can also say that you strengthen the doves by demonstrating that it is much too risky to pursue a certain course — because it could be that that is the best argument that the doves have available.

*Hawks and doves — that only means something to you in relation to your own domestic policy?*

*Kissinger:* I am not in favor of toughness for toughness' sake, or of using the Soviet leaders to demonstrate to a domestic audience what abusive language one can use or what victories one can score in a debate. But I am also opposed to pretending that the Soviets are simply misunderstood commercial travelers from the Midwest.

*Like Vice-President Nixon in his "kitchen debate"?*

*Kissinger:* That was in Moscow. I believe one should be firm in substance but polite in form.

*You once said that Brezhnev and "the war generation of Soviet leaders" had no conception of how strong the Soviet Union was militarily. What did you mean — that the younger generation, when it came to power, would have a greater sense of responsibility, or perhaps, that it would be more presumptuous?*

*Kissinger:* First of all, I don't want to confirm that particular quote. But what is certainly true is that the generation of Brezhnev, having gone through the purges, through the Second World War, and through a whole series of crises since then, is likely to be more cautious and more aware of the dangers of international complications than might be the case with a younger generation which is more technocratic, has less experience, and is possibly more familiar with the new technology.

*The Chinese are always saying that war with the Soviet Union is unavoidable. Is it propaganda, or must one have serious apprehensions that such a thing might happen?*

*Kissinger:* I think when you are dealing with a country of so much military power, of course there is always the danger that it will be tempted to use it. I think, however, we have the capability to make that prospect always look unattractive; and therefore it is entirely up to us whether there will be a war or not. If we become too weak, then there could be a war. But I do not believe a war is inevitable, and I do not believe that the Soviets are determined to start a war regardless of the opposition they will face.

*At the moment it seems that demonstrative display of the Chinese card is making the Soviet leaders very uneasy, and one wonders whether it is wise to put one's emphasis on China in this way (as Zbigniew Brzezinki in particular is said to have done).*

*Kissinger:* You know, I have very high regard for the Chinese leaders. The Chinese have been an independent country for 3,000 years. They are not going to be anybody's card. They conduct their own foreign policy according to their own interests, and we have to conduct our foreign policy according to our own interest. When those two coincide, we should cooperate. When the two do not coincide, we should pursue our own policy.

I do not think we can specifically "play the Chinese card" to suit our purposes. What we can do is to cooperate, work on parallel objectives — e.g., we both have an interest in preventing the world balance of power from being overthrown. That, I think, is a common objective. This is not "playing the Chinese card."

*Nevertheless, at the moment, the Chinese miss no opportunity of annoying the Russians, for instance by flirting with the West German Bundeswehr, making anti-Soviet speeches in Africa, or trying to buy Western arms. The nervousness of the Russians is noticeable to us, and a danger factor could develop here.*

*Kissinger:* The Chinese have the problem of not having built up their military strength for such a long time that they now have to make perhaps more rapid decisions than they would if there had been time for a more evolutionary development. But I don't think it is in our interest or the Chinese to provoke the Russians just to prove that we can annoy them.

*Should the West sell arms to the Chinese?*

*Kissinger:* I think that it is in our interest that it is not easy to overrun China.

*When you were first in Peking you spoke about "this country so mysterious to us." Was China at that time more mysterious to you than Russia, and is it still more mysterious than Russia today, or do you now know about the same amount about both countries?*

*Kissinger:* The first time I went to China, I did not know a great deal about it. And since it was a secret trip, I could not prepare myself very systematically.

*Was this secretiveness really necessary, this strange detour to China via Pakistan?*

*Kissinger:* You have to remember what the problem was. We had had no direct contact with the Chinese; we didn't know exactly what we would meet there. The reaction in the world and within our country would have been unbelievable if we had announced this was going to happen. They would have given us a list of things we had to achieve before we ever got there, and when we didn't even yet know whom we were going to talk to! We would have been negotiating with ourselves before ever meeting the Chinese. And when you do something so unusual it would be better to do it first and to see what the results would be before you announce it. If we had announced it, we would have had to testify before 500 Congressional committees explaining what we were going to do, give reassurances, submit briefs. There are some things that I think have to be done secretly.

*In Moscow you negotiated for three days without your Ambassador even knowing that you were there. Have you never been particularly frightened if things went wrong of making yourself ridiculous as a sort of unmasked Haroun al-Rashid?*

*Kissinger:* No, that was one of the risks we took. In the meantime I have learned a great deal about China. I repeat, I have always respected the intelligence and subtlety of the Chinese leaders, but I know I would not consider myself an expert on Chinese culture. I suppose I know a little more about Soviet, about Russian history; still, I think I understand both of them about equally well as far as the impact on American foreign policy is concerned.

*During your period of office one of the greatest sources of danger to world peace was the Middle East. It seems that, as time went on, you gained increasing respect for Sadat and did not think Begin's policy very profitable at the time. Is that right?*

*Kissinger:* Well, I would put it slightly differently. First, I think Sadat is a great man; I consider one of the few active spiritual and ethical qualities that I have seen is his trip to Jerusalem. You can give it a thousand pragmatic interpretations, but for somebody who has seen Arabs and Israelis deal with each other, this could not be done by just anybody, no matter how much they may have thought it might be a great stroke of genius.

On the other hand, Israel is in a different position. It is, after all, a population of only 3 million with a very precarious existence. It doesn't know, from its point of view, how long Sadat, even if he is really sincere, will stay in office. So it is harder for

Israeli leaders to make the *grand geste* than it is for a great Arab leader. It is not easy for any of these leaders.

I regret that for a variety of reasons these negotiations have got onto a legalistic level. I don't think that is the most fruitful way of proceeding.

*The greatest danger spot in the more immediate future is thought, at least within NATO, to be Yugoslavia. After Tito's death there could easily be a make-or-break test in this multinational state, during which pro-Soviet forces might call in the Red Army to help. Do you share this anxiety?*

*Kissinger:* Well, I don't want to raise any questions about Marshal Tito. According to actuarial tables his life expectancy is certainly more limited than it was at the time of his rupture with Stalin. I think that will not be excessively insulting to him if I say that.

But at that point, whether Yugoslavia will have domestic upheavals or tensions that would tempt outside intervention, I don't think even the leaders of Yugoslavia can tell today — because if they could, they would deal with them. It is generally thought that this could become a problem.

*People talk of the "self-Finlandization" of Europe and in particular of West Germany. Brzezinski used the word to a German visitor whom we both know. Is this an anxiety you share, or is it overdramatized?*

*Kissinger:* Yes, I had that concern, especially in relationship to Eurocommunism. I would not apply it to countries like the German Federal Republic, or France, or Britain. I think in countries where the Eurocommunists are gaining significant influence, it could become true.

*Does the USA, and do you, sanction a "special relationship" between the German Federal Republic and the Soviet Union's hegemony because, more than all your other allies, Bonn must be interested in good relations with Moscow — if only, though not solely, because of Berlin?*

*Kissinger:* As a theoretical question it is almost unanswerable because the Federal Republic is now strong enough and stable enough to conduct its own foreign policy, whether we approve of it or not. I would think West Germany has always had the dilemma that it has had a national concern which was not shared with equal intensity by all the countries with which it is allied. This is inevitable.

*In the early days of Brandt's* Ostpolitik, *why were you so skeptical, so obviously troubled by mixed feelings?*

*Kissinger:* Because it is, of course, understandable that the Federal Republic will pursue certain national objectives, but there is also the historic danger that a Germany conducting a totally separate or "special" policy in the center of the continent could so disquiet everybody as to bring on all the dangers that it is seeking to avoid. Now, I think that has always been inherent in any German policy, whether it is the "Hallstein Doctrine," which ran the risk of confrontations, or the *Ostpolitik*, which ran the risk of excessive negotiations. It is true that I had some doubts about the trends; and it is also true (and I think that Brandt and Bahr will agree with this), that once we had agreed on what they would attempt, I gave them a great deal of support.

*You have frequently said that in everything you did you were guided by a sense of history. History is certainly no cookbook from which one can cull recipes, but history does sharpen the perception of the structural problems of a situation. If you now look back at the years when you were active in foreign politics and as Secretary of State, what lessons would you wish to draw from them, if they can be put concisely?*

*Kissinger:* This I really am in the process of thinking through, and I don't want to do that in a few paragraphs. It is an important question and it is not that I have already thought it through and am trying to save it. I am really in the process of thinking about it all.

*One of your admirers once said that you had written about Bismarck with such "passion and brio" as to give the impression that, had you and Bismarck met, there would have been a sort of spiritual affinity. And you yourself once said that the statesman-like figure you admired most was not Metternich but Bismarck. Can Bismarck's policy still be taken as a model today?*

*Kissinger:* Popular journalism tends to describe models as if one wanted to imitate somebody on the basis of some personal admiration. This is not the case. The problem for statesmen is that the only lessons from which they can learn are those of historical experience — and then one has to be careful not to assume that they are identical.

I studied Bismarck and developed great admiration for him, even though I have to say that he is partly responsible for some of Germany's modern tragedies. I think he is the first modern statesman in this sense: that he attempted to conduct foreign policy on the basis of an assessment of the balance of forces, unrestrained by the clichés of a previous period.

What is more important is that he understood that power can be used only as an instrument of policy if you are prepared to be moderate in the political consequences you draw from it — and if you respect the right to existence of other states with whom, over an historic period, you have to coexist.

Now this had led him into a policy that was a virtuoso performance and of extraordinary complexity; and his successors simply did not have his genius to conduct such a complex policy. In simplifying it they were left only with the calculus of pure military power, without understanding the political (and other) aspects; and in this sense I think he was responsible for some of the later tragedies.

But I think in the conduct of foreign policy — in the understanding of the necessity for options — he performed masterfully.

*Yes, but even he eventually went so far with his system of "reinsurance" that he was no longer in control of it. That is only human, over so long a time.*

*Kissinger:* I would have to say that anyone who can maintain a system for thirty years is successful. His greatest weakness was the weakness of all great men: that he did not bring along his successor. Ideally if he could have passed it on to somebody who understood what he was trying to do, and if he had had an Emperor who was as willing to let his successor operate as his Emperor was, it might have gone on for a considerably longer time.

I think it is probably true that the biggest criticism one could make of Bismarck is that his system was so complex it required a genius in every generation, and that is asking too much.

*Does that apply to American foreign policy over the last eight to ten years?*

*Kissinger:* I think the biggest problem anybody has is to achieve continuity. No matter how spectacular one's successes are, if they cannot be carried on, then one has to ask oneself: Is it inherent in the nature of the policy, or inherent in the successors, or a combination of both? In any case, it is a problem.

*Bismarck, after all, spent months on his estate, which you were unable to do when you were in charge of foreign policy.*

*Kissinger:* Partly because I didn't have one.

*If you think back over the important decisions you took during your eight years in government, which decision — looked at today — do you think was wrong? What was the highlight in your political career?*

*Kissinger:* I avoid answering both of those questions because certainly mistakes were made and certainly high points were achieved. But I really would like them to be seen in more historical terms and more as a process; and for that an interview is not really the best forum. I think the most important thing I tried to do was — with what success, even I really don't know — to attempt to base American foreign policy on some fundamental principles of national interest and to avoid those oscillations between euphoria and panic which have been so characteristic. We will have to see whether that succeeded, and if it didn't succeed, somebody else will have to do it.

*What was the high spot: the ending of the Vietnam war, maneuvering the Middle East war in 1973 and the armistice mediation, or perhaps the meeting with the Chinese leaders in Peking?*

*Kissinger:* Well, each of these had tremendous qualities for me personally. Probably, what I wanted most to achieve was to end the Vietnam war under decent conditions.

*Must it not have been a great shock to you and something like a great moral defeat when you saw on television your Ambassador in Saigon running up to a helicopter on the roof of his embassy with the Stars and Stripes under his arm?*

Kissinger: It was a very painful occasion. And we did it to ourselves by reducing aid to Vietnam in each peacetime year by 25 percent. But it was still better that we had to evacuate with 1,200 men; imagine the scene if we had had to do it with 500,000 men.

*You once prophesied that the whole of Europe would possibly be Marxist in ten years' time. Was that merely a melancholy mood, or is that your conviction?*

*Kissinger:* No, there is some folklore that will never subside, and I did not say that all of Western Europe would be Marxist in ten years.

*We do not know of any Marxist country. Do you know of one?*

*Kissinger:* Certainly not east of the Iron Curtain.

*Dr. Kissinger, you are now fifty-five years old and if one thinks of your career, you have had one of the most interesting assignments a man can have in world politics. Talleyrand was Foreign Minister of France four times (the last time at the age of sixty-one). Should — or must — the world reckon with Henry Kissinger twice becoming US Secretary of State?*

*Kissinger:* We cannot demoralize the professional Foreign Service with this prospect before them.

# NELSON ROCKEFELLER

## *In Memoriam*

---

*Eulogy given at the funeral of Nelson Rockefeller,
February 2, 1979*

---

THAT Nelson Rockefeller is dead is both shattering and nearly inconceivable. One thought him indestructible, so overpowering was he in his energy, warmth, and his deep faith in man's inherent goodness. For twenty-five years, he had been my friend, my older brother, my inspiration, and my teacher.

I first met Nelson Rockefeller when, as an assistant to the President, he called me, a graduate student, to join one of the panels of experts he was forever setting up to ponder the nation's future. He entered the room slapping backs, calling each of us by the best approximation to our first name that he could remember, at once outgoing and remote. Intoxicated by the proximity of power, all of us sought to impress him with our practical acumen and offered tactical advice on how to manipulate events. After we were finished, the smile left his face and his eyes assumed the hooded look which showed that we were now turning to things that mattered. "What I want you to tell me," he said, "is not how to maneuver. I want you to tell me what is right."

"What is right?" For Nelson Rockefeller this was the quintessential question, both naive and profound, at once shaming and uplifting. It was the definition of his integrity. All that was twenty-five years ago. When that phone call came last Friday night, it seemed that our relationship had just started. And now, it was already over.

No one who did not have the privilege of experiencing Nelson's selfless dependability, his infinite thoughtfulness, can possibly appreciate how desolate our life has now become. And yet we would not trade places with anyone; his friendship will be our badge of honor so long as we live.

He permeated our lives. He was always steadfast. He took enormous pride in the accomplishments of his family, of his friends, and of his associates. He asked nothing in return except that they do their best, keep their faith, love their fellow man, and set their sights high in pursuit of honorable goals.

Nelson Rockefeller was a man of contrasting qualities: ebullient and yet withdrawn; gregarious and lonely; joyful and driven; full of the moment yet somehow marked by eternity. He could be pugnacious in asserting his beliefs but he respected those who differed with him. He could be hard but never petty; single-minded but never malicious. His enemies were the slipshod and the second-rate.

Nelson always had a marvelous time. Nothing was too trivial for his attention. He would rearrange the furniture in a friend's living room with the same enthusiasm that he rebuilt Albany or threw himself into projects to study the nation's future. He loved caviar and he loved hot dogs. He loved parties and travel and meeting people. And he loved art, not only for the sake of beauty but because it expanded the reach of the human spirit.

He was a noble man who gave strength but asked for no reciprocity. None of us ever heard him complain. He never shared his sorrow, only his inspiration. He considered himself so blessed that he felt that he had no right to burden others with the doubts and worries inseparable from the human condition even in a man so strong as himself. It was an extraordinary burden which cumulatively drained him though he would never have admitted it. Nelson was truly his brother's keeper.

Nelson could not express in glib words the wellsprings of his motivations. One had to know him well to understand the tactile manner in which he communicated — the meanings of the nudges, the winks, and mumbles by which he conveyed his infinite caring.

He was an artist. Sudden, unexpected flashes of insight startled, and sometimes astounded, one.

I have known no public figure who so often reflected about the spiritual. The Brotherhood of Man and the Fatherhood of God was not a cliché for Nelson; it was a call to action, the motive force of his life. He practiced his faith but he was too humble to preach it. He fought against injustice and fostered equality but he thought it unseemly to adopt the clamoring tone of protest. He helped the downtrodden but he thought it demeaning to publicize acts of Christian love.

Untypical as he would seem to be, Nelson Rockefeller was quintessentially American. For other nations, utopia is a blessed past never to be recovered; for Americans it is just beyond the horizon. One has to work with Americans — not listen to them — to experience their faith. One had to work with Nelson Rockefeller to sense his dauntless strength, his pragmatic genius, his unquenchable optimism. Obstacles were there to be overcome; problems were opportunities. He could never imagine that a wrong could not be righted or that an honorable aspiration was beyond reach. Self-pity, or rage, or resentment were incomprehensible to him.

He was born to leadership. Every decade, Nelson had another project: to build Rockefeller Center, to inspire a Museum of Primitive Art, to gather the nation's experts to study the problems of coming decades, to expand the state university system, to rebuild the state capital, to survey the problems of Latin America, to define our critical choices, to solve the energy problem. His faith in reason and democracy and the human personality was boundless. He never looked back. He often seemed remote because he was already living in a future which most of us had not yet understood.

He loved his family and he loved his country. In his mind, the two were connected. It is not a simple matter to be born to great wealth and power in an egalitarian society. But he was proud of his heritage, which he interpreted as a summons to honor and to duty. He deeply believed that his moral obligation was a privilege. Service was not a favor he rendered to others; they did him honor by permitting him to help.

And just as he unabashedly believed it his family's duty to serve their country, so he was convinced that it was his country's duty to vindicate its values by reaching out to the rest of mankind with the message of hope and freedom. Skeptics might scoff at his belief in America's moral mission. But then cynics do not build cathedrals.

He revered his Presidents whether or not he agreed with them. As a patriot, he sought to ease their burden. He winced when associates made unworthy comments about those who in his view had been entrusted with our future and, therefore, the hopes of mankind. One of the few times he became impatient with me was over a decade and a half ago when I had just seen President Kennedy and reported that I had told him what I thought wrong with some particular policy. Did I have a remedy, Nelson wanted to know. And when I said no, he chided me: "You should always remember that a President is overwhelmed by problems. Your duty is to offer solutions."

Nelson would be proud that two Presidents have honored him by attending this service. He would be touched at the act of grace of President Carter, who found time amidst the care of his duties for several gestures to ease the family's bereavement and then to extend the one solace that would have stirred Nelson the most: that his nation understood and appreciated his love and devotion to it. He would be grateful to President Ford, whom he loved and whom he served with unselfish dedication as Vice-President. He refuted the cynics who expected him to chafe at the limitations of the office, then stepped aside in midterm without slackening in his devotion to his responsibilities. Nelson's ambition was to *serve*, not to *be*.

Much has been said or written about the frustration Nelson experienced because he never achieved the Presidency. This misunderstands the man. His failure to reach the Presidency was, in my view, a tragedy for the country. What a great President he would have been! How he would have ennobled us! What an extraordinary combination of strength and humanity, decisiveness and vision! Yet, I never heard him express even one word of disappointment. As with everything, he sought the office with zest; but when it eluded him, he went on to new challenges — undaunted, resilient, inexhaustible.

In a sense, there was something inevitable and even noble in his gallant failure to win the nation's highest office. And, here again, the myths are wrong. He never succeeded, not *despite* the fact that he was a Rockefeller but *because* of it. His entire upbringing made him recoil before appearing to the people he wanted to serve as if he were pursuing a personal goal. Having been already so privileged he felt that he had no right to ask anything for himself as an individual. And so this superb campaigner who genuinely loved people eschewed the personal pursuit of delegates. He sought the office by trying to present to the nation the most sweeping vision of its future and the best blueprints to attain it. He had a touching faith in the power of ideas. It is not quite the way our boisterous political process works, more geared as it is to personalities than to programs.

And yet, in the final accounting, it was often Nelson who worked out the agenda which others then implemented as national policy. The intellectual groundwork for many innovations was frequently his. He continually called the nation's leaders and thinkers to their responsibility, to make their commitments and apply their best efforts to the future of the nation. Destiny willed it that he made his enduring mark on our society almost anonymously in the programs he designed, the values he upheld, and the men and women whose lives he changed.

Nelson was never quite sure that he had done enough to fulfill the moral obligations of his inheritance. This assemblage is the best testimony to how well he succeeded. Legislators and diplomats, the eminent and the humble, Americans and foreigners of all faiths and races and nations are here to pay tribute to the scope of his achievements, to the reach of his spirit, and, above all, to the greatness of his heart. This distinguished gathering would tell Nelson the one thing that, because of his humility, his friends knew better than he — how much he sustained the public life and honor of his country.

As I have thought about my gallant friend, it occurred to me that his role in our society was symbolic of America's role in the world. Like him, we are uniquely strong; like him, we are idealistic and a little inarticulate. If he were here, he would tell us: Do not look back. The future is full of exciting challenges. Do not be afraid or ashamed of your strength; neither hoard it nor abuse it; it is not a burden but God's blessing conferring an opportunity to oppose tyranny, to defend the free, to lift up the poor, to give hope to the disadvantaged, and to walk truly in the paths of justice and compassion.

When Nelson was relaxed, he did not speak about power but about love. He meant not the sentimental, demanding emotion which too often is a form of selfishness. Rather, it was the grace of the inwardly strong, an all-embracing feeling that only those who are truly at peace with themselves can dare to articulate.

In recent years, he and I would often sit on the veranda overlooking his beloved Hudson River in the setting sun. I would talk more, but he understood better. And, as the statues on the lawn glowed in the dimming light, Nelson Rockefeller would occasionally get that squint in his eyes, which betokened a far horizon. And he would say, because I needed it, but, above all, because he deeply felt it:

"Never forget that the most profound force in the world is love."

# ON IRAN

*An Interview*

Second part of an interview between *Dr. Kissinger and the editors of* The Economist, *published in* The Economist, *February 10, 1979*

D o YOU *connect events in Iran with the lack of Soviet restraint, or of American will, that you have been describing (February 3rd)?*

No one can claim that a Soviet decision started the upheavals that led to the departure of the Shah. But somebody who starts a rockslide nevertheless must be held responsible for the impact of stones that he himself did not throw. To my mind the combination of Soviet actions in Ethiopia, South Yemen, Afghanistan, plus the general perception of an American geopolitical decline, had the consequence of demoralizing those whose stock in trade was cooperation with the United States, undermining their resolution toward potential revolutionaries. To what extent and within what margin, that is of course a question of speculation.

*Did you yourself — we certainly did — underestimate the internal stresses in Iran, the degree of popular feelings against the Shah?*

In a revolutionary situation it is a very great mistake to treat the manifestations of the height of the turmoil as constant factors. A visible decline in authority generates anarchistic attitudes and disruptive tendencies that might not have occurred under different circumstances. History demonstrates that many upheavals that looked very formidable did not in the end succeed. The French student rebellion in 1968 paralyzed France for a month and then disappeared without a trace within a year.

In Iran there was a potential for unrest — produced in part by the process of modernization — which was perhaps not correctly estimated. That it burst forth into revolution is due to many more recent and essentially unforeseeable factors. It did not have to do so.

*Isn't the French case a very significant parallel? In France the turning point was when de Gaulle rallied the middle class. The Shah proved unable to rally the middle class and that's something which, speaking for ourselves, we hadn't expected and which does suggest that possibly his friends, you as his friend when in office, could have been encouraging him to build up a broader-based constituency in what has proved to be a very silent middle class — unlike the French middle class which was very vociferous.*

One has to keep in mind that the situation in Iran is sociologically substantially different from France. The fundamental difficulties were caused not by the fact that the Shah was backward, but that he was modernizing. His opponents were, in their majority, not "progressive" by Western standards; but, compared with the reactionary countries around him, he was, indeed, a progressive ruler. In every European country, the evolution from feudalism to the modern state took place over a much longer period of time and yet could not avoid substantial political instability. So, one should not pretend that modernization is a simple process.

Secondly, I accept the argument that all of us paid insufficient attention in Iran to the proposition that political construction should go side by side with economic construction. The failure was less of intelligence agencies than of a conceptual apparatus. The fashionable "progressive" view for decades has been that economic development would more or less automatically produce political stability, that a rising standard of living would reduce discontent. The enlightened view was that there was a sort of automatic stabilizing factor in economic development.

That has turned out to be clearly wrong. It would probably

have been wiser for the Shah to concentrate explicitly on a political evolution to be more commensurate with Iran's economic evolution. And perhaps we should have urged the Shah to do that, though I am not sure that we would have known what to say. Still, this failure only accounts for a kind of inchoate unrest which could easily have evolved in the direction of constitutional monarchy. And, given time, this was not incompatible with at least the stated objectives of the Shah.

What turned the inchoate unrest into a revolution was the conjunction of modernization, lack of political imagination by the Shah, American policies, demonstrations of American weakness, and assaults on American institutions perceived by those countries as essential for their survival. And clumsy tactical handling of the situation.

*You mean, by that, equivocal statements of American support?*

Our statements of support had no practical consequence and their operational content always had a caveat that in fact tended to encourage those who were fomenting unrest.

*But given the restraints which exist on American foreign policy, from Congress among other places, and which you experienced yourself, particularly in the last two or three years of your period in office, what would those practical operational measures by the United States have been?*

When we said we supported the Shah it was stated as a general objective. When we put forward concrete propositions, however, we advocated such measures as coalition government and general liberalization. Such propositions tempted the Shah, in order to maintain our support, into directions which exacerbated his problems.

The fundamental challenge of a revolution is this: Certainly wise governments forestall revolutions by making timely concessions; indeed the very wisest governments do not consider adaptations as concessions, but rather as part of a natural process of increasing popular support. However, once a revolution is in train it cannot then be moderated by concessions. Once a revolution has occurred, the preeminent requirement is the restoration of authority. These concessions, which had they been made a year earlier might have avoided the situation, accelerate the process of disintegration. *After* authority is restored there is another opportunity to make concessions.

When friends of the United States are under duress, we cannot take the curse off the necessity of that friendship by force-feeding an internal program that would have been very wise and farsighted if it had been undertaken voluntarily two years earlier, or that could again be very farsighted six months later. If we attempt to take the curse off our geopolitical necessities by placating our human rights advocates in the middle of the crisis we make a catastrophe inevitable. Ideally a country should avoid revolutions by making timely concessions. I wish that had happened in Iran, but since it did not happen the situation could not be rectified by frantic concessions in the very middle of a revolution.

*But, given the constraints an American President is under, what practical measures could he take which would tell the Shah's or any other government that there was an effective United States supporting it?*

I would think that one of the reasons for the Shah's progressive demoralization was his very real doubt whether we were actually supporting him. He certainly had the means at his disposal to resist more strenuously than he did. And he chose not to exercise them because he must have had doubts about our real intentions. Certainly those measures which we publicly proposed had their profound ambiguities. The American so-called progressive consensus deals with almost every political crisis abroad by proposing a coalition government. We were harassed for years during the Vietnam war by proposals for a coalition government that look absurd today when one sees the total inability of the Hanoi group to share political power in even the slightest degree.

What makes this faith in coalition government so incongruous is that we never practice it at home. In a country like the United States, in which the differences between the parties are not all that profound, the addition of a member of the opposition to a technical cabinet post is considered so unusual as to constitute big news. Yet in revolutionary situations the United States persistently proposes such a solution to factions who are killing each other in the street precisely because they cannot agree on the minimum necessities for a political contest. To the extent that such a proposal is taken seriously, it will be interpreted either as a clever tactic to undermine the existing government, or as an example of total irrelevance to the real issues.

*But we are living in a world where all these countries that we are talking about are developing very fast and where communications are almost instant, where educuation is rising far more quickly than even forty years ago. We are living in a world where rulers who are convenient to the United States have also, you seem to be saying, to be educated (if they haven't learned it of their own accord) in the art of creating a political class of their own.*

The transition from feudalism to the modern period has the inevitable consequence of destroying a ruling class based on landed property in favor of a ruling class of technocrats or managers or capitalists. That is a very difficult and tricky process. It is not, incidentally, identical with going from one-man rule to universal suffrage. Those are two separate issues and I feel that we in the West have not thought them through. Nor do I know the answer to this fundamental issue as well as I do the problem.

*And in preempting the sort of social unrest that is likely to happen in a situation such as you have just described, do you see human rights as being a relevant part of the United States's platform, or not? Take Iran.*

In preempting the situation a sophisticated human rights policy can help. In dealing with revolutionary situations it can be inflammatory. In Iran our human rights policy has contributed to instability. And it has had the paradoxical result that almost any government that I can foresee a year or two hence will be less free, less progressive, and practice human rights less seriously than even the government which has been replaced.

*Do you think that the many critics of the CIA's state of intelligence in Iran are really being fair? If so many were taken by surprise by the turn of events in Iran, is it surprising that the CIA was taken by surprise as well?*

What we faced in Iran was not primarily a matter of intelligence. It was a conceptual failure in understanding the impact of rapid economic development; later on, once unrest had broken into revolution, a series of policy judgments were involved. In any case, I regret the degree to which the CIA has been emasculated in recent years, and we are paying for it now and not only in Iran.

*Do you think that that contributed to any failure on this occasion?*

Emasculation of the CIA contributes in three ways. One, it makes analysts more cautious. Second, we have practically deprived ourselves of covert capabilities. This is especially dangerous in areas where there is a huge gray area between military intervention and normal diplomatic processes. Third, it has affected the psychological balance. I would have thought that as late as five years ago opponents of the United States in a country like Iran might well have feared an American reaction; they might well have concluded — overestimating the CIA's capacities — that we simply would not tolerate an assault on the political structure of so close an ally. The various Congressional investigations — which incidentally have found very few transgressions — have, however, had the practical result of exhibiting our operating procedures in so much detail that opponents have a precise idea of what we can and cannot do. And Congressional restrictions have tied our hands even more. Destroying the mystique of the CIA is in itself a psychological handicap.

*With the benefit of hindsight in Iran, is there anything that we can now do or achieve in three situations: first, Saudi Arabia and the Gulf?*

Earlier in this discussion (February 3rd) we spoke of the dangers of the 1980s entirely in terms of East-West relations. A fair assessment would show that the East-West problem is currently complicated by historical processes in many parts of the world, including the Gulf and Saudi Arabia, that are to some extent independent of the East-West conflict.

In Saudi Arabia and the Gulf we now face two distinct problems. One is the growing perception of the potential irrelevance of American power to the most likely dangers that these countries face. They are bound to be concerned lest the United States, for a variety of reasons, will accept adverse geopolitical changes provided they can be structured to appear in some way to result from internal upheavals. The second problem is the social change fueled by the tremendous resources that oil makes available. Those two factors, of course, become linked and feed on each other.

The situation in Saudi Arabia and the Gulf now will be importantly determined by the outcome in Iran: both objectively by what emerged in Iran; and comparatively by what conclusions are drawn about the relevance of the United States to the problems of the countries most affected.

Whether we like it or not, the Shah was considered our closest ally in that area for thirty-seven years. He left office under the visible urging of the United States. To explain that we had no alternative is no consolation to threatened friends because they are not interested in our motives but in our capacities. If they should conclude that at critical moments we will deal similarly with them they will seek reinsurance in Moscow or Baghdad now. So somehow we have to convince them that our policy will enable them to survive in some structure compatible with their perception of themselves.

Moreover, events in Iran are bound to create a change in the balance of power in that region. Whatever government emerges will be preoccupied with its internal problems. The balance will thereby tilt toward radical forces in ways not yet fully foreseeable. The very existence of a cohesive and strong Iran prevented Iraq from pursuing aggressive policies in the Gulf. Even under the best conceivable outcome, Iran will be absorbed for a period of years in the restoration of a minimum of domestic tranquillity. Iraq and other radical states thereby develop a freer hand. Countries like the emirates — that have the power to affect the economic prosperity of industrial democracies — will become increasingly threatened, and tempted to accommodate.

We cannot resign from the problem by renouncing the role of policeman. Of course, the term policeman has a pejorative ring. The fact remains that in a broad sense the balancer of power is a kind of policeman, whose responsibility is to prevent peaceful countries from feeling impotent and aggressors from becoming reckless. It is a responsibility we cannot avoid. So we need a complex of policies. We need a visible presence of American power in the Indian Ocean, in part as a substitute for the declining Iranian power. We must develop a political program that the Saudis and other threatened countries can believe in and that relates the inevitable political and social change to at least enough political stability to permit a legitimate government to operate. And we must be careful not to use lack of success in the one area as an alibi for failure to perform in the other.

*But in this list of things that the United States needs to do, do you include the willingness to use military force to uphold a particular regime?*

We surely should not exclude it publicly — though of course it can only be a last recourse. Having been in office, I know how extremely complicated it is to design effective policies. There are few public servants for whom I have a higher regard than Secretary Vance. I also know how futile it is for an outsider to pretend that he has tactical solutions to a situation where success depends on the subtle accumulation of nuances. So I would insist that your questions are important, even if my answers are unsatisfactory.

In office I learned that there is often an incongruity between the public debate and the responsibilities of the statesman. Journalists insist on answers; the most important responsibility of the statesman is to ask the right questions. If bureaucracies are challenged they will often produce much better answers than the political leader; he however must be prepared to insist on the fundamental course. He is not hired as a whiz-kid on technical answers; he is hired for supplying a sense of direction.

*But the fact of modern political life in America — and you could say that it was a fact for Roosevelt at the time of Hitler's war — is that a statesman has also to carry the American people and the American Congress with him. Otherwise, however subtle and however nuanced the thing that he wishes to . . .*

Without any question. But he cannot carry the Congress and the American people with him unless he explains what their problem is. In 1940 the overwhelming majority of the American people was isolationist. Still, Roosevelt succeeded in awakening public opinion to the Nazi danger. It is better to have made the effort and fail than to base policy on public opinion polls. Which in any event is the road to disaster. For the public will not forgive their leaders for calamities even if these occur in response to their presumed wishes. Chamberlain was certainly overwhelmingly popular after Munich, and was destroyed eighteen months later because of the result of Munich.

*The second particular problem I wanted to relate to this chain of events which you have been describing is Turkey. Do you think that the already unstable situation in Turkey is (again, with the advantage of hindsight in Iran) something which the United States could now help remedy?*

Let me make three points. First, from the foreign policy point of view, the estrangement of Turkey from the Alliance started in the previous Administration when the Congress insisted on punishing Turkey by imposing an embargo against any geopolitical sense. Ironically it failed completely in achieving even its immediate tactical objective of promoting a Cyprus solution. Second, I am in favor of helping Turkey. If some stopgap measures are necessary to keep Turkey from sliding into chaos, I support them. But we need less stopgap measures than to convey an impression that we are mastering the big trends. Thus the United States, confronted by a disintegrating situation in Iran, should not frantically look around for things to do elsewhere. In the so-called northern tier we need a settled view of our objectives and capabilities; only then will a crash program make sense.

*While, evidently, the United States and the Alliance need to build up a coherent strategy in such an area, you seem to be saying that there has got to be a local reimposition of authority. Would you favor in Iran — and if things got very much worse, in Turkey — the sort of local reimposition of authority that has taken place in Pakistan?*

In Turkey I think we are far from such a situation.

*In Iran?*

In Iran one has to analyze the tendency of the actual forces that exist. The chief forces in Iran are the army, the genuine and ungenuine Khomeini-type religious groups, the National Front, and the radicals who are organizing the strikes, who I believe one way or the other are given impetus from Communist (or Communist-encouraged) organizations. If I analyze the probable policies of the various groups, a combination of the National Front and the army is likely to be more sympathetic to our objectives than almost any other grouping.

*But that underestimates the very real impact in several of the countries that we have been talking about of Islam. In Pakistan we've got an army leadership which espouses a very severe, strict form of Islam. Is that not a better bridge to build, between Islam and the army, as an alliance for reimposing authority in Iran?*

Frankly, I know too little about the tactical situation in Iran to make a prescription.

*The third area that has been affected tangibly by Iran is Camp David and after. Indeed, the signing of Camp David has been affected. We have heard Americans say that after Iran the Camp David peace agreement is irrelevant. Would you go that far?*

No, I would not go that far. I think the Camp David agreement is far better than a failure under any circumstances. And therefore I strongly support the efforts of the Administration and the general trend of the Administration's policy with respect to Camp David. Nevertheless, the impact of Camp David will be crucially determined by the attitude we take to the question that you ask about the Gulf and Saudi Arabia. The policy of Saudi Arabia, or Jordan for that matter, toward Camp David will grow out of their assessment of the momentum behind the radical trend in the area and of our ability to staunch it.

No formulation of a linkage between the West Bank and the Egyptian treaty, or any of the other issues now in dispute, can overcome the fundamental impact of the conflict between the moderates and the radicals, or take from our shoulders the necessity of contributing to a stabler balance in the aftermath of Iran. In other words, until a few years ago our Arab-Israeli policy could act as a symbol of the American strategic and political dominance of the area. Now the Egyptian-Israeli agreement is an admission card to dealing with other even deeper issues. Its failure would be compounding a disaster. Its success by itself, important as it is, is only a building block.

*Could one argue the opposite, as Mohamed Heikal argued on British television the other day: namely, that the radical states, for example, Iraq, which you described a few moments ago as a radical state, and Syria, were on the way to becoming more moderate until Camp David? Now, with Iran gone, and with Iraq and Syria very much in the driving seat in that area, were Camp David just to wither away you might on this reasoning get a revival of that trend toward moderation in Iraq and Syria.*

Under the present circumstances the failure of Camp David must be perceived as a sign that the United States and all of those who have bet on the United States are incapable of shaping events. Far from spurring moderation, it would give a tremendous impetus to radicalism which could lead to the eviction of the United States from a key role in that area. I don't agree with Heikal's analysis that Iraq and Syria were triggered into a less moderate course by Camp David. If Iran had remained stable, if Camp David had been carried to a conclusion rapidly and in a dominant fashion, by which I mean the achievement of its stated objectives, the evolution would have been otherwise. Syria might well have joined the process, though after some interval. What is necessary as far as Syria is concerned (and maybe also Iraq) is a balance of incentives that make it clear we still are a decisive factor in the area. If that is lost, no amount of Arab-Israeli negotiations in the abstract can avert the advance of radicalism.

*The reason why some Americans seem to feel that Camp David is less relevant now is because Israel must feel, in the present phase of apparent American weakness, that to give up Sinai with its oil fields, having lost access to Iranian oil, is not worth a piece of paper — and that the impulse of non-signature of Camp David comes from Israel.*

Yes, but Israel has to weigh this against its position in the American Congress, and with the American public, if it should find itself blamed for the failure. My impression is that Israel is willing to sign the Egyptian agreement; the biggest obstacle to its completing the agreement is Israel's fear as to what will happen on the West Bank. It may have been a mistake to be too specific about a West Bank solution in the context of the Egyptian treaty.

*To return to your overall theme. We talked (February 3rd) of the Russians feeling that they might be encircled in the long run but that they might have an advantage during the 1980s. Do you feel that in the longer run history is on their side or on that of the West?*

Of course, fundamentally, history is neutral, and a great deal depends on the efforts that are being made. In terms of resources, social and economic trends, I would believe that history is clearly against the Soviet system. In that sense we are the wave of the future. It is this that gives the 1980s their particular urgency, because the chief element lacking in this potential coalition of countries is an organizing strategy, an organizing will. If this could ever be generated, the Soviet geopolitical position would become precarious and it would then become compounded by the disintegrating tendencies within the Soviet system, even though they may take another decade or so to develop. All of this makes the early 1980s a time of potential danger but also of opportunity, depending on how we react to the clear outlines of the future.

# THE STRATEGIC ARMS LIMITATION TREATY (SALT II)

Statement before the Committee on Foreign Relations
of the United States Senate, July 31, 1979

I N HIS ESSAY *Perpetual Peace* the philosopher Immanuel Kant wrote that world peace would come about in one of two ways: after a cycle of wars of ever-increasing violence, or by an act of moral insight in which the nations of the world renounced the bitter competition bound to lead to self-destruction.

Our age faces precisely that choice. For the first time in history two nations have the capacity to inflict on each other and on mankind a level of destruction tantamount to ending civilized life; yet they have also before them unprecedented possibilities of cooperation to harness the wonders of technology to improve the human condition.

Both mankind's hopes and fears are bound up with the relationship between the United States and the Soviet Union. These two countries possess huge nuclear arsenals; they also espouse sharply opposing concepts of justice and hold conflicting visions of the future. The ideology of Soviet leaders does not make them content to practice their preferred social system at home; they strive for its victory worldwide. Hence the Soviet Union and America clash in areas that each considers vital. We have allies whose interests we will not sacrifice. Soviet allies such as Vietnam and Cuba are quite capable of generating crises of their own, all too frequently encouraged by Moscow to do so.

The peace we seek therefore must rest on something more tangible than a hope or a fear of holocaust. It must also reflect a military and geopolitical equilibrium. The notion of balance of power has always been unfashionable in America. But it is the precondition of security, and even of progress. If the mere avoidance of conflict becomes our overriding objective, and if our own military power is disparaged, the international system will be at the mercy of the most ruthless. If the desire to conciliate becomes the sole operational basis of policy, we run the risk that the threat of war will become a weapon of blackmail; our allies and our moral values will both be permanently in danger. The desire for peace will be transformed into a caricature of itself, and become instead the beginning of appeasement. How to strive for both peace *and* our moral principles; how to avoid nuclear war without succumbing to nuclear blackmail — this is the overwhelming problem of our period.

The United States must proceed simultaneously on three fronts:

First, we must maintain a military balance that does not tempt aggression against our friends or allies, against our vital interests, or in the extreme case against ourselves.

Secondly, beyond resisting naked aggression, we have a stake in the principle that political or economic pressure, or military or terrorist blackmail, should not become the arbiter of the world's political disputes. The geopolitical equilibrium must be maintained lest radical forces hostile to the West gain such momentum that they appear as the irresistible wave of the future.

And thirdly, on the basis of a balance thus achieved and preserved, we must be ready to explore routes to genuine peaceful coexistence. The great powers, having learned that they cannot dominate one another, must practice moderation and ultimately cooperation. The creativity of a world of diversity and peaceful competition can be the basis of unparalleled human progress. A stable balance is the most hopeful — perhaps the only — basis for the control and ultimately the reduction of weapons of mass destruction.

Too often these requirements are posed in the alternative. But the quests for security and for peace are inseparable; we cannot achieve one without the other. No democracy can court conflict. Our government will have support in resisting challenges to our vital interests only if confrontation is seen to have been unavoidable. Our people have a right to expect of their government that it will explore all avenues to a genuine peace. And our allies will insist on it.

The new treaty poses a particularly complex problem for me. When I was a professor, I participated in the academic discussions of military doctrine and strategy that underlay early initiatives in arms control. I helped design the first SALT agreements in 1972. I was involved in the negotiations of the Vladivostok accord of 1974, which marked the first breakthrough of SALT II; I played a major role in the negotiations which came close to completing an agreement in January 1976. I have a longstanding personal commitment to the process of limiting strategic nuclear arms. As an historian I am conscious of the lessons of World War II when a global war resulted because the democracies disdained to maintain the balance of power. But equally we must not forget the tragedy of World War I when disaster resulted even *with* an equilibrium of power, when technology and rivalry outran the control of statesmen.

Thus SALT cannot be considered in isolation. It is one element in our overall national security policy. It must be viewed in the context of the global balance that it reflects, or purports to affect.

Thus I regret to have to say that the present treaty comes up for ratification at a time of grave danger to our national security and to the global equilibrium. The military balance is beginning to tilt ominously against the United States in too many significant categories of weaponry. The unprecedented Soviet use of proxy forces in Africa, the Middle East, and Southeast Asia, and the turmoil caused by radical forces and terrorist organizations sponsored by Moscow's friends, mark ours as a time of profound upheaval. We have learned painfully that we alone cannot be the

world's policeman. But neither our moral values nor our safety
can tolerate the Soviet Union's increasing tendency toward global
intervention. As the United States nurses its wounds after Vietnam, radical forces are threatening regional stability and attempting the violent overthrow of moderate governments friendly to the
West. If present trends continue, we face the chilling prospect of
a world sliding gradually out of control, with our relative military
power declining, with our economic lifeline vulnerable to blackmail, with hostile forces growing more rapidly than our ability
to deal with them, and with fewer and fewer nations friendly to
us surviving.

In addressing the treaty before you, I respectfully submit,
the Senate has a responsibility to examine the broader condition
of our national security. The Senate has an opportunity at least to
begin to reverse the unfavorable trends in the military balance
and to put the Soviet Union on notice that we consider the constant
probing of every regional equilibrium and the encouragement of
subversive and terrorist groups as incompatible with any definition of coexistence. Without such an affirmation, SALT will become a soporific, a form of escapism. I shall submit specific proposals to achieve this, later in the statement.


## THE SHIFTING STRATEGIC BALANCE

The basic technical facts about the current military balance have
been presented in great detail before this and other committees.
Let me concentrate first on the serious transformation, adverse to
our interests, that has taken place in the overall strategic balance
during the last decade and a half.

For about the first twenty-five years of the postwar period,
the problem of maintaining the military equilibrium was relatively straightforward. The Soviet Union was always superior in

ground forces on the Eurasian continent; we were vastly ahead in strategic striking power as well as in theater nuclear forces. The reach of the Soviet Union was limited to regions accessible to motorized ground transport, generally adjacent territories in Europe, and to some extent China. Africa, most of the Middle East, even Southeast Asia were beyond the capacity of major Soviet military intervention. And the areas which were hostage to Soviet ground armies were protected by three factors:

- first, by the American proponderance in strategic nuclear striking power capable of disarming the Soviet Union or at least reducing its counterblow to tolerable levels while still retaining large residual forces for attacks on industrial targets;
- second, by a vast American superiority in so-called theater nuclear forces everywhere around the Soviet periphery;
- and third, in Europe by substantial American and allied ground forces that posed at least a major probability that Soviet ground attack would trigger the nuclear retaliation of the United States.

Not surprisingly, the major crises in the first twenty years of the postwar period — whether in Berlin, Korea, or Cuba — were ultimately contained, because the risks of pushing them beyond a certain point always appeared exorbitant to Moscow.

This state of affairs will soon have ceased to exist. Starting in the 1960s, the military balance began to change — almost imperceptibly at first, so great was our superiority — but with growing momentum in recent years. It is imperative that we recognize without illusion the dangerous trends that are emerging. It is crucial that we begin now to rectify them.

The growth of Soviet strategic nuclear forces has been inexorable for a decade and a half. In 1965 the Soviet strategic arsenal comprised about 220 intercontinental ballistic missiles (ICBMs) and 100 submarine-launched ballistic missiles

(SLBMs). By 1968 the number had grown to 860 ICBMs and over 120 SLBMs. We had stopped our buildup at 1,054 ICBMs and 656 SLBMs in 1967. By mid-1970 the Soviets had caught up with us in numbers of launchers. Our intelligence estimates of their plans invariably turned out to be too low; contrary to popular mythology the Soviets *did* build on the scale of the "worst case" hypothesis of our intelligence community and not to the level that was defined as "most probable."[1] Instead of stopping when they reached parity with us, as the Johnson Administration expected, the Soviets *continued* their missile buildup — until they were frozen at the levels of the ceilings established by the first SALT agreement in May 1972. Then they switched energetically to qualitative improvements in their missile forces.

Our problem derives not only from the larger number of warheads on Soviet ICBMs but above all from the difference in the types of weaponry emphasized by the two sides. In the Sixties, the United States unilaterally decided to base its strategic forces on light but highly accurate ICBMs, the less vulnerable but also less accurate SLBMs, and the more versatile but more vulnerable manned bombers. The Soviets made the opposite decision, relying on large land-based missiles capable of delivering a far heavier payload. At first the crudeness of their technology and the lack of accuracy deprived these weapons of effectiveness against military targets. But as Soviet technology improved, its advantage in numbers and missile payload was bound to tell. For the land-based ICBM is always likely to be the most accurate and powerful strategic weapon, and the one most capable of rapid attack against the military targets of the other side. In short the Soviets have emphasized quick reaction forces by modernizing their ICBMs; we concentrated on slow-reacting forces like air-launched cruise missiles. Thus the asymmetry in the capacity of the two sides to

[1] See Albert Wohlstetter, "Is There a Strategic Arms Race?" *Foreign Policy* 15 (Summer 1974) : 3–20; "Rivals. But No 'Race,'" *Foreign Policy* 16 (Fall 1974) : 48–81.

destroy each other's military targets has grown with every passing year.

There is now general agreement that their improvements in missile accuracy and warhead technology will put the Soviets in a position to wipe out our land-based forces of Minuteman ICBMs by 1982. Whether this capability is ever exercised or not — and I consider it improbable — it reverses and hence revolutionizes the strategic equation on which our security and that of our friends have depended through most of the postwar period.

The revolution in the strategic balance is aggravated by a comparable buildup of Soviet aircraft and missiles that threatens to overturn the American advantage in theater-based nuclear forces. The Soviet Union has deployed scores of new missiles of 2,000-mile range — the SS-20 — which carries a MIRVed warhead of three reentry vehicles. Several hundred supersonic Backfire bombers will threaten all peripheral areas in the Eighties (leaving aside for the moment their utility for intercontinental missions). A Soviet superiority in theater striking forces is therefore upon us. The inequality is demonstrated by the fact that we have had to assign part of our strategic forces — a number of Poseidon boats — to cover targets threatening NATO. Thus in case of war we are likely to be strained either with respect to our strategic or with respect to our theater nuclear coverage.

All this has been accomplished while the Soviet advantage in conventional forces has grown, and while the reach of Soviet power has been extended enormously by the rapid development of the Soviet navy, an expanding long-range airlift capability, the acquisition of Soviet bases in countries like South Yemen and Vietnam, and the establishment of vast Soviet arms depots in such countries as Libya and Ethiopia, which will enable the Soviet Union to move its own or proxy troops rapidly to their prepositioned weapons. At the same time our Navy declines and our access to overseas bases shrinks.

Rarely in history has a nation so passively accepted such a

radical change in the military balance. If we are to remedy it, we must first recognize the fact that we have placed ourselves at a significant disadvantage voluntarily. This is *not* the result of SALT: it is the consequence of unilateral decisions extending over a decade and a half: by a strategic doctrine adopted in the Sixties, by the bitter domestic divisions growing out of the war in Vietnam, and by choices of the present Administration. All these actions were unilateral, hence avoidable. They were not extracted from us by clever Soviet negotiators; we imposed them on ourselves by our choices, theories, and domestic turmoil. It is therefore in our power to alter them.

The prevailing American strategic doctrine of the Sixties went under the modest name of "assured destruction." According to it, deterrence was guaranteed so long as we possessed the ability to destroy a predetermined percentage of Soviet population and industrial capacity. Strategy thereby turned into an engineering problem, an economic analysis essentially independent of the size of the opposing forces. So long as enough of our weapons survived to wreak the theoretically calculated havoc, deterrence would be maintained; our military effectiveness was essentially independent of the threat we faced; the vulnerability of part of our forces — such as our ICBMs — was irrelevant so long as enough warheads would remain to inflict an "unacceptable" amount of damage on the Soviet Union.

This doctrine not only took for granted continued Soviet inferiority in technology; it also ignored the psychological inhibitions in the way of implementing such a strategy. The targeting scenarios developed from this doctrine left a President with no other options in a crisis but the mass extermination of civilians, or capitulation. This strategy was morally questionable even in an era when we had superiority. In an age of strategic equality it would be a formula for mutual suicide.

The emergence of a new strategic nuclear environment should have forced a reconsideration of this targeting doctrine and a renewed attention to regional nuclear and conventional balances. Unfortunately, at the precise moment that such a reexamination became urgently necessary, *all* our defense programs came under systematic attack as a byproduct of the bitter domestic debate over Vietnam. On the one hand, the Vietnam war reduced funds available for modernization of our military forces; even more important, the wholesale assault on defense spending and programs jeopardized even those major projects for which funds were available and budgeted. New weapons were decried as excessive, as symptoms of a military psychosis, as wasteful and dangerous. "Reordering national priorities" was the slogan of the day; it was the euphemism for cutting the defense budget. The ABM passed by only one vote and was then emasculated in the appropriations process; the C-5A transport aircraft which later saved an ally in the 1973 Middle East war was challenged repeatedly on budgetary grounds; MIRVs, the only strategic system available to us to offset the Soviet numerical superiority in the 1970s, were under constant attack. In the realm of strategic doctrine, paradoxically it was those most alarmed at the arms race who clung to the most bloodthirsty targeting strategies, in the hope that these would obviate the need to strengthen or increase our strategic forces.

In this atmosphere, maintaining even the strategic forces inherited from the Sixties absorbed the energies of the Administrations up to the end of the Vietnam war; obtaining funds for new programs was enormously difficult. The best that could be accomplished in the early 1970s was to alter the older strategic doctrine and shift targeting from civilian to military objectives. (Paradoxically, however, the decline of our *capability* for a counterforce strategy turned even the more sophisticated targeting into a high-risk tit-for-tat option with no logical stopping place.)

After the end of our involvement in Vietnam, new strategic programs could at last be funded: the B-1 manned strategic bomber, to become operational in 1978; the MX ICBM, to become operational in 1983; the Trident submarine and missile, expected to become operational in 1979; various kinds of cruise missiles for the 1980s — all of which would give the United States greater options and some of which would bring about a new counterforce capability.

Every one of these programs has been canceled, delayed, or stretched out by the current Administration, so that we are at a point where only the Trident (with only the most limited counterforce capability) can be operational during the period of the projected SALT treaty. In addition, even the Minuteman production line was closed down, leaving us without an emergency hedge for rapid buildup in unexpected contingencies. We now face the challenge of the early Eighties with forces designed in the Sixties. We have been able to develop new programs in only four years out of the last fifteen, and most of them have been held in abeyance since 1977.

Furthermore, a remedy will be more difficult if the Administration intends to return to the pure "assured destruction" strategic doctrine. In his State of the Union address last January 23, President Carter proclaimed that "just one of our relatively invulnerable Poseidon submarines . . . carries enough warheads to destroy every large and medium-sized city in the Soviet Union."

But this truism demonstrates rather than solves our strategic dilemma. Even under SALT conditions we will have, in the early Eighties, at best equality in the capacity of our strategic forces to inflict civilian damage, and a clear inferiority in the ability to attack and destroy the land-based missiles of the other side. Our Minuteman missiles do not carry sufficient warheads or possess adequate throwweight for a disarming attack against Soviet ICBMs; our present strategic forces can put at risk less than one-half of Soviet ICBMs. *All* of our ICBMs will in the Eighties be vulnerable to an attack by the greater numbers of missiles and warheads, and improving accuracy, of Soviet land-based missiles.

Since our modern military doctrine and strategy have de-

pended much more on strategic forces than those of the Soviets, even overall equality revolutionizes the postwar security
and geopolitical structure. But in fact the situation is worse. My
principal worry is not only the growing vulnerability of our land-
based forces — though this must be remedied — but the growing
*invulnerability* of *Soviet* land-based forces. The deterrent effect
of our strategic forces in defense of allies will continually decline; our strategic forces will surely lose their ability to offset the
Soviet capacity for regional intervention. And this capacity will
be reinforced by the growing edge in Soviet theater nuclear forces,
a naval and airlift capability which immeasurably extends the
reach and preponderance of Soviet conventional power.

I want to reiterate that it is not necessary for present purposes to debate whether the Soviet Union would in fact run a risk
of war on the global level; it will be grave enough if the Soviet
willingness to run risks in regional conflicts is magnified. And that
seems to me the minimum consequence of what is ahead. The side
that can defend its interests only by threatening to initiate the
mutual mass extermination of civilians will gradually slide toward strategic, and therefore eventually geopolitical, paralysis.
The consequence, to put it bluntly, is that in the 1980s regional
conflicts — whether deliberately promoted or not — threaten increasingly to grow out of control unless we drastically reverse the
trend. We cannot possibly continue to gamble with inferior forces
for regional defense, a shifting balance in theater nuclear forces,
vulnerable land-based strategic forces, and invulnerable Soviet
ICBMs without courting the gravest dangers. The decline in relative power *must* be dramatically reversed.

Even more important is a strategic doctrine which answers
the following questions:

1. How in the Eighties will we safeguard our national security when we face adverse trends in every significant military
category?

2. How will we fulfill our commitments to our allies in the absence of a significant counterforce capability, when strategic parity is at best tenuous and the theater nuclear balance is turning against us?

3. How will we protect our vital interests in areas such as the Middle East with our present conventional forces, airlift, and declining naval capability?

4. How will we prevent global blackmail?

Our safety and that of all of those who depend on us depends on the response. Every day we delay in dealing with the issue magnifies our peril.

The Senate therefore cannot deal with the SALT treaty in a vacuum; it must simultaneously seek to restore the military and geopolitical balance. No responsible leader can want to face the 1980s with the present military prospects. This, and not SALT in isolation, is the principal problem facing us.


# SALT IN THE CONTEXT OF AMERICAN STRATEGY

The idea of arms control developed in the late Fifties and early Sixties. The underlying rationale derived from the indisputable fact that thermonuclear weapons and intercontinental missiles have added a new dimension of peril to the historical problem of military rivalry. In the past it could be argued that weapons were a symptom rather than a cause of tension. Indeed it is difficult to find an historical example for the cliché that arms races cause wars. (What caused World War I was mobilization schedules, not the rate of increase of armaments.) But today, indeed, the nuclear age combines weapons of unprecedented destructive power, extremely rapid modes of delivery of intercontinental range, and high vulnerability to a surprise attack.

In these new and unprecedented circumstances, the conclusion seemed inescapable that the side whose capacity for retaliation was vulnerable must react in crises in ways which would heighten the likelihood of cataclysm; a country whose strategic forces were not secure could be driven, even against its will, to strike first rather than await the opponent's attack which it would know it could not survive. In the late Fifties, one of the most brilliant students of deterrence, Albert Wohlstetter, correctly perceived that what Churchill called the "balance of terror" was perilously delicate. Arms control sought to circumscribe and if possible eliminate this danger by measures that would enhance each side's "second-strike capability," that is, its secure capacity to retaliate, thereby reducing the incentive and capacity for surprise attack.

This analysis was essentially correct. At the same time this novel military doctrine — according to which an adversary's invulnerability was thought to add to stability — was combined with "assured destruction" reasoning to produce a kind of "minimum deterrence" theory by which we allegedly had no need to consider the threat posed by the level of Soviet forces. Even theorists of arms control who valued maintaining the strategic balance only dimly perceived that the strategic stability they sought implied a strategic revolution. For if attained, it would greatly magnify the danger at levels of violence below that of general nuclear exchange. If crises no longer produced fear of escalation to all-out war, they would also grow more likely. Thus even strategic stability (not to speak of a Soviet edge) would require new major military efforts by us on the regional level or else major political weakness would result. Above all it was erroneously assumed the Soviets held a similar view. In fact, there was no evidence that Soviet strategic planners — almost all military men — subscribed to the academic subtleties of American strategic theory. As Secretary Harold Brown has said, our unilateral restraint does not seem to be reciprocated by the Soviets: "We have found that when we build weapons, they build; when we stop, they nevertheless continue to build. . . ."[2]

As one of the architects of SALT, I am conscience-bound to point out that — against all previous hopes — the SALT process does not seem to have slowed down Soviet strategic competition, and in some sense may have accelerated it. The Soviets worked hard and successfully to enhance the first-strike capabilities of their land-based ICBMs despite our restraint and within the framework of SALT. The Administration of the early 1970s of which I was a member sought to use SALT to demonstrate its commitment to easing tensions and thereby restore a public consensus behind a strong national defense; to some extent we succeeded. But we will not draw the appropriate conclusion if we do not also admit that SALT may have had a perverse effect on the willingness of some in the Congress, key opinion makers, and even Administration officials to face fully the relentless Soviet military buildup.

New weapons systems have long had to overcome the traditional objection of advocates of "minimum deterrence" that they were unnecessary (because we already possessed an "overkill" capability); they were now also attacked by arms control experts as endangering the prospects of SALT. Indeed, many new programs could be put through Congress less on their merits than as a "bargaining chip"; they were needed, various Administrations argued, so that they could be traded in a negotiation. Whatever the tactical utility of this argument, it tended to reduce the energy with which such programs were pursued. The Pentagon found it difficult to muster enthusiasm — or scarce resources — for programs which were ephemeral by definition. After a while the Soviet Union began to play the game deliberately: from ABM to cruise missiles it systematically sought to use SALT to inhibit our military and technological development; it tried to fuel our

[2] Statement of Secretary Brown before the Senate Foreign Relations Committee, July 9, 1979.

domestic debate, adding its own propaganda pressures to domestic pressures against new weapons systems.

The theory that new American weapons weakened the prospects of arms control thrived despite all evidence to the contrary. In 1967, before we had an ABM program, when President Johnson suggested to Soviet Premier Kosygin at Glassboro that both sides renounce ABMs, Kosygin contemptuously dismissed the idea as one of the most ridiculous he had ever heard. By 1970, after the Nixon Administration had narrowly won its Congressional battle for funding of an ABM, Soviet SALT negotiators refused to discuss any subject *except* ABM, and it required the most strenuous negotiating efforts to maintain the crucial linkage between offensive and defensive limitations. Conversely, neither the abandonment of the B-1 by the current Administration, nor its stretch-out of the MX missile, nor the slowdown in the Trident program speeded up SALT negotiations or improved the terms.

The SALT negotiations have always proceeded against the background of the strategic balance as it existed, and must be considered in this context.

The negotiations for SALT I grew out of the ABM debate of the 1960s: whether the United States should follow the Soviet lead and build a defense against ballistic missiles, or try to head off such a new competition by negotiating some limits with the USSR. After considerable Soviet stalling, to see whether Congress might kill the ABM without any need for Soviet reciprocity, the SALT negotiations began in November 1969. Almost from the outset it was apparent that the *only* system the Soviets were eager to limit by negotiation was the *sole* system we were building — the ABM. In the 1972 ABM treaty both sides agreed in effect to leave themselves indefinitely vulnerable to missile attacks; ABMs were restricted to a token deployment at one site (which we then unilaterally abandoned for budgetary reasons). In effect we traded our superior ABM technology for a halt to the numerical buildup of Soviet offensive forces.

To restore equality in this critical area — strategic offensive forces — proved to be enormously difficult, largely due to the unilateral decisions of the Sixties that stopped both our ICBM and SLBM programs by 1967. As I have said, in pure numbers of offensive missiles the Soviets passed the United States in 1970; in this category we had no bargaining chips. Our only active program was adding multiple warheads (MIRVs) to our land- and sea-based missiles. The Soviet numerical building program was so considerable, and Congressional opposition to comparable American programs was so unrelenting, that it was the Defense Department which in July 1970 and then again in January 1972 urged a five-year mutual freeze on offensive weapons, primarily to arrest the momentum of the Soviet buildup and to give us an opportunity to catch up.

The first SALT agreement on offensive weapons was thus a photograph of the existing balance, not an alteration of it: it froze the numbers of American and Soviet land- and sea-based missiles for five years. The numerical balance was favorable to the USSR in the same proportion that the previous decade of unrestricted arms competition had produced. Because of our MIRV program, the United States retained a substantial advantage in numbers of warheads for the lifetime of the Interim Agreement and beyond. The criticism later heard, that SALT I "gave" the Soviets unequal numbers, missed the central point: what had produced the Soviet numerical edge was not SALT I but the unilateral American decisions of the Sixties to stop our strategic building programs, and then the Congressional and public attacks on the defense budget growing out of the Vietnam war. The 1972 SALT agreement curtailed no American offensive program; it did halt the numerical growth of the Soviet strategic forces. It gave us an opportunity to catch up — which we sought to do by pushing the development of the B-1 slated to be operational in 1978, the Trident submarine and missile planned for 1979, the MX missile for 1983, and a variety of cruise missiles for the early Eighties.

But the simple Interim Agreement of SALT I could not deal with — nor did it pretend to address — the rapid evolution of technology. Modernization of existing weapons was allowed, and both sides proceeded apace with new programs. The United States funded its MIRV program, and the Soviets developed a new generation of ICBMs; in doing so they pushed to its outer limit the SALT I provision restricting conversion of "light" to "heavy" missiles. It was these larger missiles (the SS-17, 18, and 19), soon equipped with MIRVs, and with the potential of greatly improved accuracy, that were bound to give the Soviets for the first time in history a capacity to launch a first strike against our land-based missiles.

These trends, which would eventually put our force of ICBMs into jeopardy, led us first to undertake a complex but eventually fruitless negotiation to set a low, long-term ceiling on Soviet missile capabilities both in numbers and in quality. For a time these negotiations seemed promising; but they fell victim to the collapse of executive authority resulting from Watergate. In the wake of President Nixon's resignation, it seemed prudent to pick up the thread of a simpler agreement that at least consolidated numerical equality, and then to move as quickly as possible in SALT III into the more intricate discussion of the qualitative factors (missile accuracy, throwweight, number of warheads, testing limits, and so forth). Thus, in November 1974 in Vladivostok, President Ford pressed for an agreement based on equal aggregate ceilings, and the Soviet Union accepted our proposal. A framework accord was reached specifying strict equality of 2,400 missiles and strategic bombers for each side, and an equal limit of 1,320 missiles with MIRVs, in an agreement to run through 1985.

The Ford Administration had first hoped that a treaty implementing the Vladivostok accord could be completed in 1975. But two new issues intervened to slow down the talks: first was the Soviet insistence that cruise missiles be entirely banned if they had a range of more than 600 kilometers (350 miles); second was the US counterdemand that the Soviet aircraft called the "Backfire" be counted as a "heavy" bomber and thus be included in the SALT totals. Inevitably the two systems became linked in the talks. Throughout 1975 and into early 1976, the United States and the USSR made proposals to resolve the dispute. Basically, the Ford Administration was prepared to limit the range and number of *some* cruise missiles *provided* the Soviets would reciprocate by limiting the Backfire bomber in some comparable manner. In January 1976, we were close to a compromise along these lines which also would have lowered the Vladivostok ceilings of 2,400 to "below 2,300."

Two events prevented the completion of the negotiations. First, the introduction of 25,000 Cuban proxy troops in Angola raised serious doubts about Soviet motives and fueled a whole new debate in this country about US–Soviet relations. And the imminent American Presidential election convinced President Ford that it would be best to keep SALT from turning into a partisan issue and so to wait to conclude an agreement after the election.

The advent of a new Administration brought with it the obligatory new approach. The first proposal to Moscow in March 1977 abandoned the negotiations as they then stood. An entirely new proposal was submitted, immediately rejected, and quickly withdrawn. The parties returned to earlier proposals, and over two more years were spent refining the agreement. Meanwhile the presuppositions of that agreement were daily challenged by technological change, the pace of the Soviet buildup, and the unilateral abandonment or stretching out of major American weapons systems, all of which further tilted the strategic balance dangerously against us.

Three conclusions emerge: The imbalances we now face, and which concern so many, stem in essence from unilateral American decisions rather than from the SALT negotiating process. This is important when we consider the provisions of the SALT treaty.

No negotiation can achieve through diplomacy that for which we have been unwilling to make unilateral efforts.

Second, SALT by itself cannot bring about parity; it can only ratify trends which exist. SALT cannot be a substitute for defense programs. If we fall behind by our own actions, SALT runs the risk of perpetuating an inequality. But whether that comes about is up to us; and to avoid it must be a principal concern of the Senate.

Third, SALT III cannot simply be an extension of the previous process. It must be explicitly related to our long-term strategic program. Its principles must be clearly worked out between the Administration and the Congress and settled with our allies *before* we launch ourselves into it.

# THE VIENNA TREATY: HOW DOES IT AFFECT THE STRATEGIC BALANCE?

We must now ask, how does the SALT II agreement affect the strategic balance? The agreement is composed of three documents:

- The treaty itself, running until the end of 1985, would limit the total numbers of ICBM and SLBM launchers (though the term is not defined); heavy bombers; MIRVed missiles; and land-based MIRVed missiles. It also defines counting rules for MIRVed missiles and for heavy bombers equipped with air-launched cruise missiles.
- Second is a protocol that restricts cruise missiles other than on heavy bombers to a range of 600 kilometers (or 350 miles) and bans the testing and deployment of mobile ICBMs. The protocol is supposed to expire on December 31, 1981.

• Third is a set of principles to guide the negotiations for SALT III.

Any fair-minded analysis must recognize the beneficial aspects of the SALT II agreements. The overall ceiling of 2,250 will force the Soviets to get rid of 250 strategic systems, including some modern ones, while giving us the right to equalize the numbers. The permitted number of land-based Soviet MIRVs (820) is some 100 below the maximum number that they probably intended to build in the absence of SALT. There are some restrictions on missile testing procedures. There are limits on numbers of missile warheads on ICBMs and a prohibition on more than one "new" ICBM. There is for the first time an agreed baseline of information on the Soviet forces. The counting rules are a useful way of dealing with the MIRV problem.

Regrettably none of these very real achievements affects the grave strategic situation which I have described and which must urgently be reversed. The treaty does not reduce the Soviet first-strike capability against our land-based forces, or improve our ability to survive a first strike. It does not diminish the Soviet residual capability to destroy civilian targets in the United States. And it does not enhance — indeed it may slightly inhibit — the possibility for the United States to catch up in the capacity of our strategic forces to attack military targets.

To be sure, the Soviets will be obligated after 1981 to reduce the total number of their launchers by about 250. But the new ceiling of 2,250 will not limit the Soviets' ability to destroy our ICBM force or to inflict devastating damage upon the United States. The reduction in Soviet numbers is irrelevant to our strategic problem. For the danger to our security derives from warheads, not from launchers, and the Soviet total of ICBM warheads will increase from 3,200 at the time of the signing of SALT II to over 6,000 even after the reduction in Soviet launchers is supposed to take place; the total number of Soviet warheads (including SLBMs) will approach 12,000 in 1985 as compared to 8,000 at the time of the SALT signing. (In fact, if the Soviets went all out they could get 8,000 MIRVed warheads in the permitted new land-based missiles.) Moreover, the total Soviet missile throw-weight will increase from about 6 million pounds at the time of the signing of SALT I, to 7 million pounds at the signing of SALT II, to 9 million pounds (compared to our 2.5 million) in 1985. And improvements in Soviet accuracy will approach ours by 1982; the practical effect of this will be to reduce the number of warheads that *need* to be aimed at our ICBM silos, freeing a larger number of the ever-increasing Soviet warheads for other targets.

The agreed ceiling, of course, is some 200 above the 2,060 operational systems *we* now possess. We thus have some considerable room for expansion of single-warhead sytems. But given the cancellation of the B-1 bomber, the delay in the operational date for MX, and the slow pace of Trident production, there is almost no chance that the United States can reach the permitted total of 2,250 except perhaps by keeping in service ten older Polaris submarines (with 160 missiles); this the Navy is likely to oppose because of the heavy cost of operation and relatively short range of its missiles. The result, therefore, is that in practice the overall aggregate numbers will continue to be unequal.

The limitation of land-based MIRVed launchers to 820, which may be some 100 below the probable Soviet program, is equally welcome and similarly without significance to our fundamental problem. The Soviet Union can destroy our land-based ICBMs with about half of the land-based MIRVs permitted by the treaty; this would leave over 300 Soviet land-based MIRVed launchers, 380 sea-based MIRVed systems, and some 500 single-warhead systems — or well over 5,000 warheads — aimed at our civilian population and industrial potential. (By contrast, if we expended our *entire* land-based force against the Soviet ICBM silos we could destroy fewer than half.)[3]

Nor is the threat to our forces and to the overall strategic balance reduced by the provision limiting new missiles during the time of the treaty. The provision is drafted so as to permit the deployment of the MX for the United States, a comparable new missile for the Soviet Union, and the modernization of existing missiles, allowing an increase in their volume of up to 5 percent in each direction. Except for setting a precedent for qualitative restraints, these limitations have little operational effect on the Soviet program — all the less so as there seems to be no definition of baselines. The testimony of Administration witnesses seems to confirm that no known Soviet program is affected.

In short, the Vienna treaty will not diminish the threat to the strategic balance. During the life of the treaty the Soviets will complete their counterforce capability against our ICBMs. This will coincide exactly with our period of maximum danger. To be sure, a good case can be made for the proposition that in the absence of the treaty the relative numbers will be even worse. But the analysis here suggests that what is allowed to the Soviets will meet all their foreseeable counterforce and residual needs.

But I must repeat: *any* SALT treaty is likely to ratify existing strategic trends. SALT negotiators cannot produce what our military programs — for whatever reason — have neglected. The Soviets will never agree to unilateral reductions. If we want equality, we must build to equality. We must reverse the strategic trends if we are serious about an equitable SALT treaty. Nothing in the Vienna treaty diminishes the need for a substantial military

[3] Though the permitted total of land-based MIRVs is some 300 above what we possess, we cannot expand our land-based MIRVs significantly since the treaty also contains a subceiling of 1,200 permitted MIRVed vehicles. We could thus increase the number of our land-based missiles only by reducing the number of submarine-based missiles. That sublimit will also force us to dismantle either one Poseidon boat (or fourteen Minuteman III) when the seventh Trident submarine goes on sea trials, probably by 1983. If the eighth and ninth Tridents were to become operational before December 1985, three more Poseidon boats or forty-eight Minuteman III or some combination of the two would have to be dismantled.

buildup by the United States. In fact, the situation which SALT reflects makes such a buildup imperative.

In fairness, it must be pointed out that the same was true of the SALT II aggregates worked out in the previous Administration. There are nevertheless three essential differences: first, the rate of advance of Soviet technology which has been unexpectedly rapid (the estimate at Vladivostok was that Minuteman would not become vulnerable to a Soviet counterforce strike until after 1985); second, the unilateral abandonment or stretch-out of almost every American strategic program inherited by the Carter Administration, which makes the Soviet threat even more ominous; and third, the Soviet geopolitical offensive in Africa, the Middle East, and Southeast Asia which has gained momentum since. But to help a bipartisan solution I am willing to concede that the problem we face has origins going back at least fifteen years.[4]

The novel — and to me the most disturbing — feature of the current treaty is its negative impact on the theater nuclear balance. The Soviet Backfire bomber is limited to production of no more than thirty per year, through an oral agreement outside the treaty or protocol. There has been dispute about the utility of the Backfire in carrying out unrefueled attacks against the United States. There is *no* doubt of its ability to threaten all our allies as well as China and the sea approaches to Eurasia. In addition, the Soviet Union is developing a large number of SS-20 missiles each with a range of 2,000 miles and three MIRV warheads. Like the Backfire, the SS-20 is convertible to intercontinental range — in the case of the Backfire by adding fuel tanks, or an aerial refuel-

---

[4] On at least one occasion I contributed to the existing ambivalence. After an exhausting negotiation in July 1974 I gave an answer to a question at a press conference which I have come to regret: "What in the name of God is strategic superiority?" I asked. "What is the significance of it . . . at these levels of numbers? What do you do with it?" My statement reflected fatigue and exasperation, not analysis. If both sides maintain the balance, then indeed the race becomes futile and SALT has its place in strengthening stability. But if we opt out of the race unilaterally, we will probably be faced eventually with a younger group of Soviet leaders who will figure out what can be done with strategic superiority.

ing capability; in the case of the SS-20 by adding another stage, thereby converting it into the already tested mobile SS-16. These actions are prohibited by SALT II but they are not easily verifiable, and in any event they represent a rapid break-out potential should the treaty be broken or lapse.

The most immediately available American counter to these weapons has been cruise missiles. In the negotiations conducted by the Ford Administration, proposed restrictions on cruise missiles were made conditional on comparable restrictions on the Backfire. The concept was to limit the number of cruise missiles of more than 600-kilometer range in some relationship to limits on the Backfire. The protocol, on the other hand, prohibits the deployment of land- and sea-based cruise missiles and of air-launched cruise missiles of more than 600-kilometer range on other than heavy bombers altogether — even when they carry conventional warheads. The same protocol prohibits the testing and deployment of mobile ICBM launchers, even though the Soviets have already tested a mobile system (the SS-16) and we have neither tested nor developed a comparable weapon.

The provisions of the protocol with respect to cruise missiles, especially, restrict exclusively American programs; they affect not a single Soviet program. They amount to a unilateral renunciation of an American capability. The protocol also for the first time limits American weapons relevant primarily to the theater nuclear balance — thus affecting important interests of our allies — in return at best for restrictions relevant primarily to the United States. This is something we have heretofore consistently refused to do as a matter of principle in the decade that SALT negotiations have been taking place. It is a dangerous precedent.

Two arguments are advanced on behalf of the protocol: first, that it was necessary to induce the Soviet Union to go along with limits in the overall treaty; second, that since the protocol will lapse at the end of 1981 and since we will have no cruise missiles of more than 600-kilometer range before then, no real concession is involved. These propositions are mutually inconsistent; if the protocol restrains nothing we can do before the end of 1981 and will lapse, then why are Soviets so insistent on it?

The answer is that the Soviets know the history of moratoria and protocols very well; they are aware that such "provisional" agreements almost never end on their expiration date, especially if a negotiation is then taking place. At a minimum the protocol's terms will be the point of departure for the next round of negotiations. The Soviets will have the option of offering a seeming concession — for example, reducing the SALT totals to 2,150 (which we know they can accept since at one stage in the current negotiations they suggested it), or even lower. They can conversely threaten to abandon whatever negotiation is then taking place. Will we then insist on pursuing the development of cruise missiles, without which we have done for nearly three years? And if we do extend the moratorium, we will then have explicitly traded theater capabilities important to our allies in return for marginally reducing the threat against ourselves.

This deficiency of the protocol would not be cured by a proposed Senate amendment or reservation stating that it may not be extended except with the Senate's approval. Such an amendment, to begin with, implies that the protocol with its existing one-sided terms might well be extended, albeit with the Senate's consent. This will make it more difficult to appropriate significant sums for cruise missile programs which may at any moment be ended by an extension of the protocol.[5] Moreover, if the protocol comes up for extension independently of a broader consideration of the strategic balance, the temptation to extend it could easily be overwhelming.

To sum up: I have serious reservations about the protocol. As for the treaty, I conclude that its terms do not improve our

[5] Apparently the Navy has virtually abandoned the development of cruise missiles aimed at land targets — a role still considered important enough in the Ford Administration to cause the Joint Chiefs of Staff in 1976 to withhold their consent to an agreement which did not protect that capability.

strategic situation but neither do they prevent our remedying it during the remaining six years of its life. Undoubtedly it imposes some inhibitions on us — the prohibition against "heavy" missiles for the United States, for example, as well as the protocol's ban on mobile missiles through 1981. But I believe that the Senate can deal with these during the ratification process. (The issue of heavy missiles seems to me most relevant to the period *after* the expiration of the treaty since we could not build any before 1985 and since MX should take care of immediate needs.)

The crucial question is whether we can unite behind what is clearly necessary. Ratifying SALT — or rejecting SALT — makes sense *only* if it prompts dedication to our national defense and security. The Senate's judgment of the Vienna treaty should hinge, in my view, on what will be done to remedy existing trends and on the international impact of ratification or rejection.

Let me turn, therefore, to the broader political context of this SALT II agreement.

## THE GEOPOLITICAL PROBLEM
### The Soviet Union

The awesomeness of modern weapons, and the aspirations of all peoples for peace, impose the imperative of peaceful coexistence. No democratic leader deserves the public trust if he fails to make a genuine effort to reduce the dangers of nuclear holocaust, and to free national energies for dealing with the many urgent problems of mankind. The temptation is overwhelming to view this common stake in peace as a common bond between us and the Soviet Union. It should be and someday it must be if a cataclysm is to be avoided. But we cannot in good conscience say that current evidence supports the proposition that the time has yet arrived.

For a too brief period in 1972 and 1973, our insistence on restraint in the conduct of international relations seemed to bear fruit. SALT I was accompanied by a declaration of principles signed by the United States and the Soviet Union. It affirmed the necessity of avoiding confrontation, the imperative of mutual restraint, the rejection of attempts to exploit tension to gain unilateral advantage, the renunciation of claims to special influence in any region of the world. These principles, of course, reflected an aspiration, not a contract; they defined a yardstick by which to assess Soviet behavior. The strategy of détente was to encourage observance of these standards by a combination of positive incentives for constructive behavior and firm responses to block adventurism. The principles agreed in Moscow were a paradigm of conduct which the Soviet Union could violate only to its political cost.

Whether the Soviet Union ever intended to comply with them, or whether it was tempted into an adventurous course by the collapse of our executive authority as a result of Watergate (which deprived us of both incentives and penalties), or whether a combination of all these factors was responsible, will never be known.

Whatever the cause, the fact is that since 1975 there has been an unprecedented Soviet assault on the international equilibrium. That year saw the introduction of Cuban combat forces into Angola, eventually reaching 40,000, backed by Soviet financing, airlift, and policy support. By 1977 Soviet planes and pilots were flying air defense missions out of Cuba so that the Cuban air force could operate in Africa, and 1977 witnessed the spread of Cuban forces to Ethiopia. East German military and intelligence advisers have now joined the Cubans all over Africa and the Middle East. There have been two invasions of Zaire — and there may yet be a third; there have been Communist coups in Afghanistan and South Yemen and the occupation of Cambodia by Vietnam, preceded by a Soviet Friendship Treaty designed to secure Hanoi's rear during its aggression. Soviet arms depots in Libya and Ethiopia fuel insurgencies all over Africa. While the collapse of the

Shah of Iran had many causes, one contributing factor surely was the demoralization of a pro-Western leadership group by the gradual and unopposed growth of Soviet power in nearby areas.

Nor is this all. Terrorist organizations supported by Communist funds, armed by Communist weapons, and trained by Communist instructors are becoming a systematic instrument of anti-Western policy threatening countries friendly to us on several continents. They are not, to be sure, all controlled by Moscow; but someone who has started a rockslide cannot avoid responsibility by claiming that the rock he threw was not the one that ultimately killed bystanders. These tactics, reinforced by a Soviet military buildup clearly threatening the strategic, theater, and conventional balances, are incompatible with any notion of détente or coexistence.

Some argue that SALT is necessary lest we risk a return to the Cold War. This is a curious argument. Whatever label we give to recent Soviet conduct — whether "Cold War" or opportunism — it must be ended if there are to be any prospects for East-West coexistence or cooperation. No leader serves his people by pretending that SALT is needed to perpetuate an acceptable state of affairs. It is *not* an acceptable state of affairs, and it cannot be continued.

The Vienna summit recorded no progress toward a clear understanding with the Soviet Union on the key issue of political restraint. It was not possible, of course, to settle in the space of three days all the outstanding issues of Africa, the Middle East, or Southeast Asia. Nor can the Senate responsibly delay SALT until these vexing matters are settled; they must be dealt with by intelligent and patient diplomacy and firm resistance to pressure. But it would have been important to give at least symbolic expression to what is the overwhelming political challenge of our period: The ultimate test of an improved relationship — the real turning away from the Cold War — must be restrained Soviet international conduct. The refusal of the Soviets even to discuss the subject at Vienna, the reiteration by Brezhnev of the commitment to so-called struggles of liberation, are worrisome indeed.

What is involved here is a profound issue in US–Soviet relations which is both philosophical and practical. Can peace be realized exclusively by restraint in the field of arms? Or does the structure of peace require a geopolitical dimension as well? Is it possible to proceed in separate negotiations on their merits, or must there be some relationship between all the various interactions of two superpowers in the field of foreign policy? In the language of recent controversies, should there be "linkage" or not?

In my view, to seek to separate US–Soviet relations into discrete compartments runs the risk of encouraging Soviet leaders to believe that they can use East-West cooperation in one area as a safety valve while striving for unilateral advantage elsewhere. The Administration, imagining that linkage was a personal idiosyncrasy of previous administrations, decided to "abolish" it. SALT was pursued for its own sake, unaffected by Cuban troops in Ethiopia and East German auxiliaries in Mozambique; by Communist coups in Afghanistan and South Yemen; or by Soviet Friendship Treaties such as the one with Vietnam that was a prelude to the occupation of Cambodia.

This raises several problems. First of all, it is not possible to "abolish" the simple reality that the two superpowers impinge on each other on a broad range of issues and areas. Moreover, the attempt to do so produces an almost compulsive commitment to whatever particular subject seems susceptible to solution, such as SALT, thus permitting the Soviets to dictate the pace of negotiations and to use it to reduce the risks of aggressiveness. And it simultaneously overloads the issue under negotiation. If SALT must bear the whole weight of East-West relations, it runs the risk of turning into escapism; it will eventually crumble under the strain.

No serious person would maintain that nothing should be settled until all issues are settled; nor should SALT become the hostage of every passing political tension of a world in flux. What is needed, however, is a broad recognition that in an interdependent world the actions of the major nuclear powers are inevitably related and have consequences beyond the issue or region immediately concerned. A demonstration of American impotence in one part of the world erodes our credibility and hence the stability of other regions; pressures against our friends, encouraged by the Soviet Union or its proxies, cannot be compensated for by other negotiations such as SALT. If we ignore these facts we paradoxically enhance the attractiveness of such adventures. It surely is not provocative to ask the Soviet Union to accompany restraint in arms with restraint in political conduct. Attention to this kind of linkage ensures that no agreement stands alone, vulnerable to the next crisis, or turns into a soporific to lull the West while adventurism runs free.

I am inclined to agree that the failure to ratify an agreement negotiated over seven years by three administrations would have a disruptive impact on East-West relationships, creating a crisis atmosphere for which we may have little public or allied support. This is undoubtedly one of the telling arguments in favor of ratification. But the Senate will also wish to consider that to deal with SALT in isolation runs the risk of seriously misleading the Soviet Union. Moscow cannot have it both ways: the slogan of détente and the reality of the systematic undermining of the geopolitical equilibrium. We should use the SALT debate to force a decision. The Senate will want to make clear that Soviet expansionism threatens the peace and that coexistence depends above all on restrained international conduct, for which the Senate should define some criteria.

In the long run this is also in the Soviet interest, for current trends will make a confrontation inevitable sooner or later. Our country will not be defeated without noticing it and when it does take notice, it will resist. The course of inadequate defense preparation, gradual reduction of military capacity, and partial accommodation to Soviet expansionism must be reversed — on a bipartisan basis and by cooperation between the Administration and the Congress.

## The Concern of Allies

All our allies have expressed support for ratification of the Vienna treaty. But their endorsement results from a complex of factors of which approval of the provisions of the treaty is by far the least significant. Each has been urged, if not pressed, by the Administration to express support. In some cases the Soviets have added their entreaties. Refusal to comply would thus risk relations with both superpowers over an issue that is of high technical complexity and has been under negotiation for seven years. If the treaty failed as a result of their opposition, our allies might find themselves in the uncomfortable position of taking on *both* superpowers. Some governments are loath to expose themselves to domestic criticism as an "obstacle to détente" — especially over a treaty which the United States has already declared compatible with Western security. Some allies want to keep open their own individual options for détente and increased East-West trade. Some are afraid lest their objection endanger their essential defense cooperation with the United States (even while worried about the noncircumvention clauses of the treaty). Some sense the changing military balance but, unsure of our direction and unwilling to demand domestic sacrifice, seek to mitigate their perils by accommodation with the Soviet Union, staying one step ahead of us on the road to Moscow. All are reluctant to contribute to a further weakening of American executive authority, reasoning correctly that whatever their views on particulars their ultimate security depends on the self-assurance and credibility of the American President. There is no doubt that failure to ratify the treaty will shake European confidence in an American government that for seven years assured them that it knew what it was doing.

At the same time, allied endorsement should be seen in the context of a pervasive ambivalence. Our allies, especially in NATO, fear an exacerbation of tensions — but they are also deeply worried about the military imbalance on the European continent which the ratification of the present strategic relationship brings to the forefront of concern. The thoughtful leaders among them know that the basis of their security is eroding as our strategic superiority ebbs — but they fear there is not enough domestic support for a really significant defense effort, especially when American attitudes on that score are so ambiguous. They do not want to be perceived as an obstacle to SALT II, but they are highly uneasy about the inevitable SALT III, in which some limitation of theater-based nuclear weapons has already been placed on the agenda.

The United States thus stands in danger of being blamed by our allies at one and the same time for risking détente and for paying inadequate attention to security, for provoking the Soviet colossus and for jeopardizing the defense of the free world. It has ever been thus in the postwar period. The ultimate test of our leadership cannot be a poll of our allies, which will aways reflect a mixture of incommensurable motives. The test of our leadership is American willingness to give a clear-cut signal of what we understand by Western security and how we intend to maintain it. No other country or group of countries, however closely associated, can take this burden from our shoulders. None of our allies will forgive us if we fail.


## RECOMMENDATIONS

We thus return to our original problem. The Senate is in the anomalous position of being asked to ratify a treaty which is essentially peripheral to our basic security and geopolitical concerns but of which either simple ratification or simple rejection would have a profound and dangerous symbolic impact. Failure to ratify an agreement negotiated over seven years would compromise international confidence in our ability to perceive our own interests or to harmonize the various branches of our government. But it is equally true that if the custodian of free world security neglects its task, sooner or later panic will become inevitable. The Senate in considering ratification needs urgently to address our dangers in a comprehensive way:

- first, how the Senate can make concrete steps to begin redressing the military balance;
- second, how it can deal with the specific problems in the treaty and protocol; and
- third, how the Senate can put the Soviet Union on notice that continued attempts to upset the global equilibrium will not be tolerated.

Some, whose analysis I respect, have urged amendments to the treaty to accomplish these goals. These amendments are of two kinds. The first category would not require any renegotiation with the Soviet Union. They would either express the Senate's interpretation of the meaning of ambiguous clauses of the treaty, or instruct our negotiator on criteria to be applied in any follow-on negotiations, or reassure uneasy allies about our intentions in applying SALT provisions, for example, on noncircumvention. The second category of amendments would seek changes in the text. These amendments *would* require renegotiation of the Vienna agreement and they again fall into two categories: One type would alter the strategic balance during the term of the treaty, for example, by forcing a reduction of Soviet throwweight or heavy missiles. The second type would represent a claim of equal "entitlement" — such as an American right to possess 308 heavy missiles — which cannot be exercised during the life of the treaty and would therefore represent an assertion of principle rather than a contribution to the strategic balance.

The only amendments that would make any immediate difference are the kind which go to the heart of the problem: they would remove the Soviet counterforce capability against our ICBMs (by mandating a drastic reduction of throwweight, for example). Such amendments are almost certain to be rejected by the Soviets; they would be accepted, if at all, only after an actual buildup of our forces, which in turn might well be delayed by the very fact that renegotiations were under way. If we maintained current limits while negotiating, the result would be a continuation of the existing deterioration of the strategic balance. We might thus wind up without either SALT or a strengthened defense.

After much reflection I have concluded that I can support ratification only with the following conditions:

- first, if it is coupled with a defense program representing an obligatory understanding between the Congress and the President which overcomes on an urgent basis the grave peril posed by the current military balance;
- second, if it is accompanied by amendments — not requiring renegotiation — clearing up ambiguities in the treaty, defining the status of the protocol, the meaning of noncircumvention, and setting guidelines for follow-on negotiations;
- and third, if it is accomplished by a vigorous expression of the Senate's view of the linkage between SALT and Soviet geopolitical conduct.

This approach would avoid the negative consequences of a collapse of SALT. But ratification must not become an end in itself. In my view it can only be justified if the Administration is prepared to unite our country by demonstrating its determination to restore our military strength and the geopolitical equilibrium.

This seems to me the sense of what Senator Nunn among others has proposed, and it points the way to a bipartisan resolution of the issue.

## To Redress the Military Balance

With respect to the military programs, I respectfully recommend that the Senate give its advice and consent to ratification of the Vienna treaty *only* after the Administration has submitted, and the Congress has authorized and begun appropriating, a supplemental defense budget and a revised five-year defense program that will begin rectifying some of the shortcomings I have identified. The Congressional recess provides an opportunity to prepare such a program, on which work should already be far advanced as part of the normal budgetary process. If the Administration is unable to put forward such a program to this session of Congress, I recommend that the Senate delay its advice and consent until a new military program has been submitted to and authorized by the next session of Congress. I would be open-minded about other methods to achieve this end, provided they are unambiguous, and represent an obligatory commitment by both branches of our government.

Assurances that the Executive Branch intends to proceed with individual weapons systems like the MX are not enough, either for the reality of our danger or to reverse the political and psychological trends which will make the immediate future a period of great peril. Nor have the percentage figures of projected increases — such as the 3 percent increase agreed with NATO — proved effective, because of ambiguities about the baseline and how to compute rates of inflation. I am worried that if the consideration of defense programs takes place after SALT is ratified, the debate over the proposed defense programs may stifle remedial actions or delay them beyond all relevance — all the more so as the Administration seems to have a far from settled view about the need for a strengthened defense. Witness the cancellation of the B-1, the nuclear carrier, and the neutron bomb; the closing down of the Minuteman III production line; and the stretch-out of the MX, Trident, and cruise missile programs. After ratification, Soviet propaganda pressures can be expected to multiply, particularly against any MX basing system that ensures survivability. Allied doubts about the security situation — especially with respect to theater forces — will grow.

It is not a question of balancing the insistence of conservatives for higher defense with the considerations of liberals for a reduction in our military spending. The issue is what our country needs for its long-term security. The President and the Congress must choose. After fifteen years of giving inadequate priority to defense, it is time for a serious long-term effort to prevent a menacing imbalance against us. The program must include accelerated development of a counterforce capability through the MX and Trident II, air defense against Backfire, immediate steps to restore the theater nuclear balance, and urgent measures to beef up our capacity for regional defense including accelerated modernization and expansion of our Navy. Our current five-year program is deficient in all these categories. My support for ratification is *entirely conditional* on the development of a new program and doctrine given some binding form by the Congress.

The Joint Chiefs have testified that the rapid improvements required cannot be achieved at expenditures representing less than a 5 percent real increase over current programs, for at least the next five years. The burden of proof to the contrary should rest with the Administration.


## To Clarify the Treaty and Protocol

In addition to these military programs, I recommend that the Senate add the following amendments to its advice-and-consent resolution. *None* of them requires renegotiation with the Soviet Union.

- First, as far as cruise missiles are concerned, that the protocol may *not* be extended after 1981. The Senate should stipulate that its particular limitations can be submitted to the Congress again *only* as part of an equitable arrangement for theater nuclear forces. Specifically, no limitations may be negotiated for American theater weapons — such as cruise missiles — which are not matched by similar limitations on Soviet weapons performing comparable missions. This will bring cruise missiles into some equilibrium with the Backfire and the SS-20.
- Second, the Senate should specify that as part of SALT III, the United States should be entitled to *any* weapons system permitted to the Soviets in the new agreement unless the Soviets agree to some compensation by giving up a weapons system of equivalent characteristics allowed to us. This should take care of the heavy missile inequity within the framework — that of SALT III — which will give us a real option to produce it.
- Third, that the noncircumvention clause be interpreted by the Senate as not interrupting cooperative relationships with allies with respect to technology needed to modernize their forces. No technology available to us should be barred for transfer.

I also suggest that the Senate reexamine the SALT agreement every two years, specifically to determine its verifiability.

## To Address the Geopolitical Problem

Finally, I respectfully urge the Senate to use the ratification process to put the Soviet Union on notice that this country is prepared, nay eager, for peaceful coexistence that reflects true stability and equality in arms, and also political restraint. We are ready to pursue the control and reduction of arms with dedication. But we will brook no subterfuge, nor can we continue a conciliatory policy if Moscow chooses to exploit that policy as a convenient opening to Soviet predominance. The Senate should attach to its instrument of advice and consent an expression of the following principles:

- that the absence of political restraint will seriously jeopardize continuation of the SALT process;
- that the Senate understands this to include Soviet supply or encouragement of intervention by proxy military forces; the use of Soviet forces on the territory of its allies such as Cuba to free Cuban forces to fight in Africa; the support, financing, or encouragement by any member of the Warsaw Pact of groups and activities seeking to undermine governments friendly to the United States; or the exacerbation of regional conflicts;
- that the Administration be required to submit an annual report to the Senate on the degree to which the Soviet Union is living up to these criteria;
- that the Senate vote every two years its judgment whether the Soviet Union has lived up to these criteria. If the judgment is negative, the Senate should then vote whether whatever SALT negotiations are taking place should be continued.

Finally, if we thus reassess our strategic position, we must also take another look at the SALT process. Though the strategic conditions I have described result largely from unilateral American decisions, they have been reflected in the SALT process which was essentially a confirmation of them. The fact that I have participated in the process — and must share some of the responsibility — entitles me to warn against continuing it by rote. I urge that its long-term implications be carefully considered. Never in the postwar period has there been more disagreement and intellectual confusion about the requirements of strategic stability and the implications of arms control. A thorough reassessment and the fullest consultation with our allies are crucial before we launch ourselves into SALT III, which will directly affect our allies and hence may jeopardize our alliances.

## CONCLUSION

I recommend the approach outlined here because it gives this country an opportunity to address its dangers without abandoning an important negotiation that has already extended over seven years. And it gives us an opportunity to proceed as a united people. If the Administration rejects this approach, the Senate will have no alternative except to go the route of farther-reaching amendments, either holding the treaty in abeyance or forcing a renegotiation. The result will almost certainly be a diplomatic stalemate until the Soviets are convinced that we are determined to restore the strategic balance; it would be an indirect — and in my view less productive — route which, even if successful, would lead to the same results of a major new effort to meet our imperative security needs.

To be sure, the course I propose will make SALT II far from the turn in the arms race many of us hoped for when the negotiations were inaugurated. But too much time has been lost, too many weapons systems have been unilaterally abandoned, too many military adventures have been encouraged by the Soviet Union, the geopolitical balance has been too severely strained by Soviet pressures, for SALT to be much more than a base from which, one can hope, a new and serious effort at equitable arms reduction can be made. Concrete steps to rectify the global balance are urgently required. In this context a ratified SALT II treaty can play a useful role as a signpost to continuing negotiations, as a beacon illuminating the path to genuine coexistence and détente, and as a means to contain current tensions. But SALT must contribute to the world's security, not insecurity.

At this moment our major obligation is to restore the confidence of all those who depend on us; to redress the military balance; to reestablish some effective link between arms control and restrained international conduct. *All* Americans — of either party — should share these goals.

There are deeply concerned people who want SALT but doubt the need for augmented defense. Others see in SALT an obstacle to augmented defense. Let there be serious effort to reconcile these points of view before we turn to domestic confrontation. I am prepared to do my best in this effort.

Rarely is an opportunity so clearly presented to a legislative body to determine the course of national policy in a direction vital to the future of the democracies. After the 1919 Versailles treaty, misjudgments by the Senate *and* the Administration led to a debacle which undermined international security and doomed the world to another bloody holocaust. At this moment, the Senate and the Administration can point us in a different direction — toward a restoration of our national unity, toward the strengthening of the security of this nation and of its allies, and toward a more constructive relationship with our principal adversaries. This is America's responsibility, if we are to remain true to our trust and to the hopes of mankind.

# THE FUTURE OF NATO

*Opening remarks at the conference organized by the
Center for Strategic and International Affairs,
Georgetown University, and cosponsored by the Atlantic
Institute for International Affairs and the Atlantic Treaty
Organization, held in Brussels, September 1–3, 1979*

I T IS a somewhat strange phenomenon for me to talk to a NATO conference in Brussels in the presence of so many old friends, who will consider my words an unnecessary interruption in the thoughts they are getting ready to launch at the conference sessions. When I see my old colleague Ambassador de Staercke sitting here, it is almost like the old days; he functions as my conscience as he always has.

I think I speak for all of you when I thank the Foreign Minister for the extraordinary arrangements that have been made.

At the beginning of the conference, the most useful thing I can do is to outline the concerns that I have about the future of NATO, the problems that in my estimation require solution, if we are to retain our vitality and if we are to remain relevant to the challenges before us. Since the early 1960s, every new American administration that has come into office promises a new look at Europe, a reappraisal, and a reassessment. Each of these efforts has found us more or less confirming what already existed and what had been created in the late 1940s and early 1950s, with just enough Alliance adaptation to please the endlessly restless Americans who can never restrain themselves from new attempts at architecture.

Without going into which of these proposals were right, or if any of these specific proposals were necessary, I think the fact that in the late 1970s we are operating an Alliance machinery and a force structure under a concept more or less unchanged from the 1950s should indicate that we have been depleting capital. Living off capital may be a pleasant prospect for a substantial period of time, but inevitably a point will be reached where reality dominates. And my proposition to this group is that NATO is reaching a point where the strategic assumptions on which it has been operating, the force structures that it has been generating, and the joint policies it has been developing, will be inadequate for the 1980s.

I have said in the United States, in my SALT testimony, that if present trends continue, the 1980s will be a period of massive crisis for all of us. We have reached this point not through the mistakes of any single administration. Just as the commitment to NATO is a bipartisan American effort, the dilemmas that I would like to put before this group — admittedly in a perhaps exaggerated form — have been growing up over an extended period, partly as the result of American perceptions, partly as a result of European perceptions.

Nor is this to deny that NATO, by all of the standards of traditional alliances, has been an enormous success. To maintain an alliance in peacetime without conflict for a generation is extremely rare in history. And it is inherent in a process in which an alliance has been successful, in which deterrence has worked, that no one will be able to prove why it has worked. Was it because we conducted the correct policy? Was it because the Soviet Union never had any intention to attack us in the first place? Was it because of the policies of strength of some countries, or the policies of accommodation of other countries? So, what I say should not be taken as a criticism either of any particular American administration (even granting that there was one period of eight years in the past in which no mistakes were made) nor of any specific policies of European nations, but rather as an assessment of where we are today.

# THE GLOBAL ENVIRONMENT

Let me first turn to the strategic situation. The dominant fact of the current military balance is that the NATO countries are falling behind in every significant military category, with the possible exception of naval forces, where the gap in our favor is closing. Never in history has it happened that a nation achieved superiority in all significant weapons categories without seeking to translate it at some point into some foreign policy benefit. It is, therefore, almost irrelevant to debate whether there is some magic date at which Soviet armies will head in some direction or another. I am willing to grant that there is no particular master plan nor is there any specific deadline; I do not even consider that the present Soviet leaders are superadventurous. That is fundamentally irrelevant.

In a world of upheaval and rapid changes, enough opportunities will arise in which the relative capacity and the relative willingness of the two sides to understand their interests and to defend their interests will be the key element. I do not believe the Soviet Union planned Angola, or created the conditions for intervention in Ethiopia, or necessarily had a deadline for the revolution in Afghanistan. But all of these events happened to the detriment of general stability. I would consider it a rash Western policy that did not take into account that in the decade ahead we will face simultaneously an unfavorable balance of power, a world in turmoil, a potential economic crisis, and a massive energy problem. To conduct business as usual is to entrust one's destiny to the will of others and to the self-restraint of those whose ideology highlights the crucial role of the objective balance of forces.

This is my fundamental theme. And I would now like to discuss this in relation to specific issues.

## *The Shifting Strategic Balance*

First, at the risk of repeating myself, let me state once again what I take to be the fundamental change in the strategic situation as far as the United States is concerned, and then examine the implications for NATO.

When the North Atlantic Treaty Organization was created, the United States possessed an overwhelming strategic nuclear superiority. That is to say, for a long period of time we were likely to prevail in a nuclear war, certainly if we struck first and for a decade perhaps even if we struck second; we were in a position to wipe out the Soviet strategic forces and to reduce any possible counterblow against us to an acceptable level. And that situation must have looked more ominous to the Soviet Union even than it looked favorable to us.

If we think back to the Cuban missile crisis of 1962, which all the policymakers of the time were viewing with a consciousness of an approaching Armageddon, one is almost seized with nostalgia for the ease of their decisions. At that time the Soviet Union had about seventy long-range missiles that took ten hours to fuel, which was a longer period of time than it would take our airplanes to get to the Soviet Union from forward bases. Even at the time of the Middle East crisis of 1973 (the alert), we had a superiority of about eight to one in missile warheads. If one compares this with the current and foreseeable situation, we are approaching a point where it is difficult to assign a clear military objective to American strategic forces in a strategic nuclear exchange.

In the 1950s and for much of the 1960s, NATO was protected by a preponderance in American strategic striking power which was capable of disarming the Soviet Union, and by a vast American superiority in theater nuclear forces, although, as I will discuss, we never had a comprehensive theory for using theater nuclear forces. Since all intelligence services congenitally overestimate the rationality of the decision-making process which they are analyzing, it is probable that the Soviet Union made more sense out of our nuclear deployment in Europe than we were able to make ourselves. In any event, it was numerically superior. And it was in that strategic framework that the allied ground forces on the continent were deployed.

No one disputes any longer that in the 1980s — and perhaps even today, but surely in the 1980s — the United States will no longer be in a strategic position to reduce a Soviet counterblow against the United States to tolerable levels. Indeed, one can argue that the United States will not be in a position in which attacking the Soviet strategic forces makes any military sense, because it may represent a marginal expenditure of our own strategic striking force that does not help greatly to ensure the safety of our forces.

Since the middle 1960s the growth of the Soviet strategic force has been massive. It grew from 220 intercontinental ballistic missiles in 1965 to 1,600 around 1972–1973. Soviet submarine-launched missiles grew from negligible numbers to over 900 in the 1970s. And the amazing phenomenon which historians will ponder is that all of this has happened without the United States attempting to make a significant effort to rectify that state of affairs. One reason was that it was not easy to rectify. But another reason was the growth of a school of thought to which I myself contributed, and many around this conference table also contributed, which considered that strategic stability was a military asset, and in which the historically amazing theory developed that vulnerability contributed to peace and invulnerability contributed to risks of war.

Such a theory could develop and be widely accepted only in a country that had never addressed the problem of the balance of power as a historical phenomenon. And, if I may say so, only also on a continent that was looking for any excuse to avoid analysis of the perils it was facing and that was looking for an easy way out. When the Administration with which I was connected sought to implement an antiballistic missile program inherited from our predecessors, it became the subject of the most violent attacks from those who held the theory that it was destabilizing, provocative, and an obstacle to arms control; initially the ABM could be sold only as a protection against the Chinese and not against the Soviet threat. In any case, the ABM was systematically reduced by the Congress in every succeeding session to the point where we wound up with a curious coalition of the Pentagon and the arms controllers, both finally opposed to it: the Pentagon because it no longer made any military sense to put resources into a program that was being systematically deprived of military utility, and the arms control community because they saw in the strategic vulnerability of the United States a positive asset. It cannot have occurred often in history that it was considered an advantageous military doctrine to make your own country deliberately vulnerable.

Now we have reached that situation so devoutly worked for by the arms control community: we are indeed vulnerable. Moreover, our weapons had been deliberately designed, starting in the 1960s, so as not to threaten the weapons of the other side. Under the doctrine of "assured destruction," nuclear war became not a military problem but one of engineering; it depended on theoretical calculations of the amount of economic and industrial damage that one needed to inflict on the other side; it was therefore essentially independent of the forces the other side was creating.

This general theory suffered two drawbacks. One was that the Soviets did not believe it. And the other is that we have not yet bred a race of supermen that can implement it. While we were building "assured destruction" capabilities, the Soviet Union was building forces for traditional military missions capable of destroying the military forces of the United States. So in the 1980s we will be in a position where (1) many of our own strategic forces, including all of our land-based ICBMs, will be vulnerable, and (2) such an insignificant percentage of Soviet strategic forces will be vulnerable as not to represent a meaningful strategic attack option for the United States. Whether that means that the Soviet Union intends to attack the United States or not is certainly not my point. My point is that the change in the strategic situation produced by our limited vulnerability is more fundamental for the United States than even total vulnerability would be for the Soviet Union because our strategic doctrine has relied extraordinarily, perhaps exclusively, on our superior strategic power. The Soviet Union has never relied on its superior strategic power. It has always depended more on its local and regional superiority. Therefore, even an equivalence in destructive power, even "assured destruction" for both sides, is a revolution in the strategic balance as we have known it. It is a fact that must be faced.

I have recently urged that the United States build a counter-force capability of its own. The answer of our NATO friends to the situation that I have described has invariably been to demand additional reassurances of an undiminished American military commitment. And I have sat around the NATO Council table in Brussels and elsewhere and have uttered the magic words which had a profoundly reassuring effect, and which permitted the ministers to return home with a rationale for not increasing defense expenditures. And my successors have uttered the same reassurances. And yet if my analysis is correct, these words cannot be true indefinitely; and if my analysis is correct we must face the fact that it is absurd in the 1980s to base the strategy of the West on the credibility of the threat of mutual suicide.

One cannot ask a nation to design forces that have no military significance, whose primary purpose is the extermination of civilians, and expect that these factors will not affect a nation's resoluteness in crisis. We live in the paradoxical world that it is precisely the liberal, human, progressive community that is advocating the most bloodthirsty strategies and insisting that there is nothing to worry about as long as the capacity exists to kill 100 million people. It is this approach that argues that we should not be concerned about the vulnerability of our missile forces, when, after all, we can always launch them on warning of an attack. Any military man at this conference will tell you that launching strategic forces on warning can be accomplished only by delegating the authority to the proverbial "insane colonel" about whom so many movies have been made. Nobody who knows anything about how our government operates will believe that it is possible for our President to get the Secretary of State, Secretary of Defense, Chairman of the Joint Chiefs of Staff, and Director of the CIA to a conference called in the fifteen minutes that may be available to make a decision, much less issue an order that then travels down the line of command in the fifteen minutes. So the only way you can implement that strategy is by delegating the authority down to some field commander who must be given discretion so that when he thinks a nuclear war has started, he can retaliate. Is that the world we want to live in? Is that where "assured destruction" will finally take us?

And therefore I would say — what I might not say in office — that our European allies should not keep asking us to multiply strategic assurances that we cannot possibly mean or if we do mean, we should not want to execute because if we execute, we risk the destruction of civilization. Our strategic dilemma is not solved by verbal reassurances; it requires redesigning our forces and doctrine. There is no point in complaining about declining American will, or criticizing this or that American administration, for we are facing an objective crisis and it must be remedied.

## Theater Nuclear Forces

The second part of this problem is the imbalance that has grown up in theater nuclear forces. In the 1950s and 1960s we put several thousand nuclear weapons into Europe. To be sure, we had no very precise idea of what to do with them, but I am sure that Soviet intelligence figured out some purpose for these forces; and in any event it was a matter for their disquiet. Now one reason we did not have a rational analysis for the use of these factors was the very reason that led to the strategic theory of "assured destruction." Let us face it: the intellectually predominant position in the United States was that we had to retain full control of the conduct of nuclear war and we therefore had a vested interest in avoiding any "firebreak" between tactical nuclear weapons and strategic nuclear weapons. The very reasoning that operated against setting a rational purpose for strategic forces also operated against giving a military role to tactical nuclear forces. And this was compounded by the fact that — to be tactless — the secret dream of all Europeans was, of course, to avoid a nuclear war but, secondly, if there had to be a nuclear war, to have it conducted over their heads by the strategic forces of the United States and the Soviet Union. Be that as it may, the fact is that the strategic imbalance that I have predicted for the 1980s will also be accompanied by a theater imbalance in the 1980s. How is it possible to survive with these imbalances in the face of the already demonstrated inferiority in conventional forces?

If there is no theater nuclear establishment on the continent of Europe, we are writing the script for selective blackmail in which our allies will be threatened, and in which we will be forced into a decision whereby we can respond only with a strategy that has no military purpose but only the aim of destruction of populations.

I ask any of you around this conference table: If you were secretary of state or security adviser, what would you recommend to the President of the United States to do in such circumstances? How would he improve his relative military position? Of course he could threaten a full-scale strategic response, but is it a realistic course? It is senseless to say that dilemma shows that Americans are weak and irresolute. This is not the problem of any particular administration, but it is a problem of the doctrine that has developed.

Therefore, I believe that it is urgently necessary either that the Soviets be deprived of their counterforce capability in strategic forces, or that a US counterforce capability in strategic forces be rapidly built. It is also necessary that either the Soviet nuclear threat in theater nuclear forces against Europe be eliminated (which I do not see is possible), or that an immediate effort be made to build up our theater nuclear forces. Just as I believe it is necessary that we develop a military purpose for our strategic forces and move away from the senseless and demoralizing strategy of massive civilian extermination, so it is imperative that we finally try to develop some credible military purposes for the tactical and theater nuclear forces that we are building.

## The Role of Ground Forces

And third, it is time that we decide what role exactly we want for our ground forces on the continent. These forces were deployed in the 1950s, when American strategic superiority was so great that we could defend Europe by the threat of general nuclear war. And they were deployed in Europe, as I have often said, as a means of ensuring the automaticity of our response. Our forces were in Europe as hostages. Everybody had a vested interest in not making the forces too large. We wound up with the paradox that they were much too large for what was needed for a tripwire yet not large enough for a sustained conventional defense. I tried for the years that I was in office to get some assessment of just what was meant by the ninety-day stockpile that we were supposed to have, and what the minimum critical categories were. I know that my friend whom I admire enormously, General Alexander Haig, has done enormous work in improving the situation; nevertheless I would be amazed if even he believed that we can now say that our ground forces by themselves can offer a sustained defense without massive, rapid improvements.

## THE POLITICAL CONTEXT

Everything that I have said about the military situation would be difficult enough to remedy, but the situation is compounded by theories to which, again, I myself have no doubt contributed. In 1968, at Reykjavik, NATO developed the theory — which I believe is totally wrong — that the Alliance is as much an instrument of détente as it is of defense. I think that that is simply not correct. NATO is not equipped to be an instrument of détente; for example, every time we attempted to designate the Secretary General of NATO as a negotiating partner with the Warsaw Pact, it was rejected. But this is a minor problem, and détente is important. It is important because, as the United States learned during Vietnam, in democracy you cannot sustain the risk of war unless your public is convinced that you are committed to peace. Détente is important because we cannot hold the Alliance together unless our allies are convinced that we are not seeking confrontation for its own sake. Détente is important because I cannot accept the proposition that it is the democracies that must concede the peace issue to their opponents. And détente is important so that if a confrontation proves unavoidable, we will have elaborated the reasons in a manner that permits us to sustain a confrontation.

So I have always been restless with those who define the issue as "détente" or "no détente." All Western governments must demonstrate and must conduct a serious effort to relax tensions and to negotiate outstanding differences. But there is something deeper involved in the West. There is in the West a tendency to treat détente quite theatrically; that is to say, not as a balancing of national interests and negotiations on the basis of strategic realities but rather as an exercise in strenuous goodwill, in which one removes by understanding the suspiciousness of a nation that is assumed to have no other motive to attack. This tendency to treat détente as an exercise in psychotherapy, or as an attempt at good personal relations, or as an effort in which individual leaders try to gain domestic support by proving that they have a special way in Moscow — that is disastrous for the West. And it is the corollary to the "assured destruction" theory, in the sense that it always provides an alibi for not doing what must be done.

Against all evidence, we were told that the ABM would ruin the chances of arms control. The fact was that Premier Kosygin in 1967 told President Johnson at Glassboro, New Jersey, that the idea of not engaging in defense was one of the most ridiculous propositions that he had ever heard. By 1970, when we had an ABM program, however inadequate, it was the only subject the Soviet Union was willing to discuss with us in SALT. When we gave up the B-1 bomber, we asked the Soviets to make a reciprocal gesture. We have yet to see it. When we gave up the neutron weapon, we were told that this was in correlation with the deployment of the SS-20. (If so, the result was in inverse correlation with the SS-20.) And now we are told that of course we are all for theater nuclear forces, but first let us have another effort at negotiation. I saw a report about a distinguished American senator returning from Moscow the other day who said: "It is virtually certain that cruise missiles will be deployed and that NATO will undertake a build-up of its own unless negotiations to a new treaty are begun soon." If this is our position, all the Soviets have to do is to begin a negotiation to keep us from doing what they are already doing, negotiation or no negotiation.

Such a version of détente leads to unilateral disarmament for the West. I favor negotiation on theater nuclear forces, but the talks will accelerate the more rapidly as we build such theater nuclear forces. Then we can consider some numerical balance or

some deployment pattern, but we cannot defer the strategic decisions we must make for the sake of initiating a negotiation. We
must have détente, but the détente must be on a broad front in
the sense that all of the NATO nations must pursue comparable
policies. The illusion that some countries can achieve a preferential position with the USSR is theoretically correct, but it is the
best means of dividing the Alliance. The illusion that some subjects can be separated for individual treatment of détente, while
conflict goes on in all other areas, turns détente into a safety valve
for aggression.

My fundamental point is that we need a credible strategy;
we need an agreed strategy and we urgently need to build the required forces. We cannot wait two or three more years. We cannot
conduct a foreign policy, even though each of our political systems
encourages such a policy, in which we ease the domestic positions
of the individual countries by pretending that single forays to
Moscow can solve our problems.

Unfortunately, the time frame of the evolution of programs
that I have described is longer than the electoral period of most
of our leaders. Therefore our leaders in all of our countries have
an enormous temptation to celebrate the very successes that lead
to a differential détente either as to subject or as to region. How
is it possible that the states that have 70 percent of the world's
Gross National Product will not conduct a common energy policy?
This is not just because it has become a shibboleth that "we must
not have confrontation"; when have nations been confronted by
a massive decline of their economies without being willing to confront those who are contributing significantly to the decline? And
after all, it takes two to make a confrontation.

How is it possible that in the Middle East two totally conflicting theories on how to proceed are being carried out simultaneously? How can it be that both Egypt and the PLO must simultaneously be encouraged, sometimes, I confess, by our own gov-

ernment? But fundamentally the Europeans are playing one card and we are playing another, so that both the radical and the moderate elements are being strengthened simultaneously. One of us has got to be wrong, and it is just an evasion to pretend that we work one side of the street and the Europeans work another side of the street, because what is really involved in Europe is an attempt to gain special advantages. Yet it is a situation in which the market conditions do not permit special advantages, but where, on the contrary, once it is accepted that oil is a political weapon, even the moderates have no excuse for *not* using it as a political weapon.

I'm not trying to suggest what the correct answer is, but I am saying that the nations represented around this table ought to ask themselves whether the two years of special advantages that either of them might gain is worth the ten years' disaster that could easily befall them.

I know we have many alibis. We have the alibi that none of the things I said is inevitable because there is China. And we have the alibi that, after all, the Soviets have never stayed anywhere and they're in deep trouble themselves. And we have the alibi that we can make such great progress in the Third World that all of this is irrelevant.

In my view the Chinese have survived for 3,000 years by being the most unsentimental practitioners of the balance of power, the most sophisticated, and the ones most free of illusion. China will be an alibi for us only if we do what is necessary. China will not be on the barricades that we refuse to man as the victim of the forces which we have unleashed. So it is certain that we can have cooperation with China only if we create a balance of power.

Now the theory that the Soviets can never stay where they have been is amazingly widely held and supported by exactly one example: Egypt. I don't count Somalia-Ethiopia because I consider their departure from Somalia as a voluntary Soviet switch from one client to a larger client. And in Egypt the fact of the matter is that the balance of power was in favor of those that we supported and those who learned in three wars (in two of which we approached a US–Soviet confrontation) that they could not achieve their aims by Soviet arms. And only after that demonstration was there an Egyptian switch. So we are right back to our original problem.

And the final nostalgia — that of the "noble savage," the Third World, that we're going to sweep them over to our side: I have to confess I cannot give this an operational definition. As for the Third World nations now meeting in Cuba, when I was in office I never read their resolutions, I regret to tell you, which is just as well because I might have said something rather nasty. But I would think it is statistically impossible that over the years that these Third World nations have been meeting, the United States has never done anything right. Even by accident we're bound to do something right. I defy anybody to read through these documents to find one reference on even the most minor thing to something that the United States has ever done right. What are the prospects of progress in a world in which the Cubans can host the nonaligned conference?

It seems to me nostalgia, not policy, to appeal to radical elements in the Third World to change their operational politics. They cannot, because the radical element is required for their bargaining position, a position between us and the Soviets, and because its ideology is hostile to us. Therefore, paradoxically, the more we approach them the more they are likely to pull away from us.

I'm not saying we should not deal with the radical elements of the Third World or that we should not do the best we can in the Third World. All I'm saying is the Third World is not our alibi, it is not our escape route; we may not lose there but we are not likely to win there by repeating their slogans.

# CONCLUSION

This is not intended to be a depressing account of difficulties. It is not to say that we have no favorable prospects. It is simply to point out that problems neglected are crises invited.

In the thirtieth year of NATO we have come far and have achieved our principal purpose. If we do not address ourselves immediately to at least some of the problems I have mentioned, we will face the potentiality of debacles. And the weird aspect of it is that there is absolutely no necessity for it. The weird aspect is that the nations assembled in this room have three times the Gross National Product of the Soviet Union and four times the population. The Soviet Union has leadership problems, social problems, minority problems; all it has in its favor is the ability to accumulate military power and perhaps that only for a transitory period.

So if one looks ahead for ten years, and if we do what is necessary, all the odds are in our favor. The challenges I have put before this group do not indicate that we are bound to be in difficulties, but only that we can defeat ourselves. And by contrast, one can say we have an extraordinary opportunity to rally our people, to define new positive programs even for negotiations with the East if we do what is necessary.

Or to put it another way, our adversaries are really not in control of their own future. Their system and their conditions in many ways make them victims of their past. We around this table are in the extraordinary position that we can decide a positive future for ourselves if we are willing to make the effort. We are in the position to say that the kind of world in which we want to live is largely up to us.

# ON THE CONTROVERSY
# OVER THE SHAH

*Response to a request by the editors of the* Washington
Post; *published in the* Washington Post *on*
*November 29, 1979*

O NLY THE President of the United States can solve the present crisis, and I believe all Americans, of whatever party or persuasion, owe him our support and our prayers.

I have made no criticism of the President's handling of the crisis. My public comments in New York on November 7, in Dallas on November 10, and in Los Angeles on November 11 all called for national unity behind the President. A senior White House official told me at breakfast on November 21 that, on the basis of fragmentary news ticker reports, remarks I had made in Austin on the foreign policy challenges of the 1980s were subject to misinterpretation. I offered to put out an immediate clarifying statement expressing support for the President in this crisis and calling for unity. (Indeed, I suggested that Jody Powell draft it.) The offer was ignored.

Since then I have read and heard myself described by high White House officials as acting deviously and dishonorably; as advising the Shah — strangely enough — to seek the advice of our government about whether to stay in or leave this country; and as having exerted pressure to get him here in the first place.

This campaign struck me as all the more remarkable against the background of a call by me on the first day of the crisis to Deputy Under Secretary of State Ben Read, in which I told him that I would not criticize the Administration for its handling of the crisis either during its course or afterward; it could be sure that I would do my utmost to keep the crisis and its aftermath insulated from partisan controversy. The Administration was well aware that from the first I have been calling Congressional and other leaders, urging restraint in comment. In short, it is not I who have been courting controversy in the middle of a national crisis.

As for my own involvement in recent events, ironically it began at the Administration's initiative. In the first week of January 1979, a senior official of the State Department asked my help in finding a residence for the Shah in the United States. Our government had concluded, I was informed, that the Shah must leave Iran if the Bakhtiar government were to survive the efforts of Ayatollah Khomeini to obtain total power. If I could find a suitable domicile in America, the Shah might overcome his hesitation and hasten his departure. I doubted the analysis but acceded to the request. I called David Rockefeller for help. Mr. Rockefeller expressed his personal sympathy for the Shah but also his reluctance to become involved in an enterprise that might jeopardize the Chase Manhattan Bank's financial relationships with Iranian governmental or quasi-governmental organs. I then appealed to his brother Nelson; with his help, a suitable residence was located. A week later the Shah left Iran. Two weeks afterward Nelson Rockefeller died.

Thus David Rockefeller's later role was hardly spurred by economic considerations as has been alleged; it ran, in fact, contrary to his commercial interests. He was motivated by his desire to carry out the legacy of his late brother and his devotion to the principle that our nation owed loyalty to an ally who had been loyal to us. This was my view as well, and remains so.

Less than two months later — in mid-March — another senior official of the Department of State urged me to dissuade the Shah, who had spent the intervening period in Morocco, from asking for a US visa until matters settled down in Tehran. I refused with some indignation; David Rockefeller was then approached. He too refused. When Rockefeller and I inquired whether our government would help the Shah find asylum in another country, we were told that no official assistance of any kind was contemplated.

This I considered deeply wrong and still do.

Every American President for nearly four decades had eagerly accepted the Shah's assistance and proclaimed him as an important friend of the United States. President Truman in 1947 awarded the Shah the Legion of Merit for his support of the allied cause during World War II and in 1949 praised him for his "courage and farsightedness" and his "earnestness and sincerity in the welfare of his people." President Eisenhower in 1954 paid tribute to the Shah for his "enlightened leadership." President Kennedy in 1962 hailed the Shah for "identifying himself with the best aspirations of his people." President Johnson in 1964 lauded the Shah as a "reformist twentieth-century monarch" and in 1965 praised his "wisdom and compassion . . . perception and statesmanship." President Nixon in 1969 declared that the Shah had brought about "a revolution in terms of social and economic and political progress." President Ford in 1975 called the Shah "one of the world's great statesmen." President Carter in 1977 praised Iran as "a very stabilizing force in the world at large" and in 1978 lauded the Shah for his "progressive attitude" which was "the source of much of the opposition to him in Iran." Such quotations could be multiplied endlessly.

And they were correct. In my own experience the Shah never failed to stand by us. In the 1973 Mideast war, Iran was the sole American ally adjoining the Soviet Union which did not permit the overflight of Soviet transport planes into the Middle East. In 1973–74, Iran was the only Middle East oil-producing country that did not join the oil embargo against us; it continued to sell oil to the United States, to Israel, and to our other allies. Iran kept its oil production at maximum capacity (thus helping stabilize the price) and never used oil as a political weapon. The Shah was a source of assistance and encouragement to the forces of moderation in the Middle East, Africa, and Asia; he used his

own military power to ensure the security of the Persian Gulf and
to discourage adventures by radicals. He firmly supported the
peace process that culminated in the Egyptian-Israeli treaty; he
was a defender of President Sadat against radical forces in the
area. After his initial advocacy of higher prices in 1973, he used
his influence to keep the prices steady so that the real price of
oil actually declined over the period from 1973 to 1978 (due to
inflation).

The crisis we face in 1979 — the 65 percent hike in oil
prices, the radical challenges to the peace process, and the rise
of anti-American fanaticism in the whole area — is the price we
are paying for the *absence* of a friendly regime in Iran. The
conclusion is inescapable that many of the Shah's opponents in
Iran hate him not for what he did wrong, but also for what he did
right — his friendship for the United States, his support for
Mideast peace, his rapid modernization, his land reform, his
support for public education and women's rights; in short, his
effort to bring Iran into the twentieth century as an ally of the
free world.

I do not doubt that wrongs were committed by the Shah's
government in his long rule; the question is how appropriate it is
to raise them, after four decades of close association, in the period
of the Shah's travail. I have been deeply worried about the foreign
policy consequences of spurning him. What will other friends of
the United States in the area, in comparable perilous situations
and perhaps even more complex domestic circumstances — leaders essential for a moderate evolution of the whole region — conclude if we turn against a man whom seven American Presidents
have lauded as a loyal ally and a progressive leader?

My conviction that on the human level we owed the Shah a
place of refuge had nothing to do with a scheme of restoring him
to power. I have stated publicly that we should seek the best
relations possible with the new authorities in Tehran. I simply
assert that it is incompatible with our national honor to turn our

back on a leader who cooperated with us for a generation. Never before have we given foreign governments a veto over who can enter our country as a private citizen.

Between early April and early July, I put these considerations before three senior officials in phone conversations. And I called twice on Secretary of State Vance in the same period. The upshot was a refusal to issue a visa, explained by the tenseness of the situation in Iran. In April I delivered a public speech stating that I thought it morally wrong to treat the Shah as a "Flying Dutchman looking for a port of call."

In other words, I made five private approaches on this subject to the government — none after July. Such was the "obnoxious" pressure, as George Ball has called it, to which our government was subjected.

When it became apparent that our government would not help the Shah and that he was unable to stay any longer in Morocco, David Rockefeller and I did what we could to find him a place of refuge. David Rockefeller was able to arrange a temporary stay in the Bahamas. In April and May, I appealed to the government of Mexico. To its enormous credit, it had the courage to extend a visa even though — as one official pointed out to me — Mexico was being asked to run risks on behalf of a friend of the United States that we were not willing to assume ourselves.

Once the Shah was in Mexico, David Rockefeller, John Mc-Cloy, and I tried to be helpful with private matters on a personal basis. The education of the Shah's children in America was the principal issue. We did our best to find appropriate schooling; this raised the issue of visas. Contacts with our government were handled by Mr. Rockefeller's assistant, Joseph Reed, and John McCloy. Mr. McCloy repeatedly urged the Department of State to designate an official with whom the Shah's entourage could communicate on such matters without using our group as intermediaries. Such a contact point was never established.

This was the state of affairs when the Shah fell ill early in October. As it happened, I was out of the country from October 9 to October 23 and had no communication with any level of the government about the matter. While in Europe, I kept in touch with the Rockefeller office but did not intercede personally with any official or agency of the government — though I would have had it been necessary. My understanding is that Joseph Reed presented the medical records to Under Secretary Newsom and on the basis of those records the Administration admitted the Shah for treatment. I am not aware that there was any hesitation. To the Administration's credit, no pressure was needed or exercised; I gather that the medical facts spoke for themselves. All of us conceived that the reaction in Tehran would have to be evaluated by the Administration, which alone had the relevant facts.

As for advice to the Shah about whether or not to leave — the subject of other strange stories — the situation was as follows. With conflicting threats emanating from Tehran as to the impact on the safety of the hostages of a movement by the Shah, Rockefeller, McCloy, and I concluded that it was inappropriate for us to advise the Shah. Rockefeller called the President on November 15 to ask once again for the designation of an individual who could accurately convey the government's recommendations to the Shah's entourage. McCloy stressed the need for this to the deputy secretary of state on November 20; I repeated it to a senior White House official on November 21. We were told the Administration agreed with our approach. No such point of contact has yet been established. We were given no guidance; therefore we made no recommendations to the Shah as to what he should do when and if his medical condition permits him to leave the United States.

I reaffirm my support for the effort to assure a measure of decency toward a fallen friend of this country. The issue of the Shah's asylum goes not only to the moral stature of our nation but also to our ability to elicit trust and support among other nations — especially other moderate regimes in the area. I do not condone all the practices of the Shah's government, though they must be assessed by the standards of his region and, even more, the practices of those who will sit in judgment. Yes, we must seek the best relations which are possible with the new dispensation in Iran. But we shall impress no one by engaging in retrospective denigration of an ally of a generation in his hour of need. We cannot always assure the future of our friends; we have a better chance of assuring our own future if we remember who our friends are, and acknowledge what human debts we owe those who stood by us in *our* hours of need.

I hope this ends the controversy. I think it is imperative that all Americans close ranks. Nothing will more strengthen the President's hand in pursuit of an honorable outcome than a continuing demonstration of national unity now and in the aftermath of the crisis. I shall do all I can to contribute to this end.

# THE FOOTSTEPS OF HISTORY

*Remarks at the Davos Symposium 1980 of the European Management Forum, January 31, 1980*

I WANT to express my great appreciation about what Ted Heath has said. We have been friends for twenty years and fought sometimes together and sometimes separately about the future of our societies.

I had the privilege of working with Ted Heath when he was Prime Minister. The German statesman Bismarck once said (I paraphrase from memory) that the art of statesmanship is to listen carefully until one can perhaps discern the footsteps of history and follow for a brief period in their train. I am convinced that history will show that Ted Heath understood and heard the footsteps of history.

He realized that Europe needed unity and identity to make its contribution to our contemporary period. In office, he did not always share my own estimate of my infallibility, which made him not always the easiest partner to be with. But he performed the most important role of an ally, a friend, and a partner: to recall us to our duties, to advance his view of our future, and, as Winston Churchill said, he was not always wrong.

I am speaking to you today in an atmosphere quite different from the one in which I accepted your invitation. At that time, I thought that I would deliver a more or less standard speech about the major elements of international relations. But we find ourselves now in a period of tension, of some confusion: one is asked whether we are facing now a new period of Cold War, an end of détente — perhaps the prospect of a new world war. I would, therefore, like to analyze the nature of the contemporary situation as I see it, offer some suggestions, and ask some questions to which answers must be found.

First, I do not like the distinction of the postwar period into a period of Cold War and a period of détente. The Cold War was not so terrible and détente was not so exalted. In the Cold War, we had a certain amount of ideological hostility and a number of Berlin crises. In the détente period, we had a number of summit meetings and Soviet rearmament and expansionism. So we should not treat international relations as if there had been a clearly defined period in which we lived with a consciousness of harmony. Indeed, the tendency to deal with East-West relations as if they were like relations among individuals, the tendency to attempt to solve the problem of war and peace psychiatrically, as it were, by creating an atmosphere without substance, is in itself a problem of contemporary policy.

Relations between the West and the Soviet Union must be based on two fundamental principles. The first is: We must be strong enough and determined enough to resist expansionism, whatever forms it takes. Second, possessing, as we do, weapons of untold destructiveness, we are also doomed to coexistence, and we must seek means by which this coexistence can be made more tolerable and, in time, less dangerous and perhaps even constructive. The desire for peace must not be permitted to turn into a form of blackmail, but the willingness and necessity to resist expansion must not seek confrontation for its own sake.

One of the difficulties of Western policy has been the oscillation between euphoria and panic; the reluctance to accept the fact that we must be both strong and determined on the one side and prepared to negotiate on the other; the difficulty of relating negotiations to concrete objectives; and the unwillingness to face the strategic necessities of containing Soviet aggressiveness. As we go into this new period of danger, it is important to keep in mind that, if we succeed in what must now be done, we will again confront a period of negotiation — that is indeed the purpose — and we must prepare ourselves for it *now*.

Now let me discuss the international situation as I see it. I will mention briefly a number of structural, dynamic changes independent of specific Soviet actions, and then I will address the specific events that have led to the current situation.

We are living in a world which has seen a major redistribution of power. Several times, first at the end of World War II, when Europe lost its traditional preeminence, then in the decades afterward, there developed a new standard of power including Europe. The world became transformed first into a bipolar system and then into a somewhat multipolar system. But it is a curious system, because for the first time in history economic power, political power, and military power are not identical. For the first time in history, it is possible for a country to be militarily strong and economically stagnant, like the Soviet Union. It is also possible for a country to be economically very strong and yet be militarily insignificant, such as most OPEC countries. Some countries play a major political role, for a variety of reasons, without being either militarily or economically strong. So the incommensurability of the various elements of power gives a complexity to contemporary international relations that is unique.

The second is that, for the first time in history, foreign policy is truly global. Until the end of World War II, the various continents pursued their policies in isolation from each other. One could not really compare China and Europe in the seventeenth century because, to all practical purposes, they did not interact.

That condition has changed, and it is compounded by the loss of economic autarky of the various regions. Then, for the first time in history, there are many problems that affect all of humanity: environmental concerns, proliferation of nuclear weapons, for example. There is, again for the first time, a discovery of agricultural incompetence in many parts of the world that cannot feed themselves any longer, either because they do not have the technology or because the population has pressed at the margins of their resources — of which the reverse side is the near-monopoly position of small numbers of countries having scarce raw materials.

And there is a dilution of confidence in classic economic models, a challenge to the capitalist system due to simultaneous inflation and recession. But also there is a demoralization of the socialist systems, which nowhere have produced the satisfaction of the human personality. All of these changes are global and would make ours a period of turmoil — even apart from any specific Soviet challenge that we face. But we do face a specific challenge, and I would now like to talk about my assessment of what we are confronting at this moment in the Soviet Union.

We face, in the Soviet Union, a strange amalgam of ideology and bureaucratic and economic stagnation coupled with enormous ability in one limited field — the accumulation of military power.

The ideology places great stress on the objective correlation of forces. One can argue forever whether the present Soviet leaders still hold the pristine version of Leninism, and almost certainly they do not, but they do believe that they understand Western trends better than the West. Therefore, the worst method in negotiations with the Soviet Union is the psychiatric approach, the sentimental tendency to think that good personal relations are a guarantee for good interstate relations. The Soviets tend to treat our negotiators the way psychiatrists treat their patients: No matter what you say to them, they think they understand us better than we understand ourselves.

And if the correlation of forces tilts, in their judgment, in their direction, we live in a period of great danger. This is exactly what has happened in the last decade in the military field. Indeed, the fact that the economic performance of the Soviet Union is so poor compounds our danger, because it creates a temptation to use the military advantage while it still exists, and *before* the dilemmas of modernization grow overwhelming. The Soviet Union faces the dilemma that one cannot run a modern economy by central planning; but it is not clear that one can run the Soviet system *without* central planning. Before the Soviets address this issue, they may want to achieve security in the external environment; so that we may find a paradoxical combination of the modernizers and the bureaucrats — the bureaucrats, because when you have rigid structures, the one that commands large resources, like the military, with its own communications net and its own transportation system, plays a very important, perhaps decisive role.

Nobody should deny the Soviet Union its legitimate security concerns. Up to now, the problem has been that the Soviet Union is in danger of adopting a definition of security that can be satisfied only by the neutralization of everybody else. We cannot accept a definition of security for the Soviet Union which makes everybody else absolutely insecure. Nobody has the right to march with a hundred thousand men into a neighboring state that has consistently pursued a policy parallel to that of the Soviet Union, and in which no Western state ever attempted to assert a significant political influence, just to fulfill some theoretical concepts of security.

Nor is this an isolated act. Since 1975, at least, we have seen a pincer movement with Soviet proxy forces coming up through Africa from Angola, Ethiopia, into South Yemen, threatening the oil-producing regions on which the industrial democracies depend, from one direction. And we see another pincer movement in the coup in Afghanistan in April 1978 developing from the other direction, and now completed with the occupation of Afghanistan. We have seen networks of terrorist organizations, not directly controlled from Moscow, but financed and trained in part from Moscow, undermining the stability of many countries.

Nobody can avoid the responsibility for a rockslide when

he throws a rock down a stony hillside, just because the rock that finally kills somebody is not the rock which he threw. We have had Cuban soldiers in Africa and a Soviet brigade in China. Thus Afghanistan is a culmination of these events. For this reason, I want to state that even though I have not been noted in the United States for unalloyed admiration of every aspect of the foreign policy of our Administration, I believe that their fundamental decision to make clear that expansionism now must stop is correct. And those who worry about whether America is going too far or whether this or that move was tactically wise should ask themselves what would they think if the United States had taken the opposite course and had minimized what happened in Afghanistan, and had accepted it.

So I believe, regardless of whether one agrees with every tactical move, that the fundamental issue now is to have this basic policy direction succeed. Those who are worried should make their contribution by helping to give content to what will be an enormously difficult enterprise (which I would be amazed if we in America had thought through), in which we need the wisdom of many of our friends and in which a European view of the situation could now be of great importance to us all.

What are the necessities that we face? The West has neglected for too long its military strength. The Soviet Union, since 1962, has increased its defense budget by 5 percent, in real terms, every year for nearly twenty years. I do not need to tell a group of this composition what compound interest at the rate of 5 percent a year will yield over such an extended period. For a variety of reasons that are not worth now debating, the United States has not equaled these expenditures, and Europe has done even less — not to speak of Japan.

There has been a reluctance to face the geopolitical facts of life, which are: that a statesman has the choice of acting early in the evolution of events; at that time, his knowledge will be very limited and he has to trust his judgment; or he can wait, until he knows for certain what is happening. Then he may pay a fearful price. In 1936, it would have been easy for the democracies to resist Hitler physically, but psychologically it was hard. Five years later, they all knew what the danger was. They paid for that psychological certainty with twenty million lives. In 1975, when Cuban troops first showed up in Angola, it was a qualitative change in the international situation. Some of us wanted to resist. We were prevented by our domestic structure from doing so. It would have been easy then — it is more difficult now. It is better now than it will be three years from now.

So there is no way around the necessity of building up the overall military capacity of the United States, and of its allies. Indeed, I think we will find that, if we think through the problem, even the budget now submitted will not make up for the neglect of the past and that we will have to make even more sacrifices. Secondly, we must create not only an overall strength but a demonstrable local strength to resist in those areas that we have defined as vital.

Some months ago, I gave a speech in Brussels, to the effect that we must not act as if the fortunate circumstance of an atomic monopoly permits us never to adapt our strategy to the new circumstances. I said then, and I repeat now, that an attack on demographic targets, whose chief end is the destruction of populations, is demoralizing for all decision-makers, either European or American, who have no other choice. I repeat, however, that this does not have to be our strategy, that the defense of Europe and America must be linked, including in the nuclear field, and that we then jointly must address the question of other areas which are now the subject of debate.

Three require particular attention, and I will raise questions with respect to them that we must all answer — not, necessarily, that I know the answer: the Persian Gulf, Pakistan, and China. It is imperative that we harmonize our commitments and our capabilities. We cannot afford, and we must not tempt, another American setback. Before we engage ourselves, we must know what we are doing; and once we have engaged ourselves, we must prevail, or the impact will be catastrophic.

We have to decide, when we extend a guarantee to an area, first what precisely the area is we are guaranteeing. I am not saying we need to say all of this publicly, but we need to say it to ourselves. I hear, often, that ambiguity is a virtue — and it is, as long as the lower level of our response encompassed in the ambiguity is unacceptable to the aggressor. What is it we are defending, and what is it we are defending it against? Military attack by the Soviet Union? Proxy attack supported by the Soviet Union? Terrorist attack? Internal upheaval? And how do we prepare to achieve this objective for an extended period, which is what strategy is all about?

It is not necessary for me, now, to give an answer to these questions, except to say that we must answer them and that, to the extent that we leave gaps in our thinking, we are simply creating a new vulnerability. We must act decisively and we must keep in mind that the curse of democracies in the recent past, including the American democracy, has been the belief that if something is done halfheartedly, or somehow incompetently, one avoids domestic difficulties. But we also must act with prudence so that we do not provoke what we are trying to prevent. And that raises very serious considerations. There is no way we will be able to implement any guarantees of any area we decide to defend without some visible presence of American forces and, preferably, of Western forces. Even if it is theoretically possible to move forces rapidly, it will not necessarily be credible to our opponents or to the countries concerned. So before we spread our commitments, let us make sure we are prepared to extend our capabilities. And let us not confuse plans with capabilities. The transport for the rapid deployment force will not exist before 1984 at the earliest. Secondly, in defending an area, we have to understand in the name of what we are defending it, and that has two components:

one, what we tell our own people; and, secondly, what the leaders we are protecting are telling their people.

We have suffered, in my view, from a rather simplified conception of human rights. We do not defend other countries as an award for good behavior. We are defending them because we discover a vital security interest of free peoples. But equally we must have some concept of change, since history is not going to stop. What is the reform that can reasonably be asked? How can we support governments without challenging their fundamental structures and, therefore, making their defense meaningless to them — and yet have in mind some concept of adaptation to modernity? That, too, is a question we must answer. In areas like the Persian Gulf, we must, over time, respond in some fashion to the political concerns that these nations have and to which they give high priority, even if it is not a central issue in East-West relations, such as the Arab-Israeli problem.

With respect to Pakistan, we must ask similar questions. Pakistan faces three types of potential dangers: hot pursuit from the Soviet Union, a Soviet attack, or another India-Pakistan war, or a combination of all three.

Pakistan has become additionally vulnerable because it is simultaneously an ally of China and of the United States. Therefore, the symbolic effect of its disintegration on other countries would be very great. But, conversely, we must have some idea of how we are going to implement any guarantees and just what it is we are guaranteeing — protection against which of these dangers? I believe that the question of hot pursuit is relatively easy. The question of a full-scale Soviet attack cannot, in my view, be dealt with in the near future without some outside assistance. And that must be faced.

The problem of India has the component that, for India, the existence of a strong, fundamentalist, Islamic state presents problems of its own internal cohesion and may create its own incentives for war. On the other hand, if India is worried about our policies, it must give some assurances, other than rhetoric, that it will not act in collusion with the Soviet Union and that it will not cooperate in an attack on Pakistan. Here, a dialogue of European nations, and of the United States, with all the countries in that area, may be of great consequence.

To some extent, a similar problem is faced of clarifying our purposes in our relations with China. It means, of course, to me personally a great deal to see the representatives of the People's Republic of China in this hall. I welcome the opportunity of Chinese participation in forums of this kind. There is no question that China is a major factor in international relations; but I have, with all my affection for China, never believed that China is a card that America can play.

I do not think China survived with the longest uninterrupted history of self-government by being another country's tool in its own rivalries with third powers.

I do not believe we should conduct our relations with China on the basis of the fluctuations of our relations with the Soviet Union. We should have a steady policy that looks to a long-time future and does not attempt to add to the annoyance factor in Moscow when something particular happens which we do not like. Beyond the question of the rearmament of China, which I feel strongly we must support, we will also have the question of what our attitude is toward the territorial integrity of China, should it become the subject of Soviet pressure. That is an infinitely more important question than what arms are sold, and at what rate, and by whom.

As our commitments around the Soviet periphery multiply, the absence of statements about our intentions in particular areas becomes more noticeable. I am putting this forward as an issue that has to be discussed and thought about when we design a global strategy.

Even though it is not my special subject, I believe that recent events have given us a new opportunity toward the nonaligned.

They have seen that Communist advances led by Moscow are ir-
reversible and may create an incentive and a justification for the
Red Army — since the Soviet system operates under the peculi-
arity that the Red Army seems to be used only against Soviet
allies. So it becomes very dangerous to enter the Soviet orbit in
any form. I think that the issue of how the resources of the North
can be related to the needs of the South can perhaps once again
be addressed in a new environment, free of the self-righteousness
of some of the previous dialogue.

But I would like to say two more things: one about Europe
and the United States and the other about relations with the Soviets. Since I have come here to Europe, I have heard a great deal
about the question of whether détente is divisible; whether European and American interests remain identical; whether we can
still cooperate. Let me give a few answers.

First, of course, our interests are not identical in every single
respect, nor is it necessary for Europe to stand at attention every
time we develop a new policy. But our fundamental interests in
the world economy and in our mutual security are as congruent as
it is possible for those of sovereign nations to be. And for this
reason, I do not believe that what is called "détente" is divisible.
I do not believe that Europe, in a period of danger, can adopt the
posture that it will assume the monopoly of conciliation, while
America bears the monopoly of defense. In these senses, détente
is not divisible.

Europe has a vital interest that the policy that we are now
adopting succeed; but it also has a vital interest that the content
of this policy make sense. And I have raised enough questions
here, and some of you, some European leaders, will no doubt be
able to think of many other questions that I haven't raised, in
which Europe's contribution must be crucial. We need a common
assessment of the situation. With a common assessment, we can
have a division of labor: there are many areas of the world where
Europe is now playing, or can play in the future, a role that

would be difficult for the United States to play. But it is vital that we do this on the basis of similar interpretations of what we are up against and not suffer from what has been the bane of so much of the Atlantic debate — which is: When the United States negotiates with the Soviets, some accuse it of condominium; and when it resists the Soviets, it is accused of needless intransigence. Let us use this time, now, to develop a global strategy on a joint basis, with a division of labor where that is appropriate.

Let me conclude with the Soviets. In this phase, we must bring to a halt the Soviet geopolitical offensives that have been under way at least since 1975. That must be stopped, even in the Soviet interest. The American people are a vital people. We will not be defeated without noticing it, and, when we notice it, we will resist. The biggest danger of all is a series of reciprocal miscalculations. So we must stop the policy of pressure, of proxy forces, of encouragement of terrorism; but we must also show a way out, we must also give the Soviet Union an opportunity to define a real coexistence.

The last period of what has been called détente was characterized by Western euphoria and, to some extent, nonperformance of what we said we would do. It was also characterized by massive Soviet rearmament and a massive Soviet assault on the equilibrium. In 1972 and 1973, the Administrations in which I served signed some principles of coexistence with the Soviet Union — not because we believed for one moment that a legal document will restrain the Soviet Union, but because we wanted to create a yardstick by which to measure compliance with norms of international behavior.

What we now need, in this period when we are building up strength and creating walls to expansionism, is to talk to ourselves first as to what we understand by peaceful coexistence. I do not believe that SALT II is worth reviving. It has only three more years to run and weapons decisions take longer than three years. I believe that the next time we talk about arms control, we should negotiate on a ten- or fifteen-year basis, including the European weapons, and do so without sentimentality and without illusion. We should define for ourselves a genuine code of conduct. And, in such a negotiation, we must, of course, take seriously legitimate Soviet security concerns. But we cannot define those, or let them define them, as the right to move the Red Army into any territory whose government displeases them.

So this is the agenda before us, in which there is a need for Western strength and determination — but also a Western sense of justice and a realistic conciliation. What is needed, now, cannot be done halfheartedly or hesitantly, because that will multiply our dangers. But it must also be done carefully and reflectively. We ought to remember that we have multiples of the Gross National Product of the Soviet Union, multiples of the population, the more vital economic and political systems; so that whatever short-comings exist are matters of will and leadership, and are not inherent in the situation.

I would tell you that, at this moment of danger, I am actually more optimistic than I have been in many years. The American people have overcome the trauma of Vietnam; the American government reflects the aspiration of our people. Even though I am of the opposition party, I want you all to understand that on the fundamental course, there is now for the first time in many years a united America. So when I raise these questions, we are in a position, for the first time in many years, to give meaningful answers. But we cannot do it alone, either physically or intellectually. I do not believe we have thought everything through, nor could we have, after so dramatic a change. But these problems can now be thought through, and they must be thought through, lest we create the opposite of what we seek to achieve. And so we live in a moment of danger, which is also one of hope, where we can shape our own future and where, if we listen carefully, we might be able to hear the footsteps of history.

# THE FUTURE OF AMERICAN FOREIGN POLICY

*Address to the annual convention of the American Society of Newspaper Editors, April 10, 1980, in Washington, D.C.*

W E ARE at the beginning of another of our quadrennial debates over foreign policy. Its forms have become as stylized as a Japanese Kabuki play. The party in office claims that it inherited a debacle and by a near-miraculous effort has raised our prestige to new heights. The party out of office assails the current debacle and promises a radically new start.

This process courts two dangers. For our own public, it creates the impression that the foreign policy of the United States reflects only the idiosyncrasies of whoever is the incumbent. It masks a fundamental lesson which we seem to have forgotten: that the national interest of the United States does not change in years divisible by four.

And for the other nations of the world, the controversy is profoundly unsettling, whether they are foes watching in bewilderment or friends observing in dismay. America is the linchpin of the free world's security, the repository of the world's hope for progress. If every four years the basic premises of our foreign policy are up for grabs, America itself becomes an element of instability in the world. We give our friends an incentive to free themselves of the vagaries of our political process; we sow the psychological seeds of neutralism.

Therefore, our national debate must take place in a framework that permits us to work together as a united people after the election is over.

I supported the Administration on the ratification of the Panama Canal treaties, Middle East arms sales, the Camp David

agreement, the retaliatory steps in response to Afghanistan; and
I worked to find a nonpartisan basis for SALT. No doubt I did not
always ascribe to my successors the clear vision and profound wisdom that in hindsight I associate with my stewardship. Other Republicans, too, may well have strayed from the calm, disinterested
analysis which all of us normally associate with the Grand Old
Party.

But a major responsibility for setting the tone of our national
debate rests with the incumbents. And the present Administration,
frankly, has been unusually partisan. An Administration that can
claim that it "rejuvenated" a "weak and dispirited" NATO Alliance, that it is the first to have friendly relations with both Japan
and China, raises doubts about its grasp of reality. An Administration capable of the innuendo that President Ford, one of the
most decent men ever to occupy the Presidency, needlessly risked
American lives for a transient popularity in a previous hostage
situation tempts an equally unworthy examination of its own motives in the present situation. An Administration that in its fourth
year in office continues to blame its predecessors for every difficulty, and indeed seems to have made the confession of prior
error a key instrument of policy, invites the question whether anyone relying on us does not run the risk of later disavowal. One
cannot make history by rewriting it. A government's job is to find
solutions to its problems, not alibis.

Whoever is victorious in November will find that he needs a
unified people behind him because he will face a monumental
challenge in foreign affairs. I happen to agree with President Carter that the danger to our country is the gravest in the modern
period. We are sliding toward a world out of control, with our
relative military power declining, with our economic lifeline increasingly vulnerable to blackmail, with hostile radical forces
growing in every continent, and with the number of countries willing to stake their future on our friendship dwindling.

We did not arrive at this point all at once or during one administration — though I believe that this Administration has accelerated the most dangerous trends. Our peril is structural and conceptual. It requires a sustained national effort over an extended period of time, whoever shall be the next President — or the next and the next as well. There are, I believe, four interrelated issues that must be addressed: First, the military balance; second, the geopolitical equation; third, the attitude toward the process of change in the world; and fourth, US–Soviet relations.

## THE BALANCE OF MILITARY POWER

First of all, it can no longer be seriously denied that the overall military balance is shifting sharply against us. Every objective observer — such as the International Institute of Strategic Studies in London — has reached this grim conclusion. Whatever the causes, unless current trends are reversed, the 1980s will be a period of vulnerability such as we have not experienced since the early days of the Republic. In this decade we confront, for the first time, a potentially unfavorable strategic balance; a shifting balance against us in theater nuclear forces in Europe; and continuation of the long-standing Western inferiority in forces for regional defense.

Perhaps we are fortunate that the Iranian and Afghanistan crises illuminated our military deficiencies while the full extent of the danger was still in the future. Once awakened, we have the opportunity to redress the balance. If they do nothing else, these events *must* remind us of our inability to project forces quickly into vital regions, or else they will be the precursor of even graver challenges.

For thirty years the defense of the free world relied on our strategic superiority to compensate for our inferiority in conventional forces. That period has now ended — perhaps inevitably.

Once we lost the ability to destroy the Soviet retaliatory forces at acceptable cost to ourselves, a general nuclear war spelled mutual suicide. Last year in Brussels I pointed out that a strategy relying on such a threat is incredible, irresponsible, and escapist — even for NATO. I was severely criticized — today's equivalent of shooting the messenger to avoid the message. But a danger ignored is a debacle invited. A country that can defend its interests only by threatening the mutual mass extermination of civilians dooms itself to strategic, and therefore eventually geopolitical, paralysis.

Rarely in history has a nation so passively accepted such a radical change in the military balance. Never in history has an opponent achieved as large an advantage in so many significant categories of military power without attempting to translate it into some political benefit.

The danger is less an imminent nuclear attack on us than an increased Soviet willingness to run risks in local conflicts. And that seems to me the minimum consequence of what is ahead. We live in a world in turmoil; the safest prediction is continuing instability, some of it promoted by the Soviet Union, some of it only exploited by it. Since 1975, in Africa, in the Middle East, in Southeast Asia, radical forces with Soviet weapons, or Cuban proxy troops, and now the Red Army itself, have determined the outcome in almost every local conflict, to the detriment of our allies and friends. If this process continues and leads to direct US–Soviet confrontations, like that in Cuba in 1962 or the Mideast alert in 1973, it will be the *Soviet Union* which will possess the quantitative superiority in strategic weapons that *we* enjoyed when those and comparable crises were successfully resolved in our favor. And the Soviet local advantage has grown exponentially. Thus regional conflicts, whether deliberately promoted or not, threaten increasingly to exceed our ability to respond unless we drastically reverse the growing imbalance in *all* categories of military power.

We will pay a heavy penalty if we continue to take comfort in soporific assurances that our military establishment is still "second to none." It is this complacency which has brought us to our present pass over an extended period of time. In the 1960s, American strategic doctrine based deterrence largely on our theoretical capacity to inflict civilian casualties and economic damage on the Soviet Union, regardless of the size of the Soviet forces. This confused strategy with economic analysis. It not only overlooked the moral inhibitions that would surely affect an American President's willingness to launch such an attack; it also encouraged equanimity in the face of the relentless Soviet strategic buildup. Then in the early 1970s, a Vietnam-era antimilitary sentiment assaulted *every* defense program, whether or not it related to Vietnam. The antiballistic missile system (the ABM) passed the Senate by just one vote in 1969; forty senators then tried to stop all our MIRV testing; in 1971 we barely defeated the Mansfield Amendment to cut our forces in Europe by 150,000 men; in 1973 the Trident submarine program passed the Senate by only one vote. It was not until the advent of President Ford that these trends were reversed.

Fairness requires the recognition that President Carter thus inherited a difficult situation. But it must also be noted that the present Administration has compounded the problem by systematically deprecating the role of power, by canceling or stretching out every strategic program it inherited, by treating the whole defense budget more as a bargaining chip to win approval for SALT than as a serious instrument of national policy. History judges leaders by the adequacy of their response, not the magnitude of the challenge.

To be sure, in the current defense budget there are increases, somewhere between 3 and 5 percent. But the baseline for these calculations is unclear; the inflation rate is underestimated or hedged; key costs are understated. It turns out that the *real* increase is closer to 1 percent — or nearly irrelevant to the magni-

tude of the problem we face. And in any event, the adequacy of
our response is not measured by the percentage of budgetary
increase but by whether we are closing the gaps which every objective study reveals. And these gaps are simply not being closed;
in fact, many of them are still growing.

For a few weeks after the Soviet invasion of Afghanistan, it
seemed that we had learned some lessons. And I therefore made
several speeches in Europe urging hesitant allies to support the
Administration. Since then we are sliding back to our posture of
ambivalence. Despite the invasion of Afghanistan, the President
submitted precisely the defense budget that had been prepared
*before* Afghanistan and on the expectation that SALT would be
ratified. How can that possibly be adequate when in the meantime
we have undertaken a major new defense commitment embracing
the Persian Gulf? Since then even that budget appears to have
been cut further in the new anti-inflation program. Nor do the projected forces show any sense of urgency. The MX missile is planned
for 1987. The air and sea lift for the first brigade of the Rapid Deployment Force of which so much is made will not exist before
1985; that for the first division will not come into being quite
before 1987 (besides which, the force level is inadequate).

How do we propose to cope in the first half of the decade before this new capability comes into being? How does the Administration propose to relate our capabilities to our new commitments? Within two weeks of announcing the Carter Doctrine, the
President acknowledged that we alone could not defend the vital
Persian Gulf. Who then will join us? How can they help? What is
our strategy? What forces will be available near the area for its
defense? How can our current military establishment defend
NATO, much less save distant allies? Why should we be surprised
if threatened countries shy away from our protection?

These shortcomings, in my view, reflect the Administration's
profound ambivalence about the role of power in the world. Too
many of its officials give the impression of feeling ashamed of

American power and being fearful of military strength. They seem to operate on the premise that there is a guilt we must expiate rather than values we should defend.

Yet we cannot avoid the responsibilities that our power and principles confer upon us. Abdication will not purify us; it only creates a vacuum that will send to their destruction those who rely on us. At some point prudence turns into weakness, which tempts danger; the ostentatious renunciation of force has the paradoxical consequence of magnifying risks. The fate of those who have fallen under Communist rule since 1975 makes clear that such hesitations can no longer parade under the banner of superior morality. At first the price for our ambivalence will be paid by others; in time — and fearfully — it will be paid by us.

## THE GEOPOLITICAL BALANCE

This brings me to my second concern: the geopolitical balance. By this I mean the alignments and assessments that determine whether moderates friendly to us, or radicals hostile to us, dominate key regions; whether our alliances are vital or sliding toward lassitude. It determines whether peaceful solutions of problems like the Arab-Israeli dispute or Southern Africa are possible, or whether the radical tide or Communist proxy intervention dooms all prospects of moderation and progress.

This geopolitical balance is measured partly by intangibles — by whether friends of the United States believe they have a secure future; by whether they have confidence in our ability to aid them against challenges and deter outside threats to regional security; by whether, indeed, they will even risk engaging in self-defense — as illustrated by Pakistan's refusal of our offer of military aid.

And it depends as well on *our* ability to perceive trends and dangers *before* they become overwhelming. A statesman must act on judgments about the future that cannot be proved true when they are made. When the scope for action is greatest, the knowledge on which to base such action is often least; when certain knowledge is at hand, the scope for creative action has often disappeared.

In 1936, the movement of one French division could have dissuaded Hitler from his march into the Rhineland. If France had done so, the world might still be arguing today whether Hitler was only a misunderstood nationalist or really a maniac bent on world domination. By 1941 everyone knew that Hitler was a maniac bent on world domination — but the world paid for its insistence on psychological certainty with millions of lives.

We face, I would submit, a similar challenge from the Soviet Union — not because it is necessarily implementing a timetable for world conquest but in the sense that incremental challenges not resisted will lead inexorably to greater challenges, even if the Soviets are only exploiting opportunities that come their way. This was precisely the issue when Soviet-supported Cuban troops occupied Angola, intervened in Ethiopia, sponsored two invasions of Zaire, and established a base in South Yemen; when there were two Communist coups in Afghanistan; and when finally the Soviet army occupied that unhappy country. The problem was compounded and partly reflected by the collapse, for whatever reason, of a friendly government in Iran, which for thirty-seven years had been a major ally of the United States and had in turn been an important bulwark of other moderate forces in the entire region. This development is a major cause of the slowdown of the Mideast peace process, as moderates like Egypt, Israel, and Jordan feel increasingly isolated, threatened, and constrained. The increasing climate of insecurity in the Persian Gulf affects not only political decisions but economic decisions, including OPEC's behavior on oil prices.

Four years ago, after the Senate vote cutting off aid to Angola, I warned that the Soviet/Cuban military intervention in Angola was the beginning of "a pattern" which, if unresisted, "would have the gravest consequences for peace and stability, and it is one which the United States treats with indifference only at the risk of buying graver crises at higher cost later on."[1] Since then Soviet arms, Soviet proxy troops, Soviet friendship treaties, and outright Soviet intervention have determined the outcome of far too many local upheavals in the world's political alignments.

Precariously situated countries in the Middle East see the Soviet-supported Cuban advance coming through Africa to Ethiopia right across the Red Sea. They observe a Soviet base in South Yemen threatening the Arabian peninsula; they see Soviet-armed guerrillas invading Morocco, a traditional friend and moderate government; they see a Soviet arms depot in Libya — a precursor of future interventions in Africa and the Middle East. To them the Soviet invasion of Afghanistan now — coming eighteen months after an unopposed Communist coup in Kabul — overshadows the Persian Gulf like the northern arm of a great pincer. They observe Vietnam swallowing Cambodia and seeking hegemony over Southeast Asia under the protection of a Soviet friendship treaty. They notice that India and Pakistan are *both* vying for Soviet favor. Even in the Western Hemisphere they see radical upheavals rending Central America and the Caribbean, buttressed by a small Soviet combat force in Cuba. And they see no effective resistance.

This has its inevitable effect, which is to accelerate the demoralization of all moderate allies, driving friends toward neutralism and neutrals toward radicalism. The Administration has explained certain of its actions as an effort to win the approbation and allegiance of the Third World countries. But the Conference of the Nonaligned Nations in Havana last September demonstrated that such a policy was built on quicksand. Never has the conference passed such stridently anti-American, such unabash-

[1] News conference, February 12, 1976.

edly pro-Soviet, resolutions, shocking even such a pillar of the nonaligned movement as President Tito. The radicalism of many Third World countries cannot be moderated by a more "understanding" American posture; they object to our existence or social structure, not to our policies. And the closer we attempt to approach toward them, the more they are likely to move further away from us simply to maintain their ideological purity.

Even with the less radical Third World countries — and they are still the majority — the issue is misconceived if put in terms of approbation and allegiance. For hardly any of the countries immediately threatened *prefers* the Soviet system. Their problem is the pressure they face from outside military force or internal subversion, the menace of radical groups flaunting their implacable ideological hatred of America, undermining the balance of power even when they are not financed, armed, and trained by the Soviet bloc — as they often are.

Somewhere, somehow, the United States must show that it is capable of rewarding a friend or penalizing an opponent. It must be made clear, after too long an interval, that our allies benefit from association with us and our enemies suffer. It is a simpleminded proposition perhaps, but for a great power it is the prerequisite, indeed the definition, of an effective foreign policy.


## THE ATTITUDE TOWARD DOMESTIC CHANGE

Thirdly, what should be our attitude to the process of domestic change in the world? The Administration contends that by demonstrating our moral values and concern for human rights — if necessary by condemning our own previous actions — we will gain the approbation of mankind and thus outflank the Soviets.

Reality is more complex. It is true that American foreign policy must be grounded in the humane values of our people and of our democratic tradition. We would be neither effective nor faithful to ourselves if we sought to defend every status quo in an age of upheavals.

The problem, however, is to relate this truism to the national interest of the United States in concrete situations. It is a hard fact, but true, that some societies whose security is vital to us — particularly in the Persian Gulf — are governed by authoritarian conservative regimes. In the West constitutional democracy resulted from an evolution extending over centuries. Force-feeding the process in developing societies is not impossible, but it has the paradoxical result of involving us in permanent global intervention at the precise moment when we have supposedly learned our limits in the aftermath of the Vietnam experience.

At the same time we have dismantled the intelligence capability on which such interventionism would realistically depend. Ironically, many of those who have decried covert intelligence activities are urging a policy of *overt* intervention far more intrusive than was ever imagined in what current mythology pictures as the "bad old days."

Iran should teach us that humane values are not necessarily served by the overthrow of conservative regimes. If we encourage upheavals without putting in their place a moderate democratic alternative, a foreign policy conducted in the name of justice and human rights will wind up by making the world safe for anti-American radicalism. We will see new governments not only hostile to us but even more brutal toward human rights. All this tends to compound the geopolitical disintegration I have described earlier.

The acceleration of radical trends in the world, abetted by our policies, is visible to all. Nicaragua is often cited as a model of the new enlightenment. But while it is too early to pass a final judgment, one is uneasy when the latest human rights report of the State Department lists 400 summary executions and the holding of 7,200 political prisoners in the six months of the new regime. And a Sandinista delegation visiting Moscow in March applauded the Soviet invasion of Afghanistan and condemned what it called "the campaign launched by imperialist and reactionary forces . . . to undermine the unalienable right of the Democratic Republic of Afghanistan's people . . . to go the way of progressive transformation."

Moreover, each new upheaval tends to start a rockslide. In the wake of Nicaragua, radical Marxist anti-American forces are gaining in El Salvador; Castroite elements are already implanted in Jamaica and Grenada and beginning the assault in Guatemala. With such currents sweeping Central America and the Caribbean, are we identifying with the wave of the future, or are we abetting our own progressive isolation and irrelevance? Will Mexico in self-defense not be driven toward radicalism and anti-Americanism by forces we encouraged but did not know how to channel?

Similar trends exist, of course, in the Persian Gulf and the Middle East. If improved judicial procedures were a main concern of Khomeini's revolution, he has kept it well hidden — with 700 executions and "thousands" of political prisoners, according to the State Department's report, to say nothing of the illegal detention of our own diplomats. And how do we relate our human rights professions to the defense of our remaining friends in that vital area, most of whose domestic procedures fall short of our standards? Is it surprising that the few remaining moderate regimes are confused and apprehensive? Unless we get our priorities straight, external pressures will accelerate internal upheavals and produce a growing sense of insecurity and a growing trend of dissociation from the United States. Where would we be in the Middle East but for the miracle of Sadat's greatness?

Previous administrations perhaps showed too little sensitivity to the problem of domestic change. We do need a concept of change to which moderate democratic humane forces can rally. But currently there is entirely too much insouciance about a process that could easily engulf us. In too many parts of the world, we are losing our power to influence events for either good or ill. We live in a more hostile world today, in a weakened position, and the beginning of wisdom is to stop pretending that we are better off now because we have made obvious our desire to be universally loved.

## US–SOVIET RELATIONS

Finally, let me address myself to the current crisis in US–Soviet relations.

In the age of thermonuclear weapons and intercontinental missiles, the interaction between the two superpowers must always be a central concern of American foreign policy. On this relationship depend the prospects for peace, our security and survival, and the hopes of the whole world for a better future.

Our relationship with Moscow is inherently ambiguous. Ideology implies an ineradicable conflict; nuclear weaponry compels coexistence. Geopolitical rivalry produces inevitable tension; military technology necessitates the peaceful solution of outstanding issues. How to achieve both peace *and* justice, how to prevent the fear of nuclear war from turning into nuclear blackmail, is a central challenge for American statesmanship.

Coexistence with the Soviet Union has always raised moral dilemmas for Americans. Indeed, its dilemmas delayed our establishment of diplomatic relations with the USSR for over sixteen years after the Bolshevik Revolution. And the same ambivalence persists. Today, liberals fear the military buildup and geopolitical vigilance that are the only basis for a secure relationship with the USSR; conservatives are uneasy lest the very fact of negotiation with the Soviet leaders erode all moral dividing lines, sapping the West's will to resist and our public's support for the necessary level of defense.

This explains why we have lacerated ourselves for decades in a debate over whether "containment" or "détente" or something else should be the goal of our policy toward the Soviet Union. Those two concepts have indeed become epithets. In reality, a sensible long-term policy needs elements of both. We get into difficulty precisely when we misstate our alternatives.

It is no accident that an Administration that three years ago proclaimed its emancipation from "the inordinate fear of Communism" allegedly afflicting its predecessors has brought us to an historic low point in our relationship with the Soviet Union. An Administration more emotionally, even sentimentally, devoted to arms control than any other, that proudly proclaimed that arms control could stand on its own feet without linkage to other issues, now finds its SALT treaty stymied — perhaps for that very reason. No doubt the principal fault is the Kremlin's insatiable tendency to exploit every strategic opportunity. There can be no coexistence while the Soviet Union presses to the margins of the tolerable and often beyond.

But it seems to me also true that we have confused the Soviet leaders by inconsistent pronouncements and unpredictable reactions. Erratic shifts in our policy, whatever their reason — whether from one administration to another, or within the term of one administration, or from the tug of war between Congress and the Executive — run the risk of evaporating the restraints operating on Soviet conduct.

This Administration has in the space of a few years repudiated the SALT position of the previous Administration and then returned to its basic framework two months later; we canceled the neutron bomb and a year later pushed theater nuclear weapons; we proclaimed that the Persian Gulf needed no policeman and then announced a doctrine for its defense; we asserted the importance of Pakistan to the security of the area, then put forward a program incompatible with our stated objective, and finally dropped the entire project. We repeatedly rejected "linkage," which would have made progress in areas in which the Soviets had a stake — such as trade or SALT — dependent on Soviet restraint in exploiting tensions. This produced the spectacle that arms control proceeded while Soviet proxy forces moved into Ethiopia, while Soviet bases were established in South Yemen, while a first Communist coup took place in Afghanistan in 1978, and while a Soviet brigade was discovered in Cuba. And when Soviet troops moved to the Khyber Pass, we suddenly rediscovered linkage with a vengeance.

The essence of a strategic view is to see the interconnection of events, and the trend of events. Yet we have been unwilling to resist the seemingly marginal encroachments that cumulatively now amount to a major erosion of the free world's security. Paradoxically, by our acquiescence in the initial stages, the Soviets may even have felt misled when we later suddenly reacted — as we finally did after Afghanistan.

This American hesitation is not just the product of liberal inhibitions about intervention inherited from the Vietnam experience. Some American conservatives, too, at times seem more interested in building Fortress America and in patriotic rhetoric than in efforts to resist Soviet adventures overseas. This last was painfully evident in the Angola debate of 1975.

Every American should support the retaliatory steps announced by the President since January toward the Soviet Union — the deferral of SALT, the grain embargo, restriction on access to high technology, the Olympic boycott. These were the minimal response to Soviet aggression, but they are only reflex reactions; they do not constitute a strategy.

The Administration has been rightly disappointed in the conduct of many of our allies, in particular the Europeans. It is indeed dismaying that the industrial countries that are more threatened than we by the turmoil in the Persian Gulf are reluctant to accept the risks of a forward policy against the Soviet Union. The Western Alliance will surely be jeopardized by the

new theory of "division of labor" by which the Europeans seek to
retain the benefits of a relaxation of tensions while we assume all
the burdens and risks of resisting Soviet expansionism.

Nevertheless, our allies also have grounds for concern. Their
hesitation and reluctance are not an accident. They rightly complain of a failure of consultation. They have been exposed to the
same vacillations and cacophony of voices I have described with
respect to East-West relations. They therefore wonder how long
we will stick to our latest proclaimed course. If we want allies to
gear their policies to ours, they must be able to comprehend not
only the immediate punitive steps, but the long-term direction and
thrust of our policy. Are we acting now in order to punish the Soviet Union for an individual act, after which we will resume the
previous rhetoric and style? Or have we truly undertaken a new
policy of firmness? Can our allies make sense of a new doctrine
that generates additional commitments but *no* new forces? Are we
committing ourselves to a long-term strategy that our allies can
understand, that our Congress and public will sustain, and that
will be carried out by the leadership groups of both parties regardless of who is victorious in November? And what is that
strategy?

These questions must be answered, lest the Alliance wind up
with empty posturing everywhere: on our side defiance unrelated
to concept, in Europe accommodation drifting toward Finlandi-
zation.

At the same time, while I favor greater firmness and augmented defense, I view them not as ends in themselves but as the
foundation of a new strategy of East-West diplomacy. We must
never forget the lesson of World War II, when the democracies
failed to maintain the balance of power and thereby invited aggression. But neither can we risk ignoring the lesson of World
War I, when a war broke out *despite* the existence of a military
balance, when statesmen lost control over their military planning,
and shortsighted posturing allowed an apparently minor crisis to

escalate into a cataclysm that no leader intended or knew how to stop.

Some object to any negotiation with the Soviet Union, on the ground that it leads to euphoria or appeasement. I cannot accept the view that any serious dialogue with the Soviet Union must produce our moral disarmament. An attitude of rhetorical recalcitrance guarantees that we will be driven to negotiations in the worst circumstances, with our country torn apart by a debate over our "intransigence" and our allies buffeted by domestic assaults portraying America as the cause of world tensions. Our people surely understand the moral difference between tyranny and freedom and the necessity of both strength and survival; to maintain the proper balance is the task of leadership.

So let us not debate whether we should negotiate, but on what terms. Let us define an agenda that is neither sentimental nor bellicose, but is geared to the necessities of peace in our age. Let us articulate our own purposes, and not be driven into negotiations by the inevitable Soviet peace offensive. Let us transcend the labels of liberal and conservative as far as our foreign policy is concerned. They neither explain nor illuminate our necessities. We should spell out a position to which our people and our allies can repair, and negotiate at our own pace and on our own agenda.

In the thermonuclear age, it is simply too dangerous for the two superpowers not to be in contact. A stable long-term future requires, first, an American commitment to restore the balance of power; second, a perception that actions in different spheres and different parts of the world are linked in reality whatever one's theoretical aversion to "linkage"; together with, third, a willingness to settle outstanding issues on the basis of concreteness and reciprocity, not atmospheric goodwill.

After our election, whoever is in office should be prepared to open a dialogue with the USSR. But we must learn the lessons of the past. The greatest threat to peace is the Soviet tendency to exploit every tension for unilateral gain, undermining the security of free peoples. This must be stopped — even in the Soviet interest; the American people will not be defeated without noticing it, and when we react we shall resist — increasing the danger of war. Our goal in East-West diplomacy must be to determine what Soviet intentions are and spell out the limits of acceptable conduct. The era of proxy forces, military pressures, and encouragement of terrorists must be ended; it is incompatible with relaxation of tensions with the United States and must be shown to be so.

It is surely within America's capacity to establish the penalties and incentives to affect Soviet decisions and bring some measure of stability to the East-West relationship. We must avoid the temptation to identify progress with good personal relations or seek release in largely atmospheric gestures. While the men in the Kremlin do not mind playing on Western preconceptions that identify diplomacy with warm personal relations, they really do not know how to deal with a sentimental American policy. In the jungle of Soviet politics, no Soviet leader can justify conciliatory or self-denying policies toward the outside world except by stressing that such actions will eventually serve some Soviet aims or are necessary to avoid jeopardizing Soviet interests. It is up to us to establish these realities by our own purposeful, consistent conduct.

If progress is possible toward a code of restraint, we should be prepared to resume the SALT process. In my view we would be well advised, if and when we return to the negotiating table, to aim at a *new* SALT agreement to run for an extended period, say ten to fifteen years, that would limit the *next* cycle of weapons developments. In this case, we could also broaden the negotiation to include Soviet theater nuclear weapons, as well as planned NATO deployments, in consultation with our allies.

But I cannot stress sufficiently that all of this presupposes reliable assurances of an end to the current Soviet geopolitical offensive. If these are unobtainable we will have no choice except confrontation — and we only weaken our position by implying, as is so often done, that an arms race might work against our interests or that a confrontation would present us with greater problems than our adversary.

## CONCLUSION

Let me conclude, in other words, on a hopeful note. Almost all the problems outlined here are self-inflicted. We should keep in mind that we alone have twice the Gross National Product of the Soviet Union and, with our allies, five times the Gross National Product of the Soviet Union. If we are lagging militarily behind, it is through a lack of will, not of resources; it is within our capacity to rectify it.

We should remember that the Soviet system of government has never managed a legitimate succession. There have only been four leaders in the entire history of the Soviet Union in over sixty years. Two died in office, the third was replaced by a palace coup, and the fourth is determined to return to the earlier tradition.

Given the decrepitude of the current leadership, such a system cannot represent the wave of the future. Nor has any planned economy ever been able to match the performance of a market economy. Whether one compares Czechoslovakia and Austria, East and West Germany, North and South Korea, market economies have invariably outstripped socialist models. Stagnation seems inherent in the Soviet system. The Kremlin's dilemma is that one cannot run a modern economy with total planning, but it may also be impossible to run the Soviet system without such planning.

Two partly contradictory trends are thus involved. We face a period of maximum danger in the next five years, while the military balance is still tipping against us and the cycle of local revolutions is playing itself out. After that, the certainty is that Soviet domestic problems will mount, and our new defense programs can restore the equilibrium. But before then, Soviet reformers and Soviet conservatives may be able to unite on only one set of goals: to secure their international environment brutally and urgently before reassessing their domestic system. It is within our power to close off the avenue of adventurism, but the time is growing short. As is often the case, the seemingly boldest course is really the safest; procrastination will only prolong and thereby magnify our danger.

Therefore, as soon as possible we must restore the balance of military power. But once we do so, we face an historic opportunity. Let us make clear that we are ready for a more constructive future: a world free of the danger of nuclear blackmail; a world in which mankind's desire for peace does not become a weapon in the hand of the most ruthless but is allied to the determination of the just; a world of hope and of progress. With all our travail we remain the most fortunate people in the world: because we have the means, if we have the will, to solve our own problems. History will not do our work for us. But history tells us that we can help ourselves.

# THE GEOPOLITICS OF OIL

*Statement before the Committee on Energy and Natural Resources of the United States Senate, July 31, 1980*

THE ENERGY crisis touches the lives of Americans in many direct ways: in the constantly increasing price — or even unavailability — of the fuel to heat their homes or drive their cars; in the seemingly endemic inflation and recession to which it has contributed. But the energy crisis has also profoundly affected our national security by triggering a political crisis of global dimensions.

My topic is the international aspect of this crisis, which illuminates:

- how we reached this state of affairs;
- the threat to our national security that it entails; and
- the political dimension of any possible solution.

## EVOLUTION OF THE ENERGY CRISIS

The last three decades have been a history of our increasing dependence on imported energy, until today our economy and our well-being are hostage to decisions taken by a group of nations thousands of miles away.

In 1950, the United States was virtually self-sufficient in oil. In 1960, imports of foreign oil were still only 16 percent of our requirements. This figure actually overstates our vulnerability because our domestic production was far short of capacity;

our imports represented a strategic decision to leave part of our oil reserves in the ground undepleted. In an emergency we could have done without oil imports. Our surplus capacity helped stabilize the world oil market. By increasing our own production we were in a position to resist either exorbitant pricing or the use of oil as a weapon. These conditions have now changed irretrievably.

By 1973, America's imports had reached 35 percent of our requirements and, what was more important, we were producing at the limits of our capacity. Henceforth, increases in our consumption were bound to strengthen the bargaining power of the foreign oil producers. The world's rapid economic growth was spurring demand; OPEC found it had the power to restrict world supply — and thereby to drive up prices. The theoretical possibility of using oil as a political weapon became starkly real in 1973, when in response to the Middle East war the Arab oil producers embargoed the United States and certain West European countries and simultaneously restricted supply. Panic buying combined with a real shortage led to the first price explosion. The perverse twin effects of simultaneous inflation and recession which have buffeted our economy since 1973 are in large part the result of the fact that the supply and price of this vital strategic commodity are out of our control.

Since 1973, America's dependence on imports has *grown*, not diminished. In the winter months of 1977, oil imports for the first time reached a rate of 50 percent of our oil consumption. And in 1979, OPEC demonstrated our helplessness anew, doubling prices again.

# INTERNATIONAL CONSEQUENCES OF THE ENERGY CRISIS

It is questionable whether even OPEC realized in 1973 the full extent of its bargaining power. Nevertheless it soon grew used to it and triggered a global economic and political crisis that is still with us.

In less than a decade, the total annual oil bill paid to OPEC by all other countries has risen to $270 billion, or over one quarter of a trillion dollars. This represents a systematic impoverishment of the industrial democracies. In addition, the enormous surplus earnings of the oil producers now overhang the world economy and threaten financial catastrophe. Even when not manipulated for political purposes they are a factor of instability because the world's existing financial institutions simply cannot handle surpluses of this magnitude indefinitely. In unfriendly hands, the combined power to restrict production and manipulate vast financial resources becomes an ever more dangerous weapon, a growing threat to the world economic and financial system. Our ability to conduct a responsible foreign policy according to *our* values and *our* choices is circumscribed.

If the consequences are serious for the United States, the impact on other countries even more dependent on imported oil has been correspondingly greater. Economic crisis has been a rude shock to the peoples of the industrial democracies whose aspirations had been raised dramatically by the prosperity which since the Second World War had come to be taken for granted. For most of the industrial democracies, the political problem of the postwar period has been the fair allocation of an ever-increasing social product. The energy crisis has transformed this into an allocation of shortages, the management of a declining standard of living. In some countries, political and social tensions that were already at the margin of governments' ability to manage have given impetus to nondemocratic forces and subjected democratic institutions to severe strain.

The consequences for the cohesion of the democratic world have been grave. Atlantic solidarity has been severely tested. The open economic system that ensured prosperity in the postwar period has been threatened by a vicious spiral of recession, shrinking trade, and protectionist pressures. The energy crisis has undermined the political unity of the democracies as some allies, pursuing preferential arrangements in energy, have been tempted to pay in the coin of allied cohesion. Separate approaches on such vital issues as the Arab-Israeli dispute demonstrate disarray and complicate the pursuit of peace. Undertaken for the purpose of easing the pressures in the Middle East, such approaches, in fact, do the opposite. For if once the premise is accepted that oil producers can impose political terms, radical forces will see to it that the political price will escalate with the price of oil.

The oil crisis has its most devastating impact on the nations of the developing world. They have suffered most from the massive balance of payments drain caused by the tenfold oil price rise since 1973. The most severe blow to the economic development of new nations has come not from the "imperialist exploitation" so fashionably assailed in international forums but from an arbitrary price gouge by their Third World brethren. The developing countries do not possess the means, as the industrial nations have to some extent, to pass on the price rises to other nations in exports of manufactures. Their hopes of feeding their burgeoning populations depend on agricultural modernization, which has always relied on petrochemical fertilizers. The increase in their energy costs in fact far exceeds the total flow of external economic aid they receive. To the developing nations, the constantly rising energy costs represent a permanent, massive, and devastating threat to aspirations for progress.

In short, the energy crisis has placed at risk the entire range of this nation's objectives in the world. It has mortgaged our own economy and left our foreign policy subject to unprecedented pressures; it has weakened the industrial democracies economically and undermined the political unity which is the foundation of the security of free nations. It has stymied the world's economic growth and frustrated the hopes for progress of most of the new nations.

By a cruel irony, even the more moderate oil producers are now caught up in an ominous vicious circle. Their power over price and production is undermining the structure of the societies on which they ultimately depend for their security and progress. They have a stake in Western strength and stability, but the collapse of the pro-Western government in Iran has tipped the balance within OPEC in the more radical direction. OPEC's pricing decisions are now driven by radicals eager to destroy the international order. Each OPEC meeting is a stylized drama that opens with the moderates opposing a price increase; the radicals then insist on one; a two-tiered system is created as a compromise; then over the succeeding months the lower tier gradually drifts upward to the radicals' higher price. At the next OPEC meeting they go through the same process again — demonstrating that the geopolitical pressures on the moderate producers are now uncontainable, that the objective conditions enabling them to pursue what is in their own long-term interest — and ours — simply do not exist.

We are on a roller coaster to disaster. Our future is now at the mercy of a precarious political status quo in what is probably the most volatile, unstable, and crisis-prone region of the world.

With this as background, let me turn to my principal theme: the political future of the Middle East and the Persian Gulf, which are today the focus of the world's concern not only for

energy, but for the precarious conditions of international security
and peace.

## THE MIDDLE EAST AND THE PERSIAN GULF

The Middle East and the Gulf encompass a region of profound
passions, remarkable personalities, and almost perpetual fer-
ment. Its stark landscape and vast skies draw man to infinity; it
is no accident that three of the world's great monotheistic religions had their origins there — as well as several of the world's
recent wars. Even beyond the crucial concern for oil, it is a
cauldron of political and strategic conflict.

There are three aspects to the region's political turmoil: the
impact of the global balance of power; the contest between the
moderate and the radical forces in the area; and the Arab-Israeli
conflict. It is not possible to deal with the region's problems by
addressing one of these aspects in isolation — even an issue as
important as the Arab-Israeli conflict. They must be understood
and dealt with concurrently or the chaos will only multiply.

*First, the global balance of power.* Both history and personal experience endow Middle Eastern leaders with a highly
developed instinct for the nuances of the global balance of power.
They may proclaim the conventional litany of nonalignment, but
they understand perfectly well that their security depends on an
overall equilibrium of military strength. A global imbalance of
power enables expansionist countries to blackmail them, to interfere with diplomatic efforts for peace, to subvert domestic structures, or in the final analysis to repeat the pattern of Afghanistan: military intervention. They know that the only counterweight
to these pressures is American power. Understandably, some
leaders who cannot themselves contribute to a global balance

might wish to keep aloof from the day-to-day diplomacy by which the East-West contest is played out. They would be horrified, however, if the West took their statements of self-reliance at face value.

Thus it is disturbing that proclamations of nonalignment by Middle Eastern leaders are echoed by assertions of resignation in this country. We have been told for too long that the problems in the so-called arc of crisis have complex socioeconomic causes, that they are not essentially military problems, that not every upheaval is of direct concern to us, and that we do not really have that much influence over events anyway. Much of this is true but irrelevant; a posture of abdication makes such prophecies self-fulfilling. The Administration has already had to reverse its position in the Persian Gulf by 180 degrees, from announcing that the area did not need a policeman to proclaiming *ourselves* as the policeman.

The response to the crises in Iran and Afghanistan has illuminated the West's military vulnerability. The present turmoil in the Middle East has many causes; but central to it is the growing doubt that we possess either the military capability or the strategic doctrine to defend friendly governments in the area. The tendency in the field of strategic weapons is toward parity, which inevitably means that the Middle East becomes more vulnerable to the growing Soviet capacity for regional intervention. Our military buildup in these categories has been hesitant and ambivalent — much of it a redesignation of existing forces instead of the creation of additional ones. And the pace of it is too slow, in the face of the relentless Soviet armament program increasing at the rate of 5 percent a year over the last eighteen years. Among the surviving moderate regimes in the area, this has generated a pervasive sense of insecurity that threatens to alter political alignments and further undermine the forces for restraint within OPEC.

The military posture of the industrial democracies is still too much influenced by the strategic doctrine of the 1950s, when strategic nuclear weapons were considered capable of preventing every foreseeable challenge, including attacks on such regions as the Middle East. Obviously, strategic equivalence is the precondition of all security and it will require major efforts to ensure. But it must not blind us to the fact that we can never return to the conditions of the 1950s. Even if we succeed in maintaining strategic parity — or achieve a slight edge — one of the most urgent military problems of the next decade will be the vulnerability of vital regions such as the Middle East. Unless determined efforts are made to restore the regional military balances, by American power and aid to allies, the pressure on countries close to the Soviet periphery is bound to increase. The already pervasive insecurity will deepen. Radicals allied with the Soviet Union or backed by it will grow bolder. States known for their traditional friendship with the West will become demoralized, frightened, isolated, and threatened.

These fears are heightened by the continuing Communist assault on the geopolitical balance. In the last five years, beginning with the collapse of Indochina and the fiasco of Angola, almost every significant change in the world has been produced by Soviet weapons, Soviet friendship treaties, Soviet proxy troops, or outright Soviet invasion. The Cuban army has imposed solutions in at least two African conflicts, and from the Horn of Africa threatens the security of moderate governments in the Arabian peninsula. There have been two invasions of Zaire from Communist-held territory. Morocco is under pressure from Communist-armed guerrillas; Tunisia has been threatened by Libya. A strong pro-Western government collapsed in Iran, not as the direct result of Soviet pressures but with consequences devastating to the regional balance of power. In Southeast Asia the army of Communist Vietnam, stocked with Soviet weapons and backed by a Soviet friendship treaty, occupies Cambodia and threatens Thailand. The resulting sense of insecurity has affected the perceptions of many key countries — slowing down the Mideast peace process, removing Soviet inhibitions to the point that it felt safe to invade Afghanistan, driving traditional friends like Pakistan to reject our assistance and to embrace neutralism.

Symptomatic is the lack of enthusiasm with which the so-called Carter Doctrine has been received among the nations supposed to be protected by it. The principal obstacle is the pervasive conviction that we lack the means or perhaps the will to implement it. Leaders in the area, from centuries of national experience, do *not* believe that their countries' security can be maintained by declarations of nonalignment or of solidarity with other countries equally unable to protect themselves. Their dissociation from us reflects, rather, their dismal assessment of the trend in the global balance.

These shifting strategic realities are bound to have their effect on the price of oil. Even with the production cutbacks dictated by OPEC, some moderate oil producers in the Middle East are still producing more oil than their own economic necessities warrant and absorbing more revenues than their development programs require. The present exorbitant oil price would thus be even higher were not some OPEC countries willing to produce beyond their purely economic needs — as the price for Western and particularly American political and military protection. However, to the extent that the global balance of power is perceived to shift — to the extent that America's capaciy to deter foreign aggression or domestic upheaval is perceived to decline — our persuasiveness on even seemingly purely economic decisions such as the price of oil is also profoundly eroded.

For all these reasons it is imperative for the United States to move urgently to restore its overall military strength. The President was correct to declare our strategic stake in the security of the Persian Gulf. Now that he has done so, we have a bipartisan obligation to create rapidly the forces needed to give effect to this inescapable commitment.

The second dimension of the instability in the Middle East and the Gulf is the *contest between the moderates and the radicals* in the area. From Pakistan to Morocco, the region has seen a decade of turmoil and upheaval.

We are often told that domestic change is inevitable and irrepressible, that we have to get on the side of the forces of change. There is merit in these propositions. But we must never lose sight of a crucial distinction: We have a vital stake in the *nature* of that change, and in the success of those who support peaceful change and ties with the industrial democracies. We must *not* attempt to appease anti-Western radicals who are driven by ideology and will not be charmed out of their hostility to us by professions of our goodwill. At stake in the contest between these two groups is, among other things, the world's energy future.

The disintegration of the pro-Western government in Iran was the principal cause of the oil crisis of 1979: the long gas lines and the doubling of oil prices that is still wreaking havoc with the world economy. Iran has sharply reduced its oil production for many reasons: internal chaos, the departure of foreign technicians, the abandonment of the previous government's development and defense programs. And the fall of the Shah has affected the calculations of other OPEC members historically associated with us; our vacillating reaction to the collapse of a friend of four decades and the shabby personal treatment of him inevitably raised doubts in their minds about the value of American friendship. Many moderate oil producers in the area know only too well that their domestic practices are no better than — if as good as — Iran's. They fear the same fate from a combination of radical pressures and American disinterest. No wonder that OPEC meetings have increasingly seen the moderates hesitant, on the defensive, fearful of exerting their power for restraint. The definition of moderation has become the minimum price radicals would accept.

There is no doubt that there are forces at work beyond our capacity to channel. But the art of policymaking is to identify the range of effective influence available to us. No doubt we have sometimes underestimated that range. Your chairman [Senator Henry Jackson] deserves great credit for insisting throughout his public life that American foreign policy must be related to American values.

This is not always an easy matter. There is an inevitable reluctance to upset the apparent stability in strategically vital areas even if inaction risks storing up trouble for the future. But another obstacle has been a lack of understanding of the nature of political evolution. Conventional Western wisdom has taken it for granted that economic development automatically would produce political stability, as it did in Europe and Japan after 1945. But in those societies, political institutions had a long history; the threat to stability was the gap between economic expectation and reality. As this gap was closed, the underlying political cohesiveness asserted itself. In developing societies, by contrast, rapid modernization undermines traditional social structures and patterns and therefore produces political *in*stability.

Events in Iran have defied all Western liberal notions of progressive change. The assault on the Shah's rule did not come from those whom Western pundits would have identified as the forces of "progress": secular modernizing socialists or reformers. These existed, but ironically the decisive element in Iran turns out to have been the very process of modernization, led at a rapid pace by a ruler who, like his father, was perceived for years as a secular reformer in the mold of Ataturk in Turkey. The reaction came from groups threatened by social progress, such as the conservative landowning clerics who resisted land reform and

objected to mass education and women's rights; they found fertile
ground for agitation in the peasants who migrated from the vil-
lages to the industrial cities and felt rootless, isolated, and restless, cut off from their traditional family ties. They all found
moral sustenance in a religious fervor directed against the secular
modernism of the West — and, to some extent, also against the
Marxism of the East. The Shah clearly erred in not developing
his country's political institutions as Iran developed economically; he failed to give the new middle class a political stake
in the system. But no one — including eight American administrations — expected that his opposition would be led by those
who objected to what he was doing right, as well as to what he
was doing wrong.

We have thus, for most of the postwar period, been lacking
a theory of political change. Unfortunately, what has been implemented in recent years in that name has compounded the
problem. The new dispensation is that our difficulties arise because we have always associated ourselves with the wrong groups,
with leaders who lack public support, and that we should make
an effort to ally ourselves with the "popular will" — the test of
which presumably is governments not subject to upheaval. This
has tempted us into hectoring and pressuring friendly governments around the world.

Reality is much more complicated. First, in many so-called
progressive regimes, domestic order is maintained by more effective repression; by this standard the "right side" becomes that
which is not inhibited in its repression by association with us, and
is more successful at it. Totalitarian forces have been increasingly exempt from human rights strictures as currently practiced.

More important, our human rights pressures can have consequences exactly opposite to our intentions. What we consider
"normal" — constitutional democracy — is in fact a rarity both
in the sweep of history and on the breadth of the planet. This is
no accident. Constitutional democracy derives authority from an

abstraction: obedience to law. But constitutionalism can function only if law is believed either to reflect an absolute standard of truth or at least to grow out of a generally accepted political process. In most parts of the world and in most periods of time, these conditions have not existed. Law has been the product of personal authority, not of constitutional arrangements; the political process has been viewed as determining who has the right to issue orders. Personal authority has often been mitigated either by a concept of reciprocal obligation as in feudal societies, or by custom as that of kings who claimed to rule by divine right. In each case, tradition was a limiting factor; certain exactions were impossible not because they were forbidden but because they had no precedent. No ruler of eighteenth-century Europe could levy income taxes or conscript his subjects. Authoritarianism, in short, was usually quite precisely circumscribed.

It was paradoxically the emergence of popular government that expanded the scope of what authorities could demand. The people by definition could not oppress itself; hence its wishes — as expressed by elective assemblies or rulers in its name — were absolute. The growth of state power has gone hand in hand with the expansion of populist claims.

In this context, modern totalitarianism is a caricature, a reductio ad absurdum, of democracy; modern authoritarianism — a quite different phenomenon — is an aberration of traditional personal rule. This is why some authoritarian governments — as in Spain or Portugal or Greece — have been able to complete the evolution into constitutional democracies. No totalitarian system has ever navigated that passage.

The American dilemma is that in *most* developing countries, authority is either personal or totalitarian. While totalitarian states hostile to us are ruled out of bounds for our interventionism, we have recently been obsessed with "reforming" authoritarian governments friendly to us. The tragedy is that we seem to have no idea how to effectuate the delicate transition to constitutionalism — a process that in most of the West took centuries. What we do have is a predilection for harassing friendly governments, the result of which has been to encourage not the moderate constitutionalists but the radical totalitarians who emerge in the form of terrorists or guerrillas. The outcomes have been disastrous. We are in danger of making the world safe not for democracy but for totalitarian radicalism.

A vicious circle is created. When terrorists or guerrillas mark a society for assault, the government is tempted into acts of repression which undermine its authority, and the chaos polarizes the society so that the premise of the democratic process — that the loser accepts his defeat and in return is given an opportunity to win on another occasion — cannot be realized. The victims of terrorist attacks are often the ablest and most dedicated officials, leaving in place the corrupt whose transgressions multiply as they attempt to compensate for the peril of their station by accumulating the maximum material benefits.

In recent crises of this sort, the American tendency has been to force imperiled friendly countries to "save themselves" by accelerating our notion of reform. But once matters have reached the point of civil war — particularly if the assault is externally supported — concessions generally compound the disorder because they are seen as a sign of weakness. Nor, most often, do the radicals who challenge authority by violence have any interest in constitutional democracy. What they want is power for themselves, to install their own brand of tyranny. The time for concessions is *before* civil disorders break out, in order to preempt them — a lesson often neglected in recent decades and one that does not always work when the insurrection is inspired, financed, and trained from outside the country. The next occasion for reform is *after* tranquillity has been reestablished, but Western inhibitions and authoritarian incompetence usually combine to prevent the testing of this hypothesis. Concessions *during* a crisis only encourage the radicals and accelerate the assault.

I have dedicated so much space to these theoretical reflections to point out that while America has sometimes settled too readily for the status quo, recently the American pressure for change has more often accelerated the process of domestic disintegration than arrested it. And the end result has been both more oppression and greater international instability.

Convinced that our model is of universal validity, we have sought to implant it without regard to historical circumstance or the likely consequences. In truth, we know next to nothing of the dynamics of other societies, perhaps least of all those in the oil-producing areas; for all our tinkering with "reform," we have given little useful advice on how to navigate the tricky passage to more liberty without wrecking authority and increasing the scope of tyranny. Hard-pressed governments beset by an implacable domestic enemy are often reduced to paralysis by advice which they know is dangerous but which they dare not reject because they have relied on our support.

The result of these tendencies — contrary to our intention — has been a spread of regimes hostile to us in the Third World. In many developing countries Marxism has flourished, not because it fulfills economic or moral necessities — which it clearly does not — but because it provides a rationale for centralized political power once traditional structures collapse. More recently, Islamic theocracy has emerged as a reaction to modernization in all its forms, Western or Marxist. Its long-term viability has yet to be determined.

In the face of these onslaughts, traditional friends of the United States, belonging to neither of these orientations, stand bewildered, unsure of their future and confused about our purposes. Governments that have traditionally relied on us know that the various radical regimes, however different their origins and motivations, all agree in their all-out opposition to peaceful evolution, Western values, and the survival of the world economic system. The inevitable result of radical ascendancy — regardless of its origins — is to threaten the survival of all pro-Western governments that remain in the Third World, and especially in the Middle East, with obvious geopolitical consequences.

The impact in energy is immediate. Radical countries seek to drive up the price of oil to obtain resources to achieve their international objective of undermining American and Western influence. Moderate regimes have the paradoxical incentive to *reduce* production, since they fear the disruptive consequences of the process of modernization that destroyed the Shah. Both developments push up the price; together they spell disaster for the West.

The West has so far supplied no serious answer to this challenge. Clearly, we have fully analyzed neither the dynamics of political change nor our interest in relation to it. We must be clear in our own minds what our own survival requires, the scope of change we can responsibly advocate, and what countries we must defend in our own interest even if their institutions do not meet every democratic test.

Until we have thought this through, we have no possibility of a sensible dialogue with the oil-producing countries, even those friendly to us, on either oil prices or domestic reform.

Our natural allies are not radical groups and forces but the moderate groups which affirm peaceful change and sympathize with Western goals. If the moderates are not to be doomed — or to dissociate from us in self-defense — they must know, first of all, that we understand the realities of their situation. They must be given reason for confidence that we are prepared to cooperate with them and, finally, to stand by them. For their own survival, they must be willing to develop their political institutions. At the same time, we must understand the limits of our knowledge, and the price we could pay for clumsy experiments. And we must know clearly where we will draw our lines: what security interests we will not sacrifice in the name of reform, and what positions we will defend even if those who man them do not meet every definition of virtue.

*The Arab-Israeli conflict* is without doubt a principal factor in the turbulence of the Middle East. But its solution is closely connected with the factors that I have already described: the military balance and relationship between moderates and radicals in the area. If the Soviet Union emerges as the dominant outside power, moderate countries will be reluctant to support peace processes that displease it. In the face of a dominant radicalism, even more friends will disavow schemes that are in fact in their own best long-term interest.

A dangerous escapism has developed in the West. The illusion is widespread that solving the so-called Palestinian problem is the deus ex machina that will defuse all the region's other tensions. A West Bank solution is important, but whether it contributes to the solution of other problems depends on the nature of the settlement, the auspices under which it is achieved, and who benefits from it. The outcome must not be one that tempts constantly escalating demands by radical forces; it must create incentives for moderation rather than be seen as a reward for blackmail.

I do not believe that the status quo on the West Bank can or should be maintained. I do not agree with Israel's policy of continuing settlements on the West Bank during the Camp David negotiations. Other unilateral steps taken recently seem to me ill-advised. But I am not impressed, either, by the many fashionable proposals that amount to finding some subterfuge for introducing the PLO into the negotiations on the optimistic assumption that it would then moderate its goals and contribute to stability in the entire region.

Given my analysis of the strategic and ideological sources of the tensions in the area, the prerequisite to progress is that we show that pressures on us are *not* the road to success. A policy that is perceived as yielding to blackmail is bound to accelerate deterioration in the military and geopolitical dimensions of the Mideast crisis, leave our moderate friends even more vulnerable, and compound our energy problems.

I have consistently supported the Camp David process and the Egyptian-Israeli peace treaty. I hope that the Egyptian-Israeli autonomy negotiations succeed. But should the stalemate prove unbreakable, the search for alternatives must avoid illusions.

The proposition that establishing a PLO state would contribute to the tranquillity of the area lacks any factual basis; quite the opposite is likely to be true. I question the obsession with introducing the PLO into the negotiations not simply because of its rejection of the United Nations Security Council Resolution 242, but above all because of its radical anti-American and anti-Western policies: its close affiliation with and occasional leadership of all radical forces hostile to us in the Middle East (including those Iranians holding our hostages); its training of terrorists on a global basis; and its intimate cooperation with Soviet intelligence organizations. The PLO in its present incarnation, beyond its implacable enmity to Israel, supports all forces assaulting the present international structure. As long as it pursues such a course, it deserves Western opposition, not encouragement.

The prevailing theory is that the PLO would become more moderate after its demands were satisfied. I see no evidence for this; indeed, all evidence is to the contrary. An independent PLO state in current circumstances will have every incentive to attempt to subvert nearby moderate governments, especially Jordan, if only to escape the inevitable demilitarization provisions without which no Israeli withdrawal of any extent is conceivable.

Finally, I see no sign that such a group, with its ideology

and its affiliations, is waiting only for a pretext to become a group of agrarian reformers in a pacifist West Bank mini-state. But the last thing the Middle East needs is another radical state in the region attacking all existing institutions. This is not merely against the interests of the United States; it is also against the interests of moderate Arab states in whose well-being we have a stake. These countries understand this perfectly well, whatever their public statements, but the flirtation with the PLO compounds their vulnerability.

For all these reasons, negotiations with respect to the West Bank do not hinge on finding a gimmick for a fashionable negotiating forum. If another forum is developed, it should promote Jordanian participation; any other route will lead to failure. Our European allies must learn that when they push schemes incapable of realization they encourage radicalism and guarantee stalemate. All the industrial democracies indeed have a stake in diplomatic progress; but it is suicidal to identify progress with schemes that will in the long run promote instability.

The effort to solve the West Bank issue in one grand negotiation, defining all frontiers and all relationships, is almost certain to fail. And a prolonged inconclusive effort is bound, in its turn, to compound the tensions in the area. If the current negotiations based on the Camp David autonomy scheme do not produce the desired outcome, I hope other avenues will be attempted, including a Jordanian-Israeli negotiation. These should aim at the rapid achievement of some interim partial step, for example, returning Arab-populated areas quickly to the jurisdiction of Jordan; further Israeli withdrawals and final borders would be the subject of continuing negotiations to which all parties would be committed. The relationship of the Palestinian areas to Jordan would then become an Arab, not a general international, problem.

It is in the common interest that we not chase abstractions but begin a process that can lead to rapid results. In this manner

progress can be made in the West Bank that contributes to
political stability in the area and contains, rather than unleashes,
radical pressures.

# RESPONSE TO THE ENERGY CRISIS

Since the first price explosion of 1973, we have learned that the
energy crisis is not a mere problem of transitional adjustment;
it is a grave challenge to the political and economic structure of
the free world. The world's postwar financial institutions and
mechanisms of cooperation were never designed to handle so
abrupt a price rise in so vital a commodity or such massive
shifts of wealth. The problem will not go away by simply letting
inflation proceed; on the contrary, runaway inflation is part of
the vicious circle which drives up oil prices. Nor can the financial
imbalance be overcome by permitting the debt of consumers to
expand indefinitely, even though this is what has been happening.
The gradual impoverishment of the industrialized world is
certain to end in financial catastrophe, with grave political consequences. Finally, for a consumer-producer dialogue to be effective, certain objective conditions must be met, which do not
now exist.

There is no secret about what we must do. The industrial
democracies must adopt stringent conservation measures, develop
new supplies of oil and alternative sources of energy, strengthen
collaboration among the consumer nations, address the plight of
the developing nations, and seek a more reliable long-term relationship with the producers. These objectives are easy to state in
the abstract. It is devising programs to implement them which has
proved to be the obstacle. I will not get into the domestic side of
the problem here, except to point out the disastrous international
political consequences of our continuing vulnerability, and to

urge that the problem be dealt with as a matter of highest urgency. Aside from our military defense, there is no project of more central importance to our national security and indeed our independence as a sovereign nation.

The response to the energy crisis, of course, itself has an international dimension. For finally its solution depends on our fortitude and bold leadership. We have been subjected to political pressures, not only in the 1973 embargo but even more recently. We are now threatened by OPEC with production cutbacks if we seek to build up a strategic oil reserve. But we cannot tolerate being forced into a state of permanent vulnerability. No country has a right to demand that we remain eternally subject to blackmail. Building a strategic oil reserve is a sovereign decision of the United States and an essential matter of survival; the attempt to interfere with our doing it is a demonstration of why it is essential. We should fill our strategic reserve promptly, and any country taking retaliatory steps must know that it does so at the cost of its good relations with the United States.

No area of policy has been more disappointing than consumer cooperation. Since the establishment of the International Energy Agency in 1974, cooperation among the industrial democracies has not been adequate to the challenge. Instead of bold concerted action, too many of the industrial democracies have preferred currying favor with the OPEC countries, competing for some transitory special position or dissociating from our negotiating efforts in the Middle Eastern conflict. But any special position gained by one country can be rapidly transferred to another that outbids it. Such a course is in fact against the interests of the moderate oil producers, the claimed beneficiaries. Once the principle is established that a political price can be exacted, the moderates will become the target of radical pressures to raise the political price. The moderates cannot stand fast if the industrial democracies do not.

A subject in which it is urgent for the industrial democracies to develop a common approach is the plight of the developing nations. These countries are caught in an impossible bind. Higher oil prices absorb all their aid and export earnings; the bill for other imports mounts because of the global inflation fueled by the energy crisis; and their own capacity to export is reduced because of the recession in the industrialized countries, which is another result of the energy crisis. Thus a reexamination of the development needs of the new nations is imperative. The devastation of the developing world's hope for progress is a grim omen for a world of peace.

Another subject requiring urgent attention on a common basis is the recycling of financial surpluses. By 1983 the financial claims of the oil producers on the OECD countries will reach half a trillion dollars. That amount cannot be recycled by the commercial banking system; it will lead to the bankruptcy and instability of many developing nations; it will overtax the financial institutions of even developed nations. Recycling is easiest precisely into those countries that need it least; it will not abate the devastating impact of current prices on nations whose export earnings and foreign assistance are now largely absorbed by paying their energy bills.

The need for solidarity among the oil-consuming nations is plain. This has been my consistent urging since 1973. I do not accept the proposition that it is proper for the producers to organize but is a confrontation if the consumers seek to cooperate with each other. Research into alternative sources of energy could be pooled; major resources could be allocated to some joint programs to develop alternative energy sources, with clear target dates, for the reduction of the common vulnerability. Above all, a joint approach should be worked out for a comprehensive dialogue with the producing nations.

Eventually the solidarity of the industrial democracies will provide the secure basis for a dialogue between consumers and producers. There is in fact a congruence of interests. The consumer countries have a political stake in the independence of the producer nations, even those whose domestic policies are repugnant to us, such as Iran. The producers in turn have a stake in a stable and growing world economy, because many of them depend on it for their technology, for their development, and in a deeper sense for their independence. Both together must find means to enable the developing nations to fulfill their aspirations. But this cannot take place in an atmosphere of chaos and blackmail. The producers cannot continue the practice of periodically announcing, as a series of unilateral proclamations, decisions affecting the economic future of the entire world without any consultations or any apparent concern for their impact. The industrial democracies must enhance their cohesion if a consumer-producer dialogue is to give expression to the reality of interdependence.

Whoever is President of the United States next year has the duty, and the opportunity, to lead the way out of these dilemmas. The United States is better able than others to regain some mastery over events. We have the domestic resources, the technological skills, and the creative genius to transform the world's energy market. Therefore, decisive American efforts to implement an energy policy would transform the international environment — reducing the cartel's stranglehold on the world economy, restoring world prosperity, dispelling the clouds of political demoralization, and strengthening our security.

Thus will freedom be vindicated and the democracies flourish, transforming crisis into hope.

# INDEX